TOUFAH

The Woman Who Inspired an African #MeToo Movement

Toufah Jallow
with Kim Pittaway

Middleton Public Library
7425 Hubbard Avenue
Middleton, WI 53562

TRUTH TO POWER
an imprint of
STEERFORTH PRESS
LEBANON, NEW HAMPSHIRE

For information about permission to reproduce
selections from this book, write to:
Steerforth Press L.L.C., 31 Hanover Street, Suite 1,
Lebanon, New Hampshire 03766

Cataloging-in-Publication Data is available from the Library of Congress

ISBN 978-1-58642-300-1 (Paperback)

Manufactured in the United States of America

Book design by Leah Springate

1 3 5 7 9 10 8 6 4 2

To all victims whose rapists are not presidents.
To all survivors who have paid for survival with silence.
May the whispers of our mothers, their mothers and
the mothers before them rise in our throats.
I hope we find safety in speaking together.

CONTENTS

ALLEGEDLY

It is December 2020. I sit in front of a computer screen with my friend and colleague Marion Volkmann-Brandau, watching the rough edit of a short documentary we are producing together. Over the course of twenty-five minutes, clips of me competing in a 2014 Gambian scholarship pageant are intercut with images of the man who ruled my country for more than two decades, an all-powerful dictator whose death squad murdered and tortured at his command. Clips of powerful men from other countries appear as well: Harvey Weinstein, who used his position in the film industry to intimidate women into having sex with him. Jeffrey Epstein, who trafficked teenaged girls and young women. Mexican drug lord El Chapo, who declared that young girls were his vitamins because raping them gave him life.

Should I add "allegedly"?

It has been six years since I was declared the winner of a national pageant sponsored by my country's president, promised a scholarship to study anywhere in the world as my prize. Instead, President Yahya Jammeh raped me. I became a victim in The Gambia, was a fugitive in Senegal and then a refugee in Canada. At nineteen, I started my life over, a survivor of rape, separated from my family, afraid I would never see them again, worried they would suffer if I told anyone what had happened to me.

Should I add "allegedly"?

As I rebuilt my life seven thousand kilometres away from the country I'd grown up in, I struggled. With depression. With my secret. With loneliness. And then the dictator whose crimes had forced me to flee was deposed and driven out of The Gambia himself. I was able to return, to reunite with my family and, eventually, to tell my story, first to human rights investigators, then to international media like the *New York Times*, the *Guardian*, the BBC and CBC, and my country's Truth, Reconciliation and Reparations Commission (TRRC).

But people kept telling me I should always say "allegedly."

The strange thing is people and institutions aren't nearly as adamant that "allegedly" be attached as a qualifier when they speak of murders ordered by Jammeh, when they talk of torture carried out at his instruction, when they detail financial crimes committed as he drained the country's coffers. No one attaches "allegedly" even to his claims of curing cancer with herbal treatments.

This insistence on using "allegedly" when it comes to rape can't be explained away as simply protecting the rights of those not convicted, because the word isn't just attached to the person named as perpetrator; it is attached to the crime

itself. "He allegedly raped her" morphs into "she was allegedly raped." And it isn't something that happens only in The
Gambia, only with Jammeh. As I watch the news in my
small apartment in Toronto, I notice the same tendency in
reports about other crimes in Canada and abroad: when
men say they were beaten or assaulted, the word "allegedly"
is rarely inserted. When someone says they've been robbed,
"allegedly" almost never appears. But when a woman says
she was raped, her assertion is often framed as "she claimed
she was raped" or "she was allegedly raped." Whether in
The Gambia or Canada or the United States or the United
Kingdom, when women say they were raped, the men they
accuse are given the benefit of the doubt. The women? They
are simply doubted.

When my country's Truth Commission set out to tabu-
late Jammeh's crimes, they continued this cross-cultural tra-
dition. In October 2019, they published a list of themes for an
upcoming round of hearings and only attached the word
"alleged" to sexual violence: not to torture or to killings, not
to arrests or to witch hunts. When it came to witness testimony, the names of those accused of other crimes were
broadcast and published, but with the exception of Jammeh
himself, witnesses were instructed to refer to the rapist by a
number that corresponded to a secret list of names, doubt's
benefit keeping rapists anonymous while torturers and
murderers were named.

Some rape victims remained anonymous too, giving evidence under pseudonyms. A few testified under their own
names but asked that their faces not be shown. I understood

their reasons. In The Gambia, as in many parts of Africa and in Western countries too, to say you have been raped places you at risk of stigma and further harm. One of the victims testifying before the TRRC had been raped as a teenager, then forced into an arranged marriage afterwards to save her family's honour. Her rapist wasn't punished, but she was. After I was raped, I didn't tell my own mother until months after it happened. I thought it would be a secret that would die with me. Instead, it became a secret that almost killed my spirit, almost killed me. But now I want people to see me, to know my name, to see someone who has been raped stand proud, be strong. Survivors are strong, even those who remain hidden. They have to be strong, to still be here with us, to move on. I want girls like I used to be—girls who do not know what rape is, who do not even have the words to describe it—to see that you can survive this journey through the unknown. To see a visible survivor. To see I have survived. And to find strength in that knowledge.

And I want rapists to carry the shame so often placed on their victims instead.

In the days and weeks and months after I first spoke out, others in The Gambia spoke out as well, sharing their stories using #IAmToufah. As momentum built in this West African #MeToo movement, I realized the world's interest in me was not because of who I am, but because of who my rapist is—a former president, a dictator who has rubbed shoulders with the world's most powerful leaders. Ironically, the status the world has given him gives me more visibility.

And so I launched The Toufah Foundation to use that visibility to draw attention to the survivors whose rapists are not presidents, to redirect the power attached to his name to the fight for justice for all victims of sexual and gender-based violence. Because my life now stretches across two continents, bridging Africa and North America, the campaigns we are developing draw on the lessons and insights of feminists in both the West and in Africa, reflecting the strengths of women around the world.

In June 2015, Yahya Jammeh, then the president of The Gambia, raped me. He has never been charged. Never convicted. And because of that, the world thinks I should use the word "allegedly."

I won't.

He thought he would get away with it, tried to erase me. I thought I would never speak of it, that I would remain invisible.

We were both wrong, because I am here, shining like the sunrise of the melanated coast.

I am Toufah Jallow. This is my story.

1

A DICTATOR'S SHADOW

What can I tell you about what it is like to live in The Gambia? That's a big question. If people outside of Africa know my country at all, they know it as the country from Alex Haley's *Roots*, the place Kunta Kinteh comes from. It is Africa's smallest mainland nation, carved out by the British to protect their slave route along the two shores of the Gambia River. It is a gathering place, where the people of many African ethnic backgrounds mix, including my people, the Fula, nomadic herders. Alongside us are Mandinka, Wolof, Jola and even a small group of Krio or Aku people, descendants of slaves who returned to Africa from the Americas in the 1800s.

What is it like? It is noisy, loud and vibrant. In cities like Serrekunda and the capital, Banjul, families live in compounds organized around a central open area. Along at least two of the sides will be dwellings made of cement bricks, usually with two bedrooms and a living area. The kitchen is often outside, in the open area sheltered under a metal sheet or bamboo leaf blades, and sometimes the bathrooms are in a separate outside room as well. The compounds might typically house two or three wives of the same husband, and all of their children, each wife in a dwelling of her own. Or sometimes one family will rent from another and share the common space. The compound next door is right on the other side of the fence, and the opening to the road will have a high metal sheet as the gate. The roofs are corrugated metal too.

There is no soundproofing. When it rains, drops thrum on the metal roof. We don't need to pay for meditation apps of rain sounds to lull us to sleep: we get them for free. Voices carry from one home to the next. If I want to talk to my neighbour, I don't phone them—that costs credits and I'm saving those for important calls—I yell over the fence until they come. The children are laughing and playing—and yes, sometimes fighting—in the common space too, and traffic noise carries from the road just outside. If anyone is celebrating—and someone is always celebrating—the DJ will play until after midnight, and all you can do is hope he has good taste in music. You will hear drumming too, and if you are lucky, you'll hear the kora, a twenty-one-string West African harp that resonates through a calabash gourd base. Most of us are Muslim, but there are Christians and people of other faiths too, and if it's a religious holiday, we celebrate together, sharing food and finding joy in each other's company. If someone—even a stranger—comes to the gate when the family is eating, they will be called in. "Join us, join us!" And you must join—it's anti-social not to. This is the Gambian way.

Everybody speaks many languages, so conversations shift from English to Mandinka to Wolof to Fula to the pidgin English of the Akus. The concept of babysitters or nannies is foreign to most of us because children are raised by everyone: the other wives, the older children, the family next door, the grandmas. People aren't physically alone. Your brain is crowded with language. The air is crowded with sound. And it is only quiet in the small hours before sunrise.

That's when it is coolest too. The Gambia is hot. From October to June, the temperature sits at over thirty degrees Celsius and the air is dry and dusty. As you walk along the gravel roads, red dirt will mark your pant cuffs or skirt hem and coat your feet and legs. In the rainy season—what we call Nawet—it's worse: the humidity can push over 95 percent and the temperature can leap to over thirty-seven degrees. The red dust and sand turns to mud, and people often call in sick to work rather than tread through the muddy mess. And the thunderstorms: they crash and boom as if the sky is waging war with the air, and we all duck under cover as the rain pummels the earth and soaks everything in its path.

But a country is not just its weather, its buildings, its people. A country is also its government, its power structures, its leader and its way of life. And for all my life growing up in The Gambia, my country was shaped by the man who came to power two years before I was born, President Yahya Jammeh. A military man, Jammeh led a coup in 1994. He presented himself as a pious Muslim leader, a supporter of women's rights and an advocate for the poor and oppressed. But the reality of his regime was often brutal, as political opponents, journalists, human rights workers, student leaders, LGBTQIA+ people and many others were harassed, imprisoned, tortured and murdered.

I was barely more than a toddler when Jammeh's police forces opened fire on students protesting the beating death of a young man by firefighters and the rape of a fifteen-year-old girl by a man in uniform. When the shooting stopped, sixteen people were dead, including a three-year-old child. I wouldn't learn the details until many years later, but I remember the fear of those days, as teachers abandoned their posts and tried to avoid the stones of protesting students, and as parents, including mine, raced to collect their children from school and to lock their doors against the violence erupting in the streets. Like many Gambians, my family avoided conversations about politics, even among friends, even inside our own home, because a hint of criticism of the president or his regime could lead to arrest—or worse. Yes, there were those who believed Jammeh was righteous, anointed by Allah to lead our people. They didn't question his assertions that he could cure AIDS and cancer and other diseases with herbal remedies of his own making. But for those who didn't believe Jammeh was chosen by God, who thought of him rather as a soldier who waged war on his own people, silence was the safest option, because questioning a man as powerful as he was could be life-threatening.

This is the Gambia I was born in, the Gambia I grew up in, the Gambia I expected to grow old in.

—

"Hey Toufah!"

I was on my way to English class in my first year at Gambia College when one of the older girls called out to me from the group she was standing with. She and her friends lived in the college dormitory, while I lived at my mother's home. For many years, my mother and siblings and I had lived in a family compound with my father's other two wives and their families, but three years earlier, my mother had moved us into a small compound of our own. She had built the house using money she'd earned, including from marking exam papers and participating in education projects funded by foreign aid agencies at her day job for the education ministry.

"I heard you presenting at assembly," Ndeyastou said. She was an extroverted dancer whose words were as quick as her movements. We were speaking in Wolof, which, along with Mandinka and Fula, was one of the three major local languages I spoke. Like most Gambians, we slipped in English words where we needed them too. "You're really good. You should represent us at the July 22 pageant!"

"Is that still happening?"

"Yes, yes, the pageant is still ongoing," said Ndeyastou. "You should take part!" In my early teens, my sisters and I used to crowd around the television set in my father's first wife's living room to watch the pageant. (We had to stay on the carpet. We weren't allowed on the couches with our dirt and mess from the playground.) While the competition was named to commemorate the date of the coup that brought Yahya Jammeh to power, the pageant usually took place in late November, gathering senior secondary school, college and university girls from across the country to compete. For those of us watching on television, it was like The Gambia's version of *America's Got Talent*, as the smooth-voiced announcer introduced the program and one by one, the girls crossed the stage in the fancy hotel where the pageant was held. "Hello, my name is . . ." each would start, naming herself and the school, college or university she represented—"and I am here to take the crown home!" Each would describe her platform— ending child marriage or improving food and nutrition or building The Gambia's infrastructure—along with her talent: dancing or drama or journalism or even performing with fire. Each contestant had to show academic achievement, a talent in performance and a commitment to a larger societal issue, all with the goal of earning a full scholarship to the university of her choice, anywhere in the world.

The judges were impressive: business owners, university professors, past winners. Teens of many shades and sizes competed. By the end, one senior secondary school girl and one college or university student would each win a chance at a better future, as evidenced by the clips from past winners woven into the broadcasts claiming that winning had changed their lives. Some had gone on to study overseas, others had started businesses, still others had good government jobs.

"What do I have to do?" I asked my friend, who replied that I didn't have to do much for now—she'd submit my name for me. It was autumn 2014, and with a simple "Okay," I took the first step on what would be a life-changing journey.

At that point I was only in my first year of college, training to be a teacher, a job I didn't want. I dreamed of studying the performing arts, but our country's young university system had no such programs, and I hadn't qualified for direct entry to Gambia's universities anyway because I had failed to pass my senior secondary school math exams. My mother, Awa, kept telling me how fortunate I was to go to college, reminding me that her mother had been matched in an arranged marriage at thirteen with a sixteen-year-old boy who was leaving his family home in Senegal to head to work in The Gambia. My grandmother never learned to read and write, though she'd helped support her small family her whole life, selling goods in the market, making meals for workers in her husband's modest auto shop and to sell to others, and taking in washing. My mother remembered soaking the oily clothes the mechanics handed them in bucket after bucket of water and scrubbing to remove the grease and dirt. My grandmother made sure Awa went to school, asking neighbours to tell her what the school documents her daughter brought home meant.

My grandmother was the one who met the man who would become my father, months before my mother even set eyes on him. She peddled homemade breakfasts to office workers—ground boiled beans on soft bread with a sauce of tomato, onion, peppers and sometimes meat. My dad was hard to miss, with his smart shirts, small, round wire-framed sunglasses and high-top Afro hairstyle. Also, he rode a motorcycle. He became a regular customer, stopping at the market to pick up other homemade meals from my grandmother's canteen. Soon she offered to do his laundry for a small price as well. Where was his family from? she'd ask him in one conversation. Did he have a wife? she slid into another. He'd had a wife, he answered, which she interpreted as meaning he wasn't married now.

He seemed a modern man, with a good job working for an NGO, and my grandmother saw him as an ideal candidate. That he was past forty didn't concern her: better a mature husband than one too young and less established. Her daughter's good looks were attracting attention—dangerous attention, from my grandmother's point of view. The best way to keep her safe from the advances of men was to find her a husband to protect her. But not any husband would do: my grandmother was my grandfather's only wife, and that was the situation she hoped to find for her daughter. Granddad's friends teased him about only having one wife, but he took no mind of them. More wives meant more arguing, more trouble, more cost, and he didn't want the hassle, he would claim.

My grandmother also wanted her daughter to be "only wife," not "first wife," and more. She knew my mother was smart, and she was looking for a husband who would let Awa's education continue uninterrupted. Before long the casual questions my grandmother slipped into conversation with my father became serious negotiations. If he had a wife of his own, she'd point out, he wouldn't need to pay my grandmother to do his laundry or prepare his meals—his wife would look after him. But if her daughter was the one to become that wife, he'd need to look after her too, ensuring she completed school and earned her qualifications as a teacher. After they agreed to the details, my grandmother told my mother her plans—my mother really had no voice.

And so while my mother sat in her senior secondary school classroom, male delegations from each family went to the mosque and finalized the arrangements to marry the two, as was common in our community. No ceremony, no celebration. My mother went to class one morning as a schoolgirl and came home that afternoon as a wife.

But my grandmother's careful planning and negotiating didn't yield what she'd hoped for. My father hadn't been quite open. Yes, he'd had a wife; he'd actually divorced two wives already, but he still had a third he had married in Guinea— and two children too. My mother wasn't an only wife, not even a first wife. And that wasn't the only expectation unfulfilled. Her education was soon interrupted by a miscarriage and two pregnancies—first me and then my brother. Though it could have been grounds for divorce, at twenty she went on birth control pills without my father's knowledge so she could complete her college and university studies.

When I look back at pictures of my mother from that time, I barely recognize her: she is so slight, so tiny, a speck of a girl, like she could be swallowed up whole. It is strange because in my childhood memories, she is substantial, solid. Of course she did not grow taller, but maternity added weight to her slight frame; she became rounder, heavier, less easy to ignore. Perhaps I should describe her face, the gap in her teeth, her round cheeks, but those aren't the physical characteristics that stand out most when I think of Mum. At home, when we want babies to go to sleep, we carry or rock them in our arms. But when women have work to do and need to keep baby close, they strap the children across their backs, baby's tiny hands tucked inside the cloth wrapper, their little legs spread out over their mother's hips, leaving the woman's hands free to do what she needs to get done. This is how I think of my mother, who carried me on her strong, broad back, as she carried my brothers and sisters after me.

Though my mother had little choice in the decision to marry, once she was a wife, she did what she could—as my grandmother had done before her—to influence the course of her own future and that of her children. On one important issue, both women were united. Though ritual cutting of girls' genitals—removing external genitalia including the clitoris and labia—was common in African Muslim households, neither my mother nor grandmother condoned the practice. Other girls in our extended family had been subjected to it, but my mother and grandmother would not allow the women in my father's family to do it to me. As a teen, this embarrassed me. When showering with other girls at school, they would remark that I was uncut, different from them, and make fun of me. I didn't appreciate my mother and grandmother's efforts until I was older.

A few years into their marriage, my father brought his other wife and children from Guinea. Then he married again—his third wife. By the time I was in my mid-teens, we were fifteen people all together: his senior wife, Jariatou, and her children, Cherno, Hajakaddy, Hawlatou, Makka and Muctarr; my mother, Awa, me and my full siblings, Pa Mattar, Nogoi, Muhammed and Ida; his junior wife, Awa Bah, and her children, Penda and Jarrie; and Alpha, my father—one big, though not entirely happy, family.

My father split his week, spending time with each wife and her children in their own section of the compound. We youngsters competed for his attention. We would race down the block to meet him as he headed home at night or returned from a trip for one of the NGO projects he worked on, jostling to be the one who carried his bag, tumbling over each other to be near him when he sat in the courtyard. While our mothers policed us, he played with us, though we also all knew he was the one to make the final decisions on any matters of importance. He was the head of the household and that was his right. My mother was the only one of his wives to work in an office, which was a source of strength for her and resentment for the other wives, who griped she didn't do enough chores at home.

And then my brother Pa Mattar died. The sibling closest in age to me, he had stopped going to school after only a year or two in the classroom, labelled "mad" by an educational and medical system too under-resourced to provide a clearer diagnosis. Many Gambian families would have sent him to an institution, but my parents kept him at home, eventually hiring a series of minders to watch him. In the aftermath of his sudden and unexplained death at just thirteen, my mother decided it was time for us to have our own space. She had already used her own money to build her parents a small home on land my father had helped her acquire. And while she would never end her marriage to my father, now she decided we would leave the family's compound. Purchasing the land using a small sum she'd earned on a project for the education ministry and a foreign NGO, she gradually built us

where math was on the curriculum, I had chosen to attend a Muslim religious school in primary and middle grades—what we called Arabic school. Classes there ended at midday, leaving me free to help look after Pa Mattar. I missed the foundations of math. Attending the school also required wearing a hijab and body-covering clothing—long-sleeved blouses and floor-length skirts. When I switched back to a regular school in junior secondary school, I stopped wearing the hijab consistently. Even in the English school, religiously observant teachers would scold me. "You used to be such a modest girl!" one teacher said to me when he saw me without a head scarf. I argued that I did not want to be someone who wore a scarf to please people or to avoid punishment, that I should wear it only if I chose to freely, but I don't think he understood my meaning or appreciated my spiritual questioning.

Since I never did manage to catch up on math, a college where the only programs offered were agriculture, teaching or nursing seemed my sole option. And so I enrolled in the teaching courses at Gambia College. I never missed my literature class, where studying *Macbeth* continued to tap my interest in drama and language, though I wished it exposed us to more inspiring women's stories, like the ones I'd borrowed from my mother's bookshelf: Asare Konadu's *A Woman in Her Prime*, the story of a Ghanaian woman who is a successful farmer but remains childless despite three marriages, and her struggle to find happiness on her own terms; Virginia Woolf's passionate argument for women's independence, *A Room of One's Own*; Femi Osofisan's Nigerian retelling of Euripides' *The Trojan Women* in *Women of Owu*; and Kitty

Kelley's biography *Oprah*. All were books about women who met the world on their own terms. I was particularly struck by the grace and dignity of Konadu's heroine Pokuwaa and Oprah's real-life example as a survivor of sexual abuse.

Still, though I tried to be conscientious about all my classes too, I'd realized early in the school year that if I was going to make it through college, I needed to find other activities I enjoyed. I'd signed up for drama club, press club and more. Before long, I was presenting the week's news at our assemblies, which is why older girls, like Ndeyastou, recognized and remembered me. While competing in a pageant for a scholarship wasn't something I'd have sought out, when she suggested it, I thought, why not?

Even so, I almost missed it. After telling Ndeyastou to go ahead, I forgot all about the competition until a week later when I ran into her again.

"We haven't seen you at rehearsals," she said. "What happened?"

Rehearsals?

It turned out the first step was competing to represent your school. In the week since we'd spoken, a group of other potential contestants had been practising under the strict watch of Madame, an Aku woman and lecturer at the school who coordinated this round. So I followed the girls to the classroom where they were meeting for the next rehearsal and took a seat in the back: better to figure out what was going on before stepping forward. At the front of the room, some of the college's best female students practised their catwalks and rehearsed their speeches. *Nope,* I thought. *I'm not doing this today. I have to understand what I'm up against.*

By the next session, I was ready to join in, having crafted my speech on alleviating poverty and worked on my Fula costume for the part of the competition where girls represented their tribe. I wrapped material the colour of white sheep's wool around my head and hips, with traditional cowrie shell beads in my hair and around my wrists and ankles, and a calabash gourd basket I carried at my hip. For my talent, I would present a short dramatic dialogue, coming on stage in a torn and dirty kaftan, with a sleeveless romper underneath it in the five stripes—red, white, blue, white and green—of the Gambian flag. The idea was that I was Poverty—Poverty speaking in person, bragging about how I ran the country and that I would keep going until everyone was poor and stricken. "Nothing will shake me!" I would proclaim. "Not your aid, not your hard work!" At the height of my bragging, I intended to tear off the kaftan to reveal my second character: The Gambia, the country challenging Poverty. "No," I would say to Poverty, speaking now as our nation. "You lie, oh, you lie! I am going to get rid of you. I will take my boys and girls to school to be educated. I will get rid of malaria. I will boost the economy. My people are not going to suffer!"

The day before the college round, I realized that I'd spent so much time on my other preparations, I didn't have a dress for the most pageant-like part of the competition. Usually, when taking part in a drama or something special, if I had nothing of my own, I'd borrow what I needed from Mum's closet, but she had nothing suitable as a teenager's fancy dress. I called Ndeyastou. "I don't have the money for a new dress," I told her. She knew a second-hand clothes shop at the Serrekunda market, she said, not worn-out clothes but items returned from other stores or sometimes shipped from Europe. "Let's go there and see what we can find."

Serrekunda's market is the biggest and busiest in all of The Gambia. On the road leading into it, people with wheelbarrows sell oranges, bananas—all types of fruits. Others sell books, jewellery, cloth and beads. Women walk with their baskets of groceries. Cars and donkey carts manoeuvre slowly through the crowd, and dust is everywhere. In the background you can hear the call to prayers from the nearby mosque. As you walk by, boys tap you on the shoulder, offering stolen black-market goods: gold and silver jewellery, phones. Tourists push past, looking for African print clothing and beads to buy. And in a back section is the clothing store, its walls covered in second-hand dresses, only one of each style.

"Girl, I haven't seen you in a while!" the shop owner said to Ndeyastou as we ducked under the entrance flap. "You haven't bought anything for a long time!"

"Well, I've got someone with me today and I hope you're going to give her a good price, not too much," she said as he walked toward us, ready to negotiate, his fanny pack of cash and change at his waist. I scanned the walls for a dress that would work. Too flowery. Too small. Too girly. Then I spotted it: a black dress with a silver and black sequinned top, V-neck and a flared skirt slit at the side to the knee.

"You can't tell me you can't take off one hundred dalasis," said my friend.

"What?" replied the shop owner. "I will lose profit if I do that!"

And back and forth they went.

"Please!" I weighed in. "I really need the dress. I promise I will come back and buy more in the future."

Finally, we walked away with the dress after counting out seven hundred Gambian dalasis for him to tuck into his fanny pack—about fourteen American dollars.

I came second at my college competition, which was enough to qualify me for the final. Now it was December 2014, and I was watching the pageant hosts standing at the centre of the low stage in the ballroom of Paradise Suites Hotel in Serrekunda, as I waited for my cue. On the floor in front of them and in the balconies above, dignitaries, government officials, families and fellow students clapped and cheered as each of us—twenty-two in all—were introduced for the live television broadcast.

"Go Toufah! Go Toufah!" my schoolmates shouted as I stepped onto the stage. My mother, half-sister Penda, friends and aunties were also there to cheer me on. To the left of the stage, drummers and musicians in traditional garb sat ready to play, and at a table to the right, the four judges arranged their scorecards. The sponsors of the pageant had paid to replace my market-bought dress with an elegant floor-length black gown. As I stepped forward to the microphone to answer the question the judges posed to me, I was aware of the dignitaries, officials and others in the audience—the president did not attend—but I was most conscious of my mother's presence. She was usually so busy with work and caring for my brothers and sisters that she had rarely seen me on stage. Now I could feel her attention and pride.

The judge asked me, "What does 'Your attitude could break or make you' mean, and how would you explain it to your ten-year-old sister?"

I drew a breath, looked at the camera and smiled. "This simply means that for you to be successful or to fail in life, it's your attitude that determines it. You need to represent yourself in the best manner, in the way you behave, the way you think and the way you react to problems."

It seemed like I'd barely answered and my time was up. Off-stage, I watched as one girl after another answered her question, some of them phrased to prompt praise for President Jammeh and his government and others that were more general. *How had the July 22 revolution impacted the lives of women and girls in the past twenty years? What advice do you have for a friend who does skin bleaching? What were some of the challenges girls used to face in their education and how have they been addressed in the past twenty years?* And then we were done.

The hosts introduced performers and speakers to fill the broadcast time as the judges deliberated. Finally they were ready to announce their decision, and we all filed back before the cameras. The senior—and only male—judge came to the microphone.

"The first runner-up . . ."—he paused dramatically—"is Fatou A. Jallow!" (my formal name). The other girls turned to me as I stepped forward. As he announced the second runner-up, it occurred to me that the order was wrong—you either started with first place or with third place, not the girl in the middle. I could see others trying to get his attention and people chattering at the edge of the stage.

And then he stopped dead. "I have read them in the wrong order!" he declared, and he reread our names. This time, I wasn't first runner-up.

"Our winner is Fatou A. Jallow!"

Tears streamed down my face and around my shocked smile: from contestant to runner-up to Miss July 22 Queen, in the space of a few minutes. In the audience, my mother, aunties and Penda all cheered and danced.

As I accepted the crown from the previous year's winner, I realized that my dream of pursuing an education outside of The Gambia was now a possibility. But more than that, perhaps I could be a role model for other girls who wondered if their talents would open doors for them. I looked out at the cheering crowd, and the future seemed full of hope.

After the pageant was over and I had won, it puzzled me that no one really seemed to know the specifics of the prize scholarship, even the officials in the Gender Department of the Ministry of Education who ran the program. It seemed to depend on what President Jammeh decided.

As I waited for word of what would happen next, another opportunity I'd been hoping for materialized. I'd auditioned for a small role in a movie called *Tama or the Diamond* being shot in The Gambia by Nigerian director Efe Omo Igori. I'd gotten the part of the neglected wife of the lead character, a man who loses a tama, or small traditional drum, in which is hidden a valuable diamond and spends the rest of the film desperately trying to find it. The truth was I was more excited about this opportunity than I had been about winning the pageant: it was a chance to act professionally.

I made my way to the shoot, my lines memorized, prepared for my film debut. As I waited on set, my phone rang. It was Aisha, assistant to the head of the Gender Department. "We are going to the State House right away. You must join us," she said. "And wear your pageant gown and crown. President Jammeh is receiving an award, and he wants the pageant winners and runners-up to be there."

I froze. I was about to go before the cameras. I couldn't leave! But I couldn't tell the truth either, since no one would regard an acting commitment as an excuse to avoid a presidential summons. I leaned on an excuse familiar to every teenaged girl: cramps. "I'm so sorry," I told Aisha. "But I've got terrible menstrual cramps. I'm lying here on the bed. I can't move!"

Aisha hung up, and I thought I'd gotten away with it. But moments later, my phone rang again. This time, it was a woman I hadn't met yet, who introduced herself as Jimbee, a protocol officer for the president. "We all menstruate," she told me. "Take some medicine and come." Then she called Aisha and told her it wouldn't look good if I wasn't present, prompting Aisha to call my mother to tell her to make sure I came.

Soon my mother arrived on set from her office. The lead actress, Monica Davies, overheard some of my conversation with Mum and called the director over. He was sympathetic, but the choice between accommodating an unknown actress or getting on the wrong side of the president's office left little room to manoeuvre, and that room disappeared completely when Monica said she knew another local actress who could play my part. I couldn't stay; they couldn't wait. My film debut dissolved.

My lie had put me in another bind. I didn't have my pageant gear with me, and I was too far from home to return to get it and make it to the State House in time for President Jammeh's award ceremony. My mum solved the problem by asking a colleague to pick up my gown and crown at home in Yundum, the suburb where we lived. "She'll meet us at the State House," she said. An hour later, we were parked on the corner across from the State House's main gate with Mum and Auntie Kadijatou standing on either side of the car, blocking the view, while I twisted myself into my dress in the back seat just in time to be escorted inside to the ceremony.

The ceremony itself was too boring to remember, with lengthy speech followed by lengthier speech, culminating in the lengthiest of all from President Jammeh. Afterwards he left to pray, while the other pageant participants and I were escorted to a seating area and then to a large table where we were told to sit and wait. It dawned on me then that here I was at the State House, at the very table where I'd seen dignitaries seated so many times on television.

Eventually President Jammeh joined us. He was dressed in a white robe that covered his shirt and pants, as he usually was in public, with a round, flat-sided white hat on his head. He looked at us gathered around the table and started to make jokes about tribes, as casually as if he were an uncle or a family friend. While I was aware of his power and I had heard stories about what happened to those who opposed him, in that moment, he seemed friendly, even approachable. I see now how naive I was: I assumed that if I treated him with respect, I would be treated with respect as well. He knew some of the other girls through their family names and members, but my family wasn't among his circle. I was a new face. "Hey Fula girl," he said. "You did not want to come because your stomach was hurting!" He teased me in front of the others, saying that Fulas are always afraid, even of a mosquito bite. And then he turned serious, telling the whole group that we were role models. "Many people will be looking at you," he said. "Especially men. Don't let it go to your heads. The whole purpose of the Miss July 22 competition is to empower you, not to get you married right away and turn you into housewives!"

Anyway, he said, looking again at me, he had a medicine that eased stomach ache. He produced a bottle of herbal liquid and poured some out for all of us, encouraging us to take a sip of his special brew. He came from a region known for herbal remedies and he often publicly touted his herbal cures. In 2007 he had created the Presidential Alternative Treatment Program to eradicate HIV. That remedy, he said, was a "mandate from God," a cure created from seven herbs found in the Qur'an. News reports at the time quoted him saying, "Mine is not an argument, mine is a proof. It's a declaration. I can cure AIDS and I will."

In the years that followed, thousands of patients were subjected to treatments that included a yellow herbal potion they were supposed to drink twice each day and a green paste meant to be rubbed onto their bodies while prayers were chanted around them. State media often broadcast programs showing Jammeh himself administering the medicines, waving a leather-bound Qur'an over the patients as he did so. Ill, barely clothed women and men were shown in these theatrical demonstrations and gave testimonials to the treatment's effectiveness in advertisements. Later, Jammeh claimed his herbal treatments also cured diabetes, infertility and cancer. Perhaps we pageant winners were lucky to be treated only for indigestion. Like the other girls around the table, I drank the liquid and then quietly pushed the cup aside.

Soon President Jammeh moved on from herbal cures. He called Jimbee over, who turned out not to be simply a protocol officer, but the president's cousin and confidant. She and a presidential orderly handed fifty thousand dalasis—almost one thousand American dollars—to me and to the senior secondary school winner, and distributed smaller amounts to the other girls. Then she ushered us out of the room to where drivers waited to take us home.

On the way to the cars, one of the girls commented on how friendly the president had seemed, and another on the concern he'd expressed for all of us. He seemed smaller, less imposing than he did on television, but kinder too, remarked someone else, like an uncle or a father who was proud of your achievements. Even I had to admit I looked forward to seeing him again at the official functions to come.

We'd had the televised pageant and our first meeting with the president, but there was still an official televised award ceremony to come, on December 24. To prepare, we were all shepherded back to the hotel for two days of rehearsals.

The night of the ceremony, President Jammeh spoke, describing the pageant as "a noble thing," and explicitly saying that it was not haram, which means forbidden by Islamic law. He continued: "There is nothing you can do in this world that God will not see, and there is nothing that you will do in this world where God will not either reward you or punish you." Then, in a leap I couldn't follow, he moved on to attacking single mothers—"gold diggers," he called them—demonizing single mothers was a common refrain from Jammeh, one supported by Gambian Muslim clerics, who echoed his condemnation of women raising children alone, while routinely ignoring the role of those who must have fathered them. We were handed more gifts: iPhones, Mac computers, money—though still there was no talk of

the promised scholarship—and we performed the song we'd
been rehearsing, thanking the president. The lyrics were in
Wolof and translated into English as: "Thank you for what
you do, for empowering women, for everything you do."
Then, finally, it was time to go home.

2

"YOU COULD BE PRESIDENT"

A s 2014 turns into 2015, I have my first meeting with President Jammeh. Jimbee has been calling to ask about the project I'd proposed as part of my pageant platform: a debate I planned to organize in a local village to gather ideas on how to alleviate poverty, which we would then turn into a drama, engaging the community in both the discussion and the proposed solutions. She offers to help me get the project off the ground more quickly than through regular channels. "Just bring it to me," she says, "and I can take it directly to the president." I've been procrastinating. I am having trouble sorting out the budget—How much is reasonable? How much is too much?—and because the ministry hasn't set a deadline for my proposal, I keep putting it off. "Just bring it to me and we will go through it," Jimbee insists, and I acquiesce.

A driver named Landing arrives at my house in a big black State House car to pick me up for what I think is an appointment with Jimbee. Landing says little on our drive to the State House, then drops me off in front of the stairs to the president's residential area. Jimbee ushers me inside, past a man I come to know only by his nickname, "King Papa." This man seems at ease in the residence, walking around in his sock feet.

Jimbee and I climb the stairs in the huge house, making our way to a room with big sofas and a similarly large television, where we settle in. I'd thought I was coming to an office to see her about my project, but now it appears she and I are waiting for the president himself to join us. Thirty minutes or more passes, and eventually President Jammeh enters, shaking my hand and then hugging me in the way men my father's age hug their daughters. The conversation starts with talk of the competition, and the traditional instrument I'd played at one point. "How did you learn that?" he asks. I'd paid a Fula man to teach me, I reply. Impressive that I was so determined, he says and starts talking about his own childhood, how his father was treated like a second-class citizen and that he hadn't fit in as a child.

"What had made him not fit in?" I ask.

"You feel comfortable asking me such a question?" he says.

"I am nervous," I say. Still, my mother has raised me to have confidence, and my questions, direct as they might be, are couched in "sir" and "excellency." He doesn't seem disturbed by my straightforwardness—more intrigued, I think. We talk for an hour or more, as he reviews my project, making recommendations for changes and improvements, listening to my ideas.

"You are a brilliant girl. *You* could be president!" he says with a laugh. "Are you really only eighteen? You don't talk, you don't move like an eighteen-year-old." Maybe the question about my age should have struck me as odd, but from the time I became a teenager, men have said similar things to me. As well, I know Jammeh is a married man. An earlier marriage had ended in divorce in 1998, then in 1999, he'd married Zineb Suma, the daughter of a Guinean diplomat. More than a decade younger than the president, Zineb is a glamorous figure in The Gambia and beyond, light-skinned with straight hair she often wears up in a graceful chignon, and known for her charitable works. The couple have two children, a girl just three years my junior and a younger boy. Around 2010, the family purchased a $3.5 million mansion near Washington, D.C., where Jammeh and Zineb's daughter attended school.

When our conversation is over, I gather my phone and purse from King Papa, who had taken them from me when I'd entered the residence, and Landing drives me home. Energized by the president's interest, I spend the rest of the weekend working to revise the project. I've never tackled a project like this before and so I discuss the specifics with friends who are going to help, reworking the budget. When Jimbee calls a few days later, I tell her it is ready to submit.

That evening, sometime past 7 p.m., my phone rings. It is Jimbee: a car is coming to get me. "It's a bit late," I say.

"The president is free tonight," she says. "This isn't an opportunity many people have—you should come." My mum says it is fine, and so I go.

"Hey Fula girl," the president says when he joins us. "That's a lot of papers!" He flips through my submission, then asks, "How much is your budget?"

Sixty thousand dalasis, I say.

"That's little," he replies. "We can make it one hundred thousand."

"Should I take the project to the ministry to get started?" I ask.

"Easy, way too fast," he replies. Then he switches subjects, telling me not to focus on men, but on my career.

Again he questions my age. "You sound so mature and you look so mature," he says. I would do well as one of his protocol officers, he adds, offering me a job at the State House. Surprised, I refuse. In my head I am thinking that working in an office is the last thing I would be good at—I am almost as bad at organizing things as I am at math—and I don't want to do anything I can't do well. But instead I explain that I want to continue my studies. "I wish there were more smart girls like you," he says, as he gives me another fatherly hug and sends me on my way with his driver.

Over the weeks that follow, events where I'm to attend as pageant queen are scattered throughout my schedule, many with President Jammeh in attendance. Oddly, though, in public he often pretends not to know me. "Hey miss," he will say, or, "What's your name again?"

It won't be until much later that I understand Jammeh's actions for what they are: a slow grooming, building our private relationship with flattery, praise and gifts, contrasted against cooler public interactions that keep me just a little off balance. And while the job offer hasn't brought me into his immediate circle, other offers are still ahead.

Jimbee, the president's cousin, was soon a frequent visitor and caller. One afternoon when she showed up at my mother's house, she noticed that we had no running water. Jimbee made a phone call. "The president wants to talk to you," she said as she handed me the phone.

"Hello, Fula girl!" I heard him say. "I have been thinking about your project. It's really great. Jimbee tells me that you don't have running water in your home. I'm going to talk to Jimbee to settle that." Days later, the national water company arrived to install a line, and when my mother asked about paying for it, she was told the account had been settled. Later, Mum asked government colleagues who worked at the ministry overseeing the pageant whether this was normal: What kind of benefit do pageant winners typically get? They told her it was fine. Each winner was treated differently, they said. Some received cars, some were placed in jobs at banks or in ministries, others were assisted in opening businesses. Their prizes were tailored to their needs and goals.

Not long after, Jimbee took me shopping. "Help me choose some furniture," she said. "We are going to refurnish your house as a gift from the president," she said. "This is just the beginning. Winners get a lot." She paused, regarding me. "You have to push. You have to call me. It seems you don't call to ask for things unless I ask you." When I still hesitated, she explained that such gifts were so that when I went abroad to study, I would not worry about sending money home for my parents—I would know they were looked after and could concentrate on my studies. It was all part of the pageant winner's package, she confirmed to my mother later.

But then came the president's proposal. "You are very beautiful," President Jammeh said after a private dinner with Jimbee and me. We were in his private quarters, a part of the residence I'd never seen before. As on past visits, King Papa had collected our phones and handbags when we entered. "Do you ever think of marriage?" he asked.

"Oh no," I said. "I am just eighteen—I don't want to get married early!"

"But there is nothing wrong with getting married to a man who will support you. Do you have a boyfriend?"

I laughed, tried to put him off. "Are we supposed to talk about that?"

He asked again about a boyfriend, but I didn't answer. "You know I'm the president," he said. "I can find out anything."

My mind was racing, uncertain of where our conversation was going, but sure I wanted it to end.

"I have never met a young girl that has guts like you. You don't fear me. I like that," he said. "I have a surprise for you tomorrow. Jimbee will be giving you the money for your project." Now he called King Papa to join us, and the other man handed me fifty thousand dalasis. "For the bother of coming here today," said Jammeh as King Papa left the room again.

Jammeh then turned away to call his wife. They spoke briefly in French, exchanging what I believed were goodnights, and he turned back to me.

"Honestly, I cannot drag this out any longer," he said, turning back to me. "I want to marry you."

It wasn't a question. Simply a statement, said almost casually: he wanted to marry me. He was the most powerful man in our country, and so that was that.

"Why?" I managed to ask. "You are three times my age. You are almost my dad's age." I wondered if he was testing me. After all, he had told us to concentrate on our studies, to not be distracted by men. Perhaps he was joking, or when he said men, he meant every man except him? I couldn't be certain. "It's not you," I said, scrambling not to insult him. "I'm just not ready."

He looked at me as if I was just not understanding him. And I wasn't understanding him. I realize now that he wasn't asking me, he was telling me. And the choice wasn't mine, it was his.

"You are confused right now," he said. "Get back to me." He turned away and I left, eager to escape the discomfort in the room.

Even as I tried to convince myself it had been an elaborate joke, I told no one what he'd said, afraid that if his interest or word of my refusal spread, it would be humiliating to him, and I was afraid of what a humiliated president might do to my family, to me.

The next day on the way to school, I noticed a black car following me. It was there after school too. And I understood that things were not right and might not be right again.

The day after that, Jimbee sent Landing to bring me to a house she wanted to show me. It was the surprise the president had hinted at the day before. "Ta-da!" she said as we walked through the front door. "This is yours! And the president is giving you the car in the garage too. He told you something the last time he saw you, and when that happens, then this is all yours." I tried not to react, but she could tell from my face that this was something I didn't want. Jimbee began to berate me. "What is wrong with you? This will change your life!"

I didn't know it then, but Jammeh owned hundreds of properties around the world—one count put the number at 281. But no matter how large his real estate portfolio, I had no interest in having any part of it.

My guarded reaction was still not to Jimbee's satisfaction. "Why are you acting dumb?" she said.

"I would like to go home," I replied.

She turned away from me, calling out to the driver, "Take her back!"

Landing was quiet as we pulled away from the house. He'd always been quiet with me—but nice. "Are you all right?" he asked at last. I didn't answer. "You should be careful," he said. "Jimbee is a very powerful person in the State House." We made the rest of the journey in silence.

I still hoped I could shut the danger out. I thought that if I met it with silence, it, too, would remain silent. Others might have asked a friend for advice or told a parent about the proposal, but I'd always been reluctant to pull others into my dilemmas; I tried to solve my own problems. I locked the door after I stepped into my mother's house, where I was surrounded by the furniture Jimbee—or rather, the president—had bought to fill our rooms. On my phone, I blocked Jimbee's number and any others that I didn't recognize.

I told no one what had happened.

3

"THIS WILL BE MY SECRET"

"Three peppers for five dalasis!"

"Get my onions for ten!"

"Hey, pretty lady, come buy my stuff!"

The air in the neighbourhood market is full of dust and exclamation marks as I hurry from one vendor to the next under the hot June sun. Around me, sellers have spread their wares over corrugated metal and cardboard balanced on wooden platforms: a display of fish there, salad greens at another, rice at another still. As vendors hawk their wares, they flap fans back and forth to keep flies from settling on their goods.

"No, no, that's too much," I say to the man selling onions, before agreeing on a price we can both swallow. The plan for my family's meal that day is a full chicken stuffed with onion, ginger and other seasonings, served with boiled potatoes, eggs and marinated salad. Today, the greens are cheap because the rainy season has begun and water is plentiful, yielding both crops and market bargains.

Covered head to toe in a black niqab, I look like many other women in the market, more of us observant than usual because of Ramadan, when even those (like me) who go scarfless on normal days don a hijab, niqab or veil to imbue our fast with more purity, more devotion. Though the purpose of my garb likely differs from theirs: I wish for anonymity more than purity. Near the entrance to the market are the two men who have followed me on the fifteen-minute walk from my mother's home. In their black pants and navy blue shirts, they look too formal to be market-goers, and so they hang back, secure that they can see me over the half-fallen cement wall near the main road as I go from vendor to vendor.

My basket is nearly full, almost all of my shopping complete, as I make my way to the destination I've been aiming for from the outset, the shop that sells cooking oil. Tucked against the perimeter of the market, the store's corrugated side panel provides a place just out of view of the entrance. As the vendor passes me my oil, I tuck it into the basket at my feet and sneak a look at the entrance. I can't see the men, making it likely they can't see me. I know the oil seller will recognize my sister or mother when they come looking for me and that the basket of food I am abandoning here will be passed on to them. And so I leave it behind, ducking out the back of the shop to where the taxi drivers gather. I slide into the front seat of the closest one.

"I need to go to Banjul," I tell the driver, handing him five hundred dalasis.

After the visit to "my" house, Jimbee had continued to call me. I tried to go on with my life, though as I walked to the market or travelled to school, I often saw the same car following me or noticed well-dressed men in black loitering nearby. Even though I'd blocked her number and others I didn't recognize, still Jimbee got through, demanding my presence at official events. When I declined two in a row, telling her I wasn't feeling well, she sent a driver to take me to the hospital for a checkup. The results from the blood and urine tests done that day were never shared with me.

Then Jimbee called again.

"Hey, it's been a while," she said in the casual tone of a friend. My stomach lurched. "There's an event at the State House on the day before Ramadan starts. As the winner, you have to come." It was part of Gamo, a religious celebration of the birth of the Prophet Muhammed, and she said I couldn't refuse.

"Will the other girls be there?" I asked.

Yes, yes, she assured me. "Landing will pick you up."

That day, I dressed for the event in a gold floor-length dress, my hair lengthened and straightened with a weave, a scarf draped over it in deference to the religious holiday.

I could see the State House's two-storey columns and sloped peak framing the front entrance. As we passed through the main gate, I saw guests gathered in the garden for the religious ceremony. Landing continued on through the second gate and then pulled to a stop at the private residence. Jimbee was waiting. She brought me into the front hallway, where we both sat. Eventually she led me to another room, where she told me to wait before she made her excuses and disappeared. I could hear voices as religious leaders led prayers nearby in the garden.

And then he was there. I hadn't seen him since he had asked me to marry him. Now his approach was different: no more fatherliness, no more flattery, no more persuasion. Instead, he radiated impatience, even anger. Gone, too, was his formal white robe. He was dressed in a simple white shirt and pants.

"There's no woman that I want that I cannot have," he said, as he crossed the room toward me. My mind scrambled to find words that might placate him, but before I could, he dragged me to a bedroom next door.

"Who do you think you are? I can get any woman I want in the entire world. Let's see if you're a virgin or not." His words seemed directed as much to himself as to me, perhaps affirmations of his power, though who knows what goes through a rapist's mind?

Terror gripped me, as he struck me across the face with the back of his hand and then pulled my right arm to him, jamming a needle into me. I started to scream. His hands felt big and leathery as they covered my nose and mouth. I heard Jimbee knock on the door of the bedroom and say something. "Get out," he ordered.

There is no word for rape in the Fula language. This isn't because it doesn't happen. It's because we are supposed to believe it is so rare that no word is necessary for it. If it does happen, we are not supposed to speak of it.

How much do I tell you of what happened next? A missing word isn't the only barrier. English has the words, and still women struggle to speak of it—and when they do, they often aren't heard. And so, even as I speak in the language of the West, I struggle: to be clear, to be heard, to be believed. I'm not giving it words for me. I don't need these words to remember it, to feel it. I can't choose to turn off these words and forget. What happened next is with me always, whether I drape it in words of any language or not.

But the shame of it is not mine. And telling you what happened next places that shame where it belongs: with Yahya Jammeh and those who facilitated his crimes.

Jammeh gripped my face with one hand as he pushed me to my knees, pulling his penis out of his pants with his other hand and rubbing it on my face like someone smears dirt on you—to degrade and overpower you. He stroked himself to arousal. And then he shoved me halfway onto a bed, my feet dangling over the edge, and he raped and sodomized me.

Anger came off him in waves as he grunted and panted.

My face was crushed into a pillow. When I could get air, words wept from me.

"I'm sorry. I'm sorry. I'm sorry." A woman's apology for a man's crime.

I know that I struggled. I know that I begged for help. I know that I screamed. I could hear the Imam's prayers broadcast through the speakers in the garden outside.

He told me no one would hear me.

And at some point, I knew I was screaming but I couldn't hear myself, my ears gone deaf too. Like theirs. I don't know if it was the injection, or the shock, or . . . I don't know. Strength drained from me as chills rushed up my spine. I stopped fighting back, something that even now still fills me with shame. I hate that I stopped.

And then he came. His sweat dripped onto me. He pulled away.

I passed out.

I don't know how long it was before I woke again. He was still there, sitting on the couch in his boxer shorts, staring at me. My dress was pulled up, my leggings and underwear gone. My body ached. Later I would wonder how long he'd watched, what he saw. Did he take photos or film me? Images of my degradation were carried in his brain. Perhaps in his electronics too.

"Get out of here," he ordered, but then he left instead.

I pulled my dress down. As I stepped into the hallway, King Papa was there. He handed me my bag and my phone. As I passed him, he spoke. "He is our president, and we will do everything to protect him."

Jimbee stood at the side of the hallway, bent over her phone, and then led the way for me to leave.

Landing was waiting with the car when I stepped out of the building. I cried in the back seat for the hour it took to drive home.

He didn't ask me what happened.

—

It was 3 a.m. by the time I got home. As I passed the curtain that covered the entrance to Mum's room, she peeked out at me, calling, "It's late!" That wouldn't have worried her so much, since Gamo celebrations often continue into the early morning hours. But I know she only caught a glimpse of me. If she had seen me fully, she would have known something was terribly wrong. I closed the door to my room, dropped my handbag on the floor and wrapped my hair up with a piece of cloth.

After the house went still, I went into the bathroom and turned on the shower. The water was cold, cold, cold. But I didn't care. I just sat there in its frigid flow, the only warmth coming from the pee running down my legs and the sticky fluid seeping from me. As I scraped and tugged at my skin, I wanted the water to wash him away.

I stayed in bed the whole next day, my body numb, waves of disgust washing over me, thinking of all the things I could have done differently. Why hadn't I left the country immediately after his proposal? What made me think life was going to just go on? What could I do now?

I wanted to remove my genitals from my body, to hide them someplace no one would ever see, to separate them from my *self*. I felt as if people could see his mark on me.

I could hear my little sister Ida and the other children playing outside. I sat on the couch next to my bed and listened. I couldn't tell anyone, especially my mother—not because she would blame me, but because she would fight back. She would not let it slide. She would not be quiet about it. She would tell my father and her family. She would tell her boss. That would be dangerous for us all. Because President Jammeh wasn't going to let anyone speak out about it. And she wouldn't be able to put him on trial, to see him jailed, to beat him. She wouldn't be able to do anything.

My silence wasn't because I didn't trust my mother. My silence was because I trusted my mother so much that I knew she would fight for me. And she would lose. And when she lost, my siblings would lose her, too.

And so I thought, okay, grown-ups have secrets. This will be my secret. No one will ever know about this.

Part of me hoped I would never hear from them again, that he had done what he wanted to do and I would be left alone. But a few days later, Jimbee called, speaking as if nothing had happened. "Hey, girl, how are you? Are you feeling good? There's an event happening in three days in Kanilai." This was the president's hometown. "All of the pageant winners will be there. A driver will pick you up."

I remember saying okay, knowing now for certain that the rape hadn't been a one-time thing. Jimbee was going to keep calling me. This was going to be my life. This attack on my body would keep happening. That's what I would be—a thing to be raped until my noes turned into yeses.

I sat on the couch in my bedroom, and through the open window, I could hear my siblings fighting over toys. I could hear my sister Nogoi pounding the mortar and pestle, preparing some pepper for cooking. I was surrounded by people I loved. Yet I was completely alone.

I felt as if I was living in two worlds. In one world, I was a pageant winner. People congratulated me when they saw me, told me how proud they were of me, asked me about when I would be leaving home to study abroad. They thought this must surely be the best time of my life.

In the other world, I worried about the men in the black sedan watching me, about Jimbee summoning me. And I knew I had to begin planning my escape.

To leave, I had to go through Senegal, the country that surrounds The Gambia on three sides; our fourth faces the Atlantic Ocean. As I considered who to turn to for help, I thought about my mother's younger sister, Marie. She and my mother were at the same time alike and very different. Both were smart, but where my mother made her plans and moved with quiet resolve toward them, Marie was a louder presence, more vocal, more directly defiant. Like my mother, Marie had been pushed into an arranged marriage. But when her husband proved abusive, she abandoned him and returned to my grandmother's home with her young son. My grandmother had tried to convince Marie to return to her marriage, but Marie held firm, even going so far as to petition Muslim officials to dissolve the relationship. Eventually the families agreed the union should be broken. Marie's son was sent to a Muslim boarding school, and Marie lived with us in my family's compound before she eventually moved into a dormitory at college as she pursued her education.

To me, Marie was a radical presence: the divorced auntie who wore pants and went to college. That reputation was solidified when her brother, my uncle, came for a visit. He didn't approve of how Marie was living her life; he told her she should be home at a certain hour, shouldn't wear the clothes she was wearing. His views weren't unusual in a traditional African Muslim household, where dresses and skirts were viewed as more appropriate feminine attire, but Aunt Marie was having none of it. When she came back to our family's house late one evening after eleven, wearing pants, her brother shoved her against a wall and told her she needed to obey him.

Marie struggled free and stormed out of the room. A few minutes later, she returned in a T-shirt and shorts. "Today is the last day you put your hands on me," she told him.

My eyes grew wide as I took it all in: Marie, her brother, the voices of our other family members. "Marie, you cannot fight your brother!" someone said. But Marie wouldn't be dissuaded. "No, today we are going to see who can beat up who," she shouted as she confronted him. "It's done, it's done," yelled my uncle, refusing to fight her. But each time he backed away, she came at him again; each time things seemed to settle down, she would threaten him again. In the end, they didn't fight physically, but Marie had won the battle of wills. My uncle never laid hands on her again.

In the years since that night, Marie had moved to the U.K., where she ran a small export business sending goods from Turkey and Europe into The Gambia. And in our family, female stubbornness and independence became synonymous with her name, so much so that if I stayed out late or refused to back down on something, family members would say, "Are you sure Marie isn't your mother? You're as stubborn as she is." But where others saw stubbornness, I saw fierceness, a determination to defend the people she cared for—starting with herself.

That night, I texted Marie in the U.K., telling her I had an emergency. Could she send me five thousand dalasis? My request was unusual: I'd never asked my aunt for money before. "Does your mother know you're asking me?" she replied. I told her she didn't, but that I would tell her the next day. Marie said she'd send it right away.

The next morning, I said to my half-sister Penda, "Hey, I'm going to get the groceries today." This was usually her task, and my volunteering to do it was completely out of character. She looked at me in disbelief.

"No, really," I said. "Give me the money Mum gave you." Even as she handed the bills to me, she continued to give me a look. I could almost hear her thoughts: *What is going on?* with a dose of a younger sister's *You're so weird* mixed in as well.

Though I'd worn a hijab when I'd attended Arabic Muslim school, it had been some time since I'd donned one. This day, though, I knew both the hijab over my hair and a niqab hiding my face and clothes would help me make my escape. I had a passport I'd gotten the year before, when I'd applied to two schools in the U.S. I'd been accepted to both but hadn't been able to afford the costs of the airfare or tuition, so my passport's pages were fresh and stampless. I tucked it into my waistband along with my Gambian ID card and set out just before noon.

In the soccer field next to Mum's house, the two men I'd seen loitering near me in the days before sat on a cement block. I hurried past them with my basket, sure they would follow, since they'd seen me leave the house with my hijab wrapped around my arms. The market was three intersections away, and as I glanced back, I could see them in the distance. I ducked into the MoneyGram office to pick up the cash my auntie had sent, and hurried on to the market.

I entered the market like it was a normal day. Though it was anything but.

Half an hour later, I was in a private taxi travelling along South Bank Road from the market in Yundum near the Banjul International Airport, through Serrekunda and into Banjul. As we drove, I phoned Mum at work. At first she didn't pick up, so I called again. By the background noise, I could tell that she was in a meeting. "Hello?" she said, knowing it was me from the caller ID.

"You're not going to understand this right now," I said quickly. "And I'm sorry. I hope one day I can explain myself."

"You're so foolish. It's very noisy in here," she said. "It's hard to hear you." It wasn't unusual for me to joke with her on the phone, and she must have thought that's what was going on now. "Did you get the groceries?"

Yes, I told her. She wasn't understanding, and I was afraid to say more, worried my phone might be monitored.

"Okay, good," she said. "I'll talk to you later."

And so I let that be our goodbye. Almost an hour had passed, and I knew the men who had followed me to the market would have realized I had slipped away. I slid the SIM card from my phone and broke it in half, tossing it out the window just as I'd seen people in the movies do. If my phone was being tracked, I hoped that would throw them off my trail.

As we approached the ferry terminal, the smell of rotten fish discarded from fishing boats near the dock filled my nostrils. Cars full—some overfull—of people, trucks jammed with goods, and pedestrians lining up for tickets all crowded the entrance area. Women dressed in traditional African printed cloth dresses and head wraps carried baskets and bags, some balanced on their heads. Men hefted shopping bags and backpacks; one or two led goats on board. Young men wandered through the crowd, offering to sell tickets for less than the twenty-five dalasis the ticket office charged. "Hey, we aren't going to be travelling so I'm selling my tickets," they said. Were they genuine, counterfeit, stolen? I had no idea. Boys and girls as young as twelve or thirteen moved through the crowd as well, balancing plates of deep-fried dumplings, corn, peanuts or small plastic bags of water on their heads as they tried to sell their goods.

Vendors with wheelbarrows full of mangoes and watermelon circulated too. Off to the side, one woman sat on an overturned plastic bucket next to her cart of oranges, offering passersby slices of the cut-up fruit. I could tell she was Fula, and we exchanged greetings in my language as she offered to sell me her wares. "Not yet, not yet," I said. "I'm just waiting for somebody." I settled onto a cement block next to her, blending into the crowd as I watched the ticket lineup inch forward. I was scared but focused: I had come this far; now I had to figure out how to get across the river.

If the men in black had reported me missing, I reasoned, the Gambia Ports Authority security may have been notified: the ferry was the obvious route for crossing to Barra and then travelling to the Senegal border. To get on, I'd have to buy a ticket and they might ask me for identification. As well, I wasn't sure when the next ferry was due. What if I bought a ticket and then ended up stuck in the pedestrian holding area for hours?

My mother didn't know where I was, nor did anyone else in my family or among my friends. Without the SIM card, I couldn't make calls on my phone. If I was caught here, maybe I'd end up in prison. Or worse. The official story would simply be I'd disappeared. My family would never know what happened to me.

My gaze swept past the terminal entrance, down toward a section of shore. Rotting fish pocked the sand at the water's edge; nearby, men sat, knitting fibre unspooling from a pile between their feet into nets. Small, open fishing boats called pirogues bobbed in the water, and in one, a man with a green fishing net appeared ready to set out. He looked Wolof, which was my mother's tribe. Perhaps this was the solution to my river-crossing dilemma.

"Hey!" I called in Wolof as I made my way toward him. "Can you help me cross over? I will give you a bit more than what I would pay for the ferry." That would be a substantial sum for a single passenger on a small motorboat.

"Okay, okay," he said. There were no life jackets. "Sit in the middle here. You'll be fine." Water splashed into the boat over the gunwales. As dangerous as it looked, the tiny boat still felt safer than the ferry.

"Are you married?" he asked as he pulled the starter cord on the tiny motor. "I'm guessing you're married because you're wearing the niqab. That's good, that's good. More girls should dress like this—it's more modest." It was the kind of remark that under normal circumstances would have launched me into fierce debate, but this day I bit my tongue. Whatever he had to say, I would agree with. He could have told me I was crazy, and I would have just nodded.

And so for thirty minutes or more, the small boat slapped across the Gambia River estuary toward the opposite shore, the sun beating down on us, me agreeing with whatever he said. Finally I climbed ashore on the sandy beach close to the Barra terminal. Nearby, private taxis and passenger vans waited for fares. I slid into a taxi, and fifteen minutes later, I was at the Gambia-Senegal border.

I could see the chocolate-brown building that housed the Gambian Immigration Office, and just beyond it, the metal barricade separating it from the corresponding Senegalese Immigration Office. Though French was the official language of Senegal and English was The Gambia's official tongue, at the border you were as likely to hear Wolof, because the African language, like the tribe, spanned both countries.

So far, I had made three escapes: from the market, across the river, and from the river to the border. Now I faced the most daunting barrier of all. Here I would almost certainly be asked for my identification, and if my departure had been noted, Jammeh's agents at the border would likely already have been alerted to watch for me. I hadn't been sure what I'd face when I got here, and I hadn't planned what my next steps would be. So, as I had at the ferry terminal, I sat. I watched.

I had been to Senegal to visit relatives as a teenager but had always travelled with my mother or other adults. Otherwise, I had never travelled outside The Gambia. I'd never had to navigate the passage myself. Over to one side, I could see town trip taxis—the kind that you hire individually, rather than piling in with other passengers. Could one of them get me across? I wondered. The official border crossing was in front of us, but I was certain these drivers would have other routes as well, jungle roads and paths without customs officers.

I approached one of the drivers. "What would a town trip to the other side cost me?" I asked.

"Ten thousand dalasis," he said. I felt deflated: it was so much more than I had with me that negotiating wasn't an option. I thanked him and moved back to my perch by the side of the road, watching the traffic flow across the border.

The line was a mixture of cars, vans and trucks, including livestock trucks carrying hay, cows or sheep in the back. I had enough money for a bus or shared taxi, but I could see that the passengers in these vehicles were being asked for their papers as they crossed. Not every vehicle faced the same scrutiny. For instance, I saw that the livestock trucks moved through quickly. Those drivers didn't even disembark at the crossing, since the immigration officers just waved some of them on.

Nearby a cattle truck had pulled over to a gas pump. This was my chance, I thought—I could see the driver was Fula, like the orange seller. And so as I walked toward him, I slid into a new character underneath my coverings: a more mature Fula woman with a dying relative in Senegal and no money to pay for a bus. I wasn't sure it would work, but desperation fuelled my pretense. I told him my tale, pleading for him to take me across.

He looked over his shoulder to the truck cab. Inside was room, barely, for three: the driver himself, his apprentice, and if I squeezed in between them, me.

"Are you all right being in the middle?" he said.

Yes, yes, I assured him, my heart pounding with hope that this would work. I just needed to get to the other side and my family would pick me up there, I said.

"Okay, sure," he said. Before he could change his mind, I pulled myself into the middle seat, the gear shift jammed against my thigh, and he climbed into the driver's seat. He turned the key and the engine coughed to life, black smoke pouring out of the exhaust pipe as we joined the line of traffic heading to the crossing.

Through the grimy windshield, I could see the checkpoint over the cars in front of us. The line seemed to have slowed, with officers checking every cab, every car, every shared vehicle, requesting paperwork for all the passengers. Still they seemed to be letting the trucks pass through with less scrutiny.

"Nakala," shouted the driver in greeting to an immigration officer. As the word left his mouth, part of me wanted to reach into the air and grab it, suffocate it, but it floated away across the road. The driver waved. "How are you?" he shouted to the officer. My whole body shrank inside the niqab. I could hear my every breath, feel my gut dropping—not stopping, just dropping and dropping and dropping.

"Good, good, you know," replied the officer with a smile.

And then he waved us through. Past a tiny metal barrier. The longest distance I have ever traveled. Out of The Gambia. Into Senegal. Away from a dictator. Into the unknown.

"Where's your guys at?" asked the driver as he pulled into the parking lot on the Senegalese side of the border.

I felt like I was operating in slow motion, trying desperately to catch up with real time. "Thank you, thank you," I kept repeating as I scrambled out of the truck. "My guys should be here, they'll be here, thank you, thank you."

I waved as he drove away, my palms sticky with sweat. I was here. Now what?

Nearby a tree offered shade from the sun's heat, and three women were sheltering under it. One boiled peanuts in a pot over an open fire. Two others slow-roasted the nuts in sand in a frying pan perched atop a charcoal grill. I made my way over to them and sat. As the warm, nutty scent drifted past me, I was swamped by relief and regret.

What had I done? I'd escaped, but to what? I'd left behind everything I'd ever known in The Gambia. And I could never go back. Jammeh had been president since before I was born.

I couldn't picture the possibility of anyone other than him in power. Robert Mugabe had ruled Zimbabwe since 1980—he was ninety-one and still in control. Jammeh was only in his fifties. I might be forty before I could go home. Or sixty.

I might never be able to go home again.

When I'd left the house, my four-year-old sister, Ida, had been asleep in my bed. Now, I realized I hadn't said goodbye. When she woke up, she would ask where I was. And no one would know. My brother Muhammed wasn't much older than Ida, and he'd be puzzled too at my absence. I had cared for both these children their whole lives, had been almost a second mother to them, Ida especially. My sister Nogoi was almost a teenager. I'd always been a little jealous of her, thought she was Mum's favourite, a feeling that had solidified after Pa Mattar died and Mum became even more watchful over Nogoi and the younger children. Penda, my half-sister, had lived with us since her mother—my father's third wife—had passed away. She and I were close enough in age that friction was more common than affection between us: I thought she didn't give me the kind of respect I tried to show to my older half-siblings, though in retrospect, I see how my bossy big-sisterness must have chafed her. In our extended families, it was common to attach "Sister" or "Brother" to the name of a half-sibling to emphasize the connection, but Penda refused to call me Sister Toufah, the kind of slight between teens that led to constant squabbling between us—and frustrated sighs from my mother. Still, as the reality of my situation sank in, and the possibility of not seeing any of them again started to seem real, I realized how much I loved them all, how small our disagreements now seemed and how important our connections were.

But I'd left to keep them safe as well; I'd left to keep my mother with them. And either way, it was too late to turn back.

Most of my money was gone, used for the taxis and paying the fisherman. What little I had left was still in Gambian dalasi, a currency I knew Senegalese drivers would be reluctant to accept. I could see a small currency exchange office, and so I changed my money to Senegalese francs and bought a cheap SIM card for my phone before heading back out to where the taxis waited.

It had been more than three hours since I'd left the market, and the heat of the day hadn't yet started to cool. Because it was Ramadan, I hadn't had water since before sunrise, and now thirst overwhelmed me. I bought a bottle of water from one of the vendors and gulped it down. I could feel eyes on me: a woman in a niqab breaking fast in public. The only acceptable reason for doing so would be if I were menstruating, but even that was something a pious woman would have hidden, drinking her water out of sight of others so that no one would realize that she was exempt from fasting. But I was past caring.

I pulled out my phone, slid the new SIM card into place and dialed Ahmad Gitteh, a schoolmate a few years older than me who now was at school in Canada. Gitteh had been my older half-sister Hajakaddy's friend when I was younger. Hajakaddy was the eldest daughter of my father's first wife, and I had always admired her, mimicking her tastes: she loved Celine Dion, so I loved Celine Dion; she listened to the Backstreet Boys, so I listened to the Backstreet Boys. She loved theatre and performance, spoke English eloquently and stood up for herself—you always knew what her opinions were.

Gitteh had been a constant presence around our home. At almost six and a half feet tall, he was like a giant, towering more than a foot over my five-foot-four frame, and his personality was big as well. He had a kind of vibrancy that made you notice him. Though he came from a humble background, he was a brilliant student, with top marks in maths and sciences. He had worked briefly as a reporter for The Gambia's state television before Jammeh provided him with a scholarship to study in Canada.

One result of travelling beyond your country's borders and seeing it from the outside is that you discover things you weren't aware of while living inside the bubble of state-controlled media. At university, Gitteh read about President Jammeh's cruelty, the accusations about those he had had killed, the journalists who disappeared during his time in power—crimes that were only whispered about in The Gambia. Perhaps Gitteh asked too many questions, but whatever the reason, Jammeh cut off his scholarship and stranded him penniless in Canada. Gitteh managed to continue his studies, and in the process he became an active advocate against Jammeh and his government, writing for online sites that reported on The Gambia from outside the country.

Thankfully he answered his phone. "I'm in Senegal," I told him. "Do you know anyone who can help me, someone you really trust who doesn't work for the government?" I hadn't spoken to Gitteh in months, but I knew he might have connections outside The Gambia. In my desperation, I hoped he would help me.

"Are you all right?" Gitteh asked.

"I'm fine now," I said. "I promise I'll explain more later, but please, can you put me in touch with someone?"

"Don't you have family in Senegal?" he asked. It was true: there were relatives of my mother here, but, I told him, I didn't know who I could trust.

"I'll text you a name and number," he said.

The ping of his text followed swiftly: Ebrima Chongan. I had heard of Chongan before but didn't then know his whole story. Chongan, who had been a deputy inspector of police at the time of the coup that put Jammeh in power in 1994, had tried to rally police to help keep the democratically elected government in place. As Jammeh solidified his power, he'd had Chongan and other police officers arrested and held in Mile Two Central Prison, The Gambia's nearly one-hundred-year-old central state prison. The sprawling, bleak cement structure near Banjul was notorious as a rat- and mosquito-infested hellhole, and under Jammeh's rule it became synonymous with state-sponsored torture and abuse of political prisoners. Over the next 994 days, Chongan was one of them: at one point, an interrogator placed a gun in his mouth, telling him to say his final prayers. Chongan was eventually put on trial by Jammeh's regime, and then in the late 1990s, was exiled to the U.K. He had gone on to study law and now worked as a policy adviser in the British Home Office.

I tried Chongan's number and got no answer, so I called Gitteh back.

"Get to Dakar and try him again when you get there," he advised.

Off to the side, I could see a taxi called Sept Places—French for "seven places," the number of passengers it would carry. A regular shared taxi might take three or four, but this vehicle, the cheapest option, squeezed in an extra row.

I climbed into the back row as men filled the seats around me. One other lone woman sat at the front of the vehicle. I sank inside myself, trying to disappear. Around me, the others chattered. Dakar was a seven-hour drive away.

And then I heard his name. To most Senegalese, Jammeh was the butt of a joke: the crazy man on the other side of the border. Now someone in the car had brought up the latest story from the Gambian side, about a Christian cemetery that Jammeh had expropriated as he targeted minority Christians. Voices erupted around me, hands waving in the air, as a Gambian passenger defended Jammeh.

I did my best to be invisible.

"Hey, aren't you Gambian?" said the man next to me, trying to reel me in to the conversation.

"Yes, yes," I said. "But I don't know anything about political issues."

He laughed. "Who doesn't know about Jammeh? Do you work for him? That's why you are scared to talk about him. Are you a supporter?"

The irony. One part of me wanted to say, well, let me tell you about President Jammeh. That would quiet the car. The other part of me slid into another character.

I giggled. I made myself stupid. "We just pray it will get better someday," I squeaked out. And I made myself invisible again. For the rest of the drive, I was like a pebble at the bottom of a stream, the conversation flowing around and over and past me. I drifted in and out of sleep.

And then we arrived in Dakar.

It was almost midnight as I uncurled myself from the back seat, stretching the kinks and cramps out of my aching muscles. As soon as I stood, I needed to pee, and so I ran over to the public washroom at the side of the garage where the buses and taxis disgorged their passengers. I paid the attendant some coins to enter and went inside to relieve myself.

When I came out, I stood near the well-lit building. It would be 1 a.m. in England. Under any kind of normal circumstances, it was too late to call Chongan.

But my circumstances weren't normal. As I slid my back down the wall and looked at my phone, I hoped a man who knew what it was like to end up somewhere you couldn't come back from would be willing to help me connect with those who might protect me.

4

"I HAVE THE GIRL RIGHT HERE"

The two men in the SUV stare ahead. Around them, people jog and exercise along the beachfront in Dakar's Almadies neighbourhood, a popular destination for relaxing near the ocean or working out using the outdoor exercise machines and weightlifting benches that dot the beach. Young people especially come to the area after work. It is early evening, but the sun has already dipped below the horizon and the moon is up.

The man in the driver's seat is compact and clothed in suit pants and a crisp white shirt buttoned up to the neck, his hair closely cropped, eyes hidden behind reflective sunglasses. The man in the back passenger seat is taller, leaner, his long-sleeved shirt untucked and the buttons on his shirt cuffs undone as well. Anyone watching might think the men are focused on the activity outside the vehicle, but the scene beyond the windshield is of little concern. They could be businessmen, discussing a deal, though they aren't: the driver is a Senegalese security officer, the other a police chief.

From the front passenger seat, I stare ahead too, not really seeing the beach or the people going about their normal end-of-day activities, but also trying not to see what I am describing to these two officers. I've already told the driver some of this. Now he wants me to share it with the man in the back seat. I stammer my way through my story, trying to balance clarity with self-protection as I describe the horror of my assault to strangers. My words are inadequate, incomplete. *He did this to me . . . He put his hands here . . . He did this with his thing, and he did that . . .* And now I'm crying, the tears salting my words.

Until this point, I have shed my tears alone as I revisited what happened in my head, trying to make sense of it. But now I'm talking to these two men. Two strangers in whom my hope for the future and my safety lies.

I gulp around my tears. The men are silent. And then the man in the passenger seat just starts saying "Non." And he says it over and over: "Non, non, non, non, non." I don't speak French, but I know what this word means: no. A word I used. A word Jammeh ignored.

I panic. Does this mean he doesn't believe me?

"I can't stay in The Gambia," I say, my words spilling over each other, racing to convince these men to help me. "I need your help." I try to make my request small, simple, easy to say yes to. "Am I safe here in Senegal? Can I live here quietly on the down-low?" I feel my desperation rising in my chest.

The driver cuts me off. "Don't even think about it," he says. "Nowhere in Senegal is safe for you because Jammeh has his agents here too. You're safe here for a short time, but you'll never live a normal life here. You'd be a prisoner."

My thoughts spin. *What now?* I'm not thinking about where else I can go; my brain can't process the possibility of other options. I'm just stuck: *What now? What now?*

And then the passenger's phone rings. I don't understand all he's saying because he's speaking in French, but I can tell from the tone of his voice that he's speaking with respect. He switches to Wolof and I grasp his words. "I have the girl right here. She's not some teenager that went missing whose parents are looking for her." I can hear frustration in his voice, rising anger. "He violated this girl. She is sitting right here."

I don't think he's angry at me. I think he's angry *for* me. Inside my spinning thoughts, hope blooms.

I'd arrived in Dakar two days earlier. As I climbed out of the taxi, it sunk in that I was in a foreign country, alone on a city street past midnight, with little money and just my phone as my lifeline. I couldn't call home in case President Jammeh's police were monitoring my mother's phone calls. (I had no way of knowing how well founded my fears were: I would later find out that my mother was already being questioned by police at the station, the officers confronting her with a log of her cellphone calls.) Gitteh had given me Ebrima Chongan's WhatsApp contact details, but he wasn't online, so my messages were going unanswered. I didn't have enough credits to call him via normal long-distance. I texted Gitteh again. "I cannot reach Chongan. Can you notify him to come on WhatsApp?"

I was crouched against the wall of the garage where the buses and taxis congregated. I'd peeled off my niqab earlier as I tried to shed the dust and sweat of the day's travel and anxiety, ducking into a public toilet to clean up. An old man sat outside the door, collecting money for entry: two francs for a pee, five for "using the toilet." I laughed: How would he know? The toilet was an open hole over which you squatted, no running water inside. Then I realized the extra charge was for water from a kettle to wash yourself afterwards, and so I paid extra for water to pat under my sweaty armpits and wash the dust from my legs and feet. I was tired, dirty, afraid. No longer a college-going, scholarship-winning drama and stage performer. Now just a girl, alone in a city I did not know. Trying to be invisible. And as devastating as that identity shift was, as lonely as the night felt, I comforted myself by repeating that this was the best of my limited options. No one knew where I was, for now. I was safe, for now.

Around me, the city was quieting as the minutes ticked past midnight. I tried to calm myself by concentrating on the sights and sounds and smells around me. The scent of ripe mangoes, sold from wheelbarrows by hawkers on the street during the day, their pits and peels discarded in the gutters, mingled with the odour of gasoline that had spilled on the pavement as taxi drivers topped up their tanks. There was the hint of café Touba in the air as well, the strong black coffee flavoured with djar—Guinea pepper—and sometimes cloves, revered by many Senegalese for its connection to Sheikh Ahmadu Bamba Mbackeh. The Shaikh, a Sufi saint and Islamic founder of Senegal's holy city of Touba, had led a pacifist struggle against French colonial powers while preaching the value of hard work, civility and the virtue of overcoming negative instincts.

I watched as end-of-shift taxi drivers cleaned their cars, but even as I tried to stay calm, the street, the scene all seemed to be rotating in slow motion around me. Tears rolled down my cheeks. Why had I left? Maybe there had been other options. Maybe what happened to me wasn't so bad. I'd never been away from home alone before, never spent a night outside my country's borders on my own. And I kept thinking about Mum. What was she thinking? In that moment, everything I thought I'd done right in my escape seemed wrong.

I tried Chongan again.

"Hello?"

"Hello, Uncle Chongan. You don't know me," I said quickly, before he could hang up, adding "uncle" to his name as a sign of respect for an elder. "My name is Toufah Jallow."

"Ah, I know you," he said. "I watched you on TV and know you just won the pageant." I was both surprised and not: friends and relatives far from The Gambia watched the pageant online as a way of staying connected to the home they'd left behind, but it hadn't occurred to me that Chongan might have been one of them.

"That's great," I said. "I'm in Senegal and no one really knows. Ahmad Gitteh gave me your name and number. I thought I could trust you. I really need to get help. I don't know how or who—do you know anyone here who can help me? Or make sure that I get to a safe place to talk to safe people?"

I could hear curiosity in his voice. "What happened?"

I couldn't bring myself to say it, not over the phone, not to a strange man. "I can't really explain it all, but my life is in danger." There was a pause on the other end of the line, as I think he started to put things together. He didn't push me for more.

"I know a lot of people in Senegal," he said, "but there's one that I trust. He's high up in the ranks. I'm not going to tell you what job he really does because that is up to him, but he is someone that can maybe help you meet other Gambians that are seeking asylum, other refugees. I'll call him."

A few minutes later my phone pinged. Chongan hadn't been able to reach his contact but had left him a message and passed his name—Omar Topp—and number on to me. I dialed the number: no answer.

I put the phone on speaker and dialed again, hoping that staring at the screen would make him pick up. Seeing it ring seemed more powerful than just hearing it in my ear. The ringing stopped: he'd rejected the call. I called again. Rejected again. And then my phone rang as he called me back. His voice sounded like someone who has just woken from sleep.

I rushed to explain that Chongan had given me his name and number. "Yes, yes," he said. "It's very late. Chongan did tell me about you. I'll get back to you tomorrow."

I felt a moment of elation, but as he hung up, I crashed back to earth. I'd hoped he'd come get me, but now it was clear I wouldn't see him for hours. I drew a breath. *I can do this,* I thought.

By now, it was almost 3 a.m. I remembered that a friend who had moved to the United States had said he had a brother in Dakar. It was hours earlier in America, so I wouldn't be waking him. I called on WhatsApp, told him I was in Senegal and needed a place to stay.

"Yeah, yeah," he said. "I can get my brother to pick you up, but he lives with two other boys. It's really late there—what are you doing in Senegal?" I didn't tell him much, just that I needed a place to stay, and he gave me his brother's number.

The young man answered my late-night call and came to get me. His willingness didn't surprise me: his brother was older and perhaps helped him by sending money home to Senegal; in our community, a request to welcome a distant relative or friend wasn't uncommon. His place was a room shared with two other young men who worked construction, all three sharing two mattresses on the floor. When I arrived, I took a shower and then sat outside, where my friend's brother found me. He held a towel wrapped around some bedding he'd fashioned into a sleeping pad. "I'll sleep here," he said. "You can have my bed." The other two boys had moved their mattress to the corner of the room and put up a cotton sheet, efforts designed to respect my space. As I lay down to try to sleep, my feet stretched past the bottom of the small mattress and touched the floor. *What have I done?* I kept asking myself, as tears started to flow again. Exhaustion finally won, and I slipped into unconsciousness.

The two roommates left for work at dawn, while my friend's brother stayed with me. My phone rang not long after. It was Topp. "I'm just on my way to work. I can see you at 5 p.m. when I'm finished. Where will you be?" We agreed he'd call me and we'd figure out where to meet then.

Barely twenty-four hours had passed since I'd left my home.

As five o'clock approached, I waited for Topp's call, worrying as the minutes ticked past that he'd forgotten me. My phone rang near six. "Where are you?" he asked. I stumbled to explain my location, but since I didn't know the landmarks or streets of Dakar, my directions made little sense. I handed my phone to my friend's brother: "Can you explain where I am?"

Minutes later, a white SUV pulled up. The tinted passenger window rolled down. The driver's dark sunglasses shielded his eyes. He was dressed in what we called British style, like a businessman, in a red suit and white shirt. He told me to get in. I strained to see into the back seat to ensure no one was there. "Are you Topp?" I asked. He nodded and I climbed in.

"Do you still have your phone?" he asked.

I looked down at the iPhone in my hand, the one that had been one of my pageant gifts. "Yes."

"You cannot have it," he said. "It can be tracked."

"But I took out the SIM card."

"Still."

"I turned it off."

"Still."

He pulled the car into traffic, accelerating into the flow, darting in and out and around. In minutes, we were weaving through a marketplace like the one at home in Serrekunda, where jewellery stalls sat shoulder to shoulder with clothing and electronics shops. We pulled to a stop in front of a phone shop. Topp held out his hand for my iPhone and disappeared into the store. Fifteen minutes later he was back and handed me a compact black Nokia phone. No apps: just a game and a contacts folder. It wasn't for me to call others with; it was so that he could call me. "Don't call anybody. If you want to talk to anyone, I can call them for you. But now we need to talk."

For the first time, I had a sense of what my situation must look like to someone outside of it. Who was I? Why should he trust me? Did I look traumatized? Was I putting him at risk somehow?

He pulled back into the early evening flow of traffic. "We've got a long ride," he said. "The traffic is tough. Why don't you tell me what happened?"

I began to explain, still wary of sharing too much detail, struggling to put it all into words, but feeling I owed him the truth for whatever risks he might be taking to assist me. I wanted to earn his trust—and keep his help. My French was poor, his English poor as well, so we spoke in Wolof, another of the languages in the region that has no direct word for rape, its closest a word that, translated into English, means something like "inappropriate touching" or "leaning over" or even "stealing a tie." And so I told him President Jammeh had harassed me, that he'd touched me, and though the words were inadequate, though they cloaked the hideousness of what had happened in words that are easier to hear, he knew what I meant.

"How old are you again?" he finally asked, shaking his head when I said, "Nineteen."

"You know, I've received a lot of Gambians here," he said. "Political opponents, you know, journalists escaping because they wrote an article that wasn't in favour of him and he put them in jail, businessmen that he took their businesses from. But this . . . You kind of hear about it, but you don't. Maybe women come but they keep quiet. I've never talked to a victim."

He paused. "How old are you again?" he asked. I repeated my age, not sure why he was asking. From the time my hips, behind and breasts had started to curve from my flatter child's body, men had asked me how old I was, trying to measure whether they could safely cross whatever age barrier they maintained in their minds. It was a tactic so familiar to me that I had difficulty trusting he wasn't doing the same. It wouldn't occur to me until much later that he was measuring the gap between my age and Jammeh's.

We drove for a while in silence, finally pulling up to a motel. "You are going to stay here for the night," he said as I climbed out of the vehicle. "I have to make some phone calls because I don't really know what to do with you. I will get back to you in the morning." His words emphasized again that my situation, my claim, was unique, that this was, for him, a new landscape to be navigated. That awareness made me feel even more at risk, more alone. He showed me how to lock the door, warning me not to open it for anyone. "No one should be knocking on this door. If they say room service, you say you don't need room service. If I'm coming, I'll call you and I'll be on the phone with you and tell you to open the door when I am here. Do not call anybody. Do not go on Facebook. Do not . . ." His warnings piled up and my fear ratcheted up as well.

I needed to let my family know I was safe. Now that I had a new phone, I asked how I could get a message to my mother. It was still too dangerous to call her directly, he told me, because her phone was likely monitored. Perhaps later I could reach my mother through an app such as Viber, he said, to leave her voice notes, but for now we agreed I could call my aunt Marie in the U.K., the one who had sent me the money I'd used to escape.

"Toufah? What's going on? Your mum called me to say she couldn't find you and she doesn't know where you are." Her voice was panicked.

I told her I was in Senegal.

"When you asked me for money, I didn't know it was for leaving the country!" Her concern for me was mixed with irritation at the distress I had caused my mother and unease with having been the one who had unwittingly paid for my journey. "The National Intelligence Agency questioned her and Penda," she said. "What the hell is going on? What did you do? Your mum is going through so much hell right now!"

While I knew I was in danger, it was still shocking to hear that my mother and half-sister had been questioned by the

NIA. They were rumoured to torture people, and some who were detained by them simply disappeared.

The police had a call log from my cellphone, she said, and it showed that I'd talked to Mum the day I escaped. "They keep telling her, 'The call was five minutes long, she must have told you something,'" said my aunt, and no one believed Mum when she said that most of the call had been us trying to hear each other over the background noise of the meeting she had been in.

As well, my aunt told me, an online Gambian news site had published an article saying I had run away because the president wanted to marry me and I had said no, framing my disappearance as a foolish response by an irresponsible young woman. "Did he really ask you to marry him?" she asked.

"It's not the whole story," I told her, sickened that what had happened to me was being publicly framed as a rejected marriage request. "Just tell Mum that I am fine. I am in Senegal in a safe house. I'll call her on Viber when I can. Your calls from the U.K. won't be questioned—you're her sister. Just let her know I'm okay, that I'm in Senegal and I had to run away because my life is at risk."

Why hadn't I contacted family in Senegal? Marie asked.

"I cannot do that," I said. "I am safer where I am."

She paused, I think because she realized what this could mean—that it was safer for them and for me for us not to be in contact. "For real," she said, her tone serious, the anger and blaming gone. "What is going on?"

"I was hurt," I said. "I am an exiled person now. I cannot go back home." Before I'd gotten the last words out of my mouth, she started to speak. "Oh my God, oh my God." She repeated the phrase again and again. "My little girl who was just born yesterday is exiled. A refugee. Just like that?"

We were talking in my language, and I tried to find a word that would express what had happened. "He violated me," I said, though the word I used in our language was closer to "he troubled me." It was as if we were speaking in code, all these not-quite-right words offering what looked like protection but was really a cloak of shame worn by the victim rather than the rapist. Details remained unspoken and perpetrators were never confronted with the reality of what they had done, their brutality hidden behind words designed not to offend a listener's ear. But in that moment my aunt grasped something of what had happened. It would be years before she would know the full truth of it.

"Please, just tell Mum I'm all right. I will tell you more later. If I stayed in that country, I was going to be killed. He drugged me. That's why I had to run. I ran because I had to run."

As we hung up, guilt washed over me. I'd run away to protect my family, taking steps at each stage that I thought would keep them safe: not telling them what had happened, what I was going to do, where I was going or where I was. But my silence hadn't shielded them in the way I had wanted it to. It wouldn't have been safe for them or for me had I stayed, but by running away, I'd still put them in harm's way. And I couldn't hold those two thoughts together in my head: that I was protecting them, but that protecting them also put them at risk. It didn't make sense to me. I felt like there was no way to win.

All I could picture was Mum and Penda at the police station, so confused about what had happened to me, being interrogated, being screamed at to answer these questions. What if Mum shouted back at them? What if they didn't believe that she didn't know where I was? Was she better off in the dark, as I had left her, or should I have told her more? If I had told her, maybe she would have known what to say to them, what stories to tell. Maybe I had underestimated her. Maybe I'd made wrong decisions every step of the way.

But at the same time, I knew my mother wouldn't pretend or lie; she'd simply fight her battle even if winning seemed unlikely. I'd seen her do it when she'd discovered that a family friend had molested some of the children in our extended family home. When others tried to convince her to keep it quiet, to treat it as a family matter, she'd taken all of the children to the medical centre for examinations. Community elders begged her not to take it to the police, but she marched to the station. She didn't let it go. This wasn't a woman who would be silent knowing that her daughter had been raped, even if her rapist was the president. And I was convinced her protests would have gotten her killed.

Topp left me alone with my thoughts, telling me he'd be back the next day, warning me again not to call anyone. I turned the lock after he left. And then the tears came. I've heard people say, "It was like a dam broke." The river that flowed through me wasn't clear and cool and soothing, though. It was full of muddy, swirling rage, polluted by the memory of the foul stench of Jammeh—all the anger and sadness and fear and despair that had accumulated inside me in the days since he'd attacked me, the emotions I'd had to lock up and hide as I'd tried to survive and then escape. I'd been so focused on the next step and the next step and the next step that I hadn't lifted my head up to see the horizon I was facing. I was now a fugitive in a foreign country, relying on strangers to help me survive.

It was a night of screaming and crying and hitting walls. Alone. Like a prisoner in a cell, punished for a crime that was not mine.

When Topp returned the next day, he told me, "We're going to meet someone." He'd spoken to a friend, a senior police officer who wanted to speak to us privately, outside of his office.

We drove to a nearby beach in Almadies, pulled off the tarmac onto the sandy shoulder of the beach and waited. Just after 7 p.m., a car pulled up and parked a few car-lengths away. The driver, a tall, fit Senegalese man, unfolded himself from behind the wheel and walked toward us, climbing into the back seat.

The two men exchanged familiar greetings—the equivalent of "Hey buddy, how you doing?" here in North America. Then the stranger turned to me and asked, "How are you? Topp told me about you, but I think I missed some things, because I'm a bit confused. First, what's your name and how old are you?"

I repeated my name and age.

"I'm the head of the police, you know?" he said.

I was impressed: I can't get better help than this, I thought.

He asked me what had happened, and it all started to spill out of me. I described the whole incident, crying and talking and crying some more.

When I finished, he was silent for a few moments. And that's when he started repeating in French, "Non, non, non, non." Over and over.

Couldn't I just stay here quietly in Senegal? I asked. And that's when Topp told me I wouldn't ever be safe here.

The other man's phone interrupted us. He spoke French at first and then switched to Wolof. "No, no, no, that is not what happened," he said, and told whoever was on the line that he had me with him and that I was not some teenager who had run away from home—I was a girl who had been violated by the president of The Gambia. "If you like, I can come to your office tomorrow to talk more about it." He hung up.

The caller was Senegal's minister of the interior, relaying a request that the president of Senegal had received from Jammeh's office: a silly teenager had gone missing, a pageant winner. Could the Senegalese authorities at the border and elsewhere keep a watch for her and return her immediately should she be found? Her parents were worried.

"Does the president of The Gambia call the president of Senegal every time a girl goes missing?" the police officer said in disbelief after ending the call. While Senegal and The Gambia shared many cultural ties, relations between the two governments were often strained, especially since Senegal had elected Macky Sall as president three years earlier. Much to President Jammeh's irritation, President Sall allowed Gambian dissidents based in Senegal to amplify their criticism of Jammeh and his regime. Jammeh in return turned a blind eye to Gambian-based Senegalese rebels fighting for the independence of his neighbouring country's Casamance region. "What is so special about this girl that you're not only sending your police but you're calling us to have the girl returned?" the officer asked, rhetorically.

My heart pounded. Yes, yes! "Degala," I said, a Wolof word meaning "exactly." It was clear what I had told him allowed him to see the request through a different lens: a president desperate to control a girl with damaging information. I realized in that moment how lucky I had been, to find Topp, to talk to this officer before the other story made its way to him, to have the chance to tell my story in a situation where it didn't sound like an excuse or a fabrication.

The police chief announced that he had to think this through as he exited Topp's car. He'd be back in touch soon.

That night sleep wouldn't come, and I paced from the washroom to the bedroom, pausing every now and then to sneak a look through my curtains to the street outside. Would Jammeh's people find me before I found safety?

The next day word came from the police chief: he'd had a meeting with the minister of the interior. In their initial conversations with the Gambian authorities, assurances had been given to Jammeh's people that I would be returned, but now that the Senegalese knew what had actually happened, they wouldn't send me back. Neither, though, could they let me stay in Senegal. "Find a country willing to accept the girl," the minister had told the police chief. I was safe from Jammeh for now, but my future depended on whether another country would be willing to grant me refugee status.

I was moved from the motel to a small apartment. The days that followed were punctuated with meetings with embassy staff, human rights organizations and lawyers. In between, I slept—hours and hours of sleeping, as if my body couldn't drink in enough unconsciousness. When I awoke, I cooked. Topp or one of his security men would pick up groceries for me, and I distracted myself by preparing meals like the ones I had cooked at home for my siblings and mother, even as I tried not to think about when I might see them again. Still I barely ate what I made. Worry filled my stomach instead.

And one specific worry tormented me. Maybe I was sleeping so much because I was pregnant? The possibility sickened me. In The Gambia, being pregnant and unmarried was shameful—ironically, horribly, more shameful than being a rapist. In my mind, I bargained with God: please, I'd rather have a sexually transmitted infection than be pregnant. I examined myself in the mirror, looking for signs. My stomach ached from anxiety and all I could picture was a child inside me, kicking. Rationally, I knew that even if I had been pregnant, the fetus would have been a tiny collection of cells with no feet to kick with yet, but fear magnified my every ache, my every twinge. The trauma Jammeh had inflicted on my body spread through my cells, invading me. My guts were in my throat. When I ate, I vomited. With this fear coupled with the anxiety of not knowing what my future held, I felt myself spinning into a kind of mania.

And oh my God, I hated this imaginary baby.

I started planning how I would disappear from the world— not simply finding a safe haven as a refugee in another country, but erasing myself, changing my name, pretending I was dead. The possibility of abortion floated at the edges of my awareness, but I didn't even really know what that meant or how it happened. Disappearance, erasure—of myself—was all I could imagine. All I wanted.

Looking back now, I'm not sure what I thought erasure would actually mean. But the weight of shame that a pregnancy outside of marriage brought with it, the sinfulness my Muslim faith judged abortion to be . . . At the Muslim school I had attended as a youngster, we'd been taught women's bodies were sources of sinfulness, responsible for tempting men, causing them to behave in sinful ways. The results of those sins were at least in part our fault—and pregnancy would be further proof of my responsibility for Jammeh's sins. I felt as if my choices were hemmed in by darkness, and in that darkness, the voices of clerics and culture grew louder, all whispering that I was to blame for what had happened. It wasn't really an option to change my name and disappear. I think it was a literal erasure of myself I was actually contemplating: suicide. A sin I couldn't bring myself to even name, scurrying like a rodent at the edges of my consciousness in the darkness Jammeh had brought into my life.

It would be years before I could admit to myself that shame had pushed me that far, and even as I look back on myself now, a part of me fears my admission.

Because I do not know what would have happened if I had been pregnant.

And so I stared at my reflection in the bathroom mirror, examining my body from all angles, ignoring the lingering physical pain of Jammeh's assault and trying instead to see if my body showed signs of a child growing inside me. As the days passed, I tried to push the idea away, even as fatigue continued to overwhelm me. One afternoon, I fell into a deep sleep on the couch, only waking when Topp arrived with more groceries and shook me out of my slumber. "You are sleeping your life away," he teased me, not meaning anything by it. But his words shook loose my worry as well.

"To be honest, I think something is wrong," I said. "I think I might be pregnant."

He didn't ask me any questions or offer any advice; he simply arranged for a clinic appointment the next day for pregnancy and STI tests. When all the tests came back negative, relief overwhelmed me and the thoughts of self-erasure faded.

"She's a gold digger!" The commentator's voice on the Gambian radio station was emphatic. "She ate all the man's money and then left when he wouldn't give her more!"

The "she" he was talking about was me. In the empty hours between appointments with embassies and human rights organizations, as we searched for a country that would accept me as a refugee, I listened to Gambian online radio stations, my anxiety and frustration notching up with each inaccurate report about where I was, each rumour-filled talk show speculating on my motives for leaving. I'd said nothing publicly about Jammeh's assault, and so my reasons for fleeing remained a mystery to people at home. With rumours circulating that he had proposed marriage, my disappearance seemed even more incomprehensible: in a country where marriages were frequently arranged, where a woman's success was measured by her husband's wealth and power, a proposal from the country's most powerful man was like winning the lottery. Who in her right mind would say no?

"Honestly, Toufah is not a smart girl," one of my older half-sisters had said, I learned later, as the rumours swirled about where I was and why I'd left.

In the days just after I'd arrived in Senegal, Ahmad Gitteh had called to put me in touch with Fatu Camara, a former Gambian television star who had hosted the country's first television talk show in the early 2000s. *The Fatu Show* became one of the most watched programs in The Gambia. She had gone on to work for President Jammeh as a press secretary, but in 2013 had been arrested and detained without contact with the outside world for twenty-five days, accused of passing information about Jammeh to a Gambian news site in the U.S. After being released, Camara had escaped to Senegal and made her way to America, where she'd launched the Fatu Network, an online news site about The Gambia with a wide audience among the Gambian diaspora. Gitteh worked for the network as a program host, and Fatu, he said, could perhaps help me with contacts and getting my side of the story out.

When I first spoke with her, Fatu gave me names of human rights workers to contact for help. Later, she called back to ask if I would do an on-air interview, catching me just as Topp and I left for a meeting with an embassy official. "Yes, yes," I said. "Call me back later and I'll do the interview."

I didn't really have any idea of what I would say, and I hadn't thought through the implications of speaking publicly about what had happened. I put the interview out of my mind and went off to the embassy meeting, not knowing that over the next few hours, Fatu's network would promote my upcoming interview as a tell-all where the world would finally hear the real reasons I had left and the secrets I had been keeping.

Those promos prompted Jammeh's fixer, Jimbee, to call my mother. "Why would Toufah do this?" she asked Mum.

"Do what?" My mother hadn't heard the Fatu Network announcements.

"Toufah is about to come on the radio," Jimbee told her. "I don't know what she's going to say. It's awful!" Tell Toufah she doesn't have to do this, Jimbee told my mother. Tell her she should *not* do this. But my mother had no way of reaching me.

Though I was unable to speak to my mother and hadn't heard about Jimbee's orders, as the time for the interview grew close, I realized on my own that I couldn't go through with it. As long as my family was still in The Gambia, I couldn't say anything. Someday, maybe, I could sponsor my family to join me in whatever country I lived in, and perhaps then I could speak out. The idea that Jammeh might lose power didn't occur to me.

I sent Fatu Camara a message. I was backing out of the interview. And into the gap my silence left, a new picture of me was painted as other news outlets covered the story. Commentators said I was a whore. They said that Jammeh's wife, Zineb, was so glamorous and beautiful, he would never be tempted by someone like me. Over the days that followed, instead of hearing me on the radio, my mother heard radio hosts talking about how the land she'd worked extra jobs to buy, the cinder-block house built on land we had cleared with our own hands, had been a gift from the president, as if we did not exist before him and all we had came from him. The stacks of exams she brought home to mark so she would be paid pennies for each graded paper, the long hours into the night when she studied by candlelight for her own university exams so that she could qualify for a better job? The extra contract she'd taken on with a foreign NGO, paid in American dollars, that had allowed her to buy her land in the first place? The hours spent working away from her children? In trying to erase me, they erased my mother's accomplishments too.

While it would be easy to say it was just Jammeh's supporters who painted me this way, in truth, many in The Gambia believed the worst about me. Later I would hear from friends and family who supported me, but even some of them were puzzled. Why would I reject marriage to my country's most powerful and wealthy man? My culture—like so many patriarchal cultures around the world—left no space to imagine I might have other reasons to flee. And I had no way to safely speak out to counter the image of me that bloomed in the soil of misogyny, fertilized with rumour. It didn't escape my notice that these were judgments made about me even though I hadn't publicly accused him of rape. I couldn't imagine what backlash I'd face if I told the truth.

And through it all, I couldn't help but think this was somehow my fault. The guilt was overwhelming, even as I ranted to Topp about the lies that were being broadcast. "You know, you don't have to listen to those programs," he told me. But I couldn't stop tuning in. I thought, *I haven't even said anything about the president, and this is what I'm faced with?* And though the broadcasts filled me with rage and confusion, listening to them was a kind of self-punishment, numbing the pain I carried by focusing on these hurtful words. I knew I wasn't what they were saying I was, but maybe I deserved all of this for choosing to run away, or for not somehow avoiding being raped in the first place.

I veered between wanting to confront them and wanting to rise above it all. I thought about the ways the women I admired might react. I imagined my aunt Marie intimidating them with her fierceness—and a few carefully thrown "fuck offs" as well. I pictured Oprah taking the high road, gazing down at the small, angry men who had once harmed her but who now could only envy her success and wealth. And I thought of my mother. Unlike her sister Marie, she wasn't likely to hurl swear words or throw punches. But neither would she allow herself to be pushed out of the way. She would plant her feet firmly, wait for the right time to act and then do what she had to do, always putting her family's safety first.

But my problem was I didn't know what to do. And so I stayed silent, while anger bubbled inside me at the injustice, and Topp and I continued to search for a country that would take me in.

Through it all, Topp was steady at my side. He smiled often, his outlook frequently lifting my mood. When posing a question, he would lower his glasses with a finger and peer over the top. We were both products of the society in which we had been raised, and sometimes his questions or comments reflected that, but if I told him something was hurtful, he was never reluctant to apologize. "I am a constant student," he told me, "forever in a learning state." I appreciated his openness, his willingness to reflect and reconsider.

The human rights organizations we visited were supportive but cautious. Some, like the United Nations High Commissioner for Human Rights and Amnesty International, said they would investigate my claims if I wished them to do so, but it would take time. I fell outside the mandate of Article 19, an organization geared to helping journalists under threat. Their executive director, Fatou Jagne, who I later came to see as a mentor, had done so much for refugees of the regime over the decades. She provided me with money to help pay for some personal items and expenses, a kindness I welcomed. The embassies were equally cautious: the Americans interviewed me but told me investigating my claims could take months or longer. The interviewer at the British embassy—a man named Nigel—was friendly and supportive, and I left that meeting feeling hopeful even as he said he needed to send his report of our conversation to his superiors in order to move the file forward. I didn't hear from him again.

Each interview terrified me. Topp came with me to them all. Though the embassy interviewers often asked me if I wanted him to leave, I always asked him to stay: I wanted someone on my side. I'd never been in offices like these, never been in situations where one person asked me questions while someone else took notes and a third person simply watched it all. What were they writing? What were they thinking? What if I said something wrong? Sometimes I didn't understand the questions, and I wasn't always sure they understood my answers. I found it hard to meet their eyes, the confident young woman who had spoken her mind to a president replaced with a timid girl afraid of saying the wrong thing.

And there was a lot of crying.

As the meetings continued and I was called back to answer more questions, fill in more blanks, Topp raised another possibility: perhaps I could be accepted into a refugee camp in a friendly West African country while waiting for word from the embassies we'd visited. The Senegalese government wouldn't indefinitely pay for the apartment they'd moved me into in Dakar. Ghana and South Africa were both possibilities, but there were concerns there as well. Because my accusations were so serious, it would be dangerous for me to be in a refugee camp with other Gambians, some of whom might be Jammeh supporters. The United Nations High Commissioner for Refugees (UNHCR) representative was concerned my safety in the camp couldn't be guaranteed. He told us he'd take the file back to his committee again to see if there were other options.

The call to come in for an interview with a Canadian representative seemed like just another on a growing list of
appointments, though the woman who spoke with me
seemed colder than the American and British officials I'd
already met. Her office was tucked in the back corner of the
UNHCR's five-storey white office building in the Almadies
neighbourhood, not far from where Topp and I had met with
the police chief. The front of the building featured photos of
mothers and children, smiling faces filled with hope. At the
entrance, topped with barbed wire, a security guard swapped
our ID for visitor passes and waved us into the air-conditioned
building. The woman who met us was older and unsmiling.
She took us to her office where she asked me question after
question, her face showing no encouragement or sympathy
as she made notes of my answers.

"All right," she said, pushing back from the table and turning to the door. "Give me two minutes."

When she returned, she still looked stern. "You didn't tell
me about the furniture he bought for your family. Why did
you leave that out?"

My stomach turned and tears filled my eyes. I assumed
she thought I was a liar. It's true, I'd left that out. Part of
me wanted to argue it wasn't relevant, but it was also true
I'd skipped over those details because I didn't want to have
to explain the logistics of the gifts: which were pageant gifts,
which were personal gifts, who bought them and when. My
palms were sweaty and I rubbed them on my legs to calm
myself as I tried to fill in the gaps she pointed to in my story. I
don't remember all of her questions, but every few minutes

she'd exit the room, then return to ask for more information. Did I think I was safe in Senegal? What were the names and ages of all of my family members? And then she asked whether I still had the dress I was wearing the night of the incident.

Yes, I told her, I had the dress. I didn't share with her the details of how we had gotten it to Senegal; she didn't ask. I had arrived with just the clothing I was wearing, as I'd been afraid that carrying anything unusual to the market would tip off the minders who were following me. But once I was in Dakar, Topp had arranged for a complicated pass-along to get the dress as well as official documents such as my birth certificate and educational diplomas, the laptop computer I'd won in the pageant, and other clothing to me. Mum packed it all into a suitcase that was handed off to someone with no obvious connections to my family. That person brought it to the border, where a relative of my mother's picked it up and arranged for it to be placed in the trunk of one of the Sept Places taxis. On arriving in Dakar, the taxi driver called a number and the young man who had let me stay in his room on my first night picked it up and passed it on to a contact of Topp's, and that person handed it off to Topp's driver, who brought it to me. Hand to hand to hand to trunk to hand to hand to Topp's officer to me. So yes, I had the dress.

She left the room again. As I sat there, all I could think was that my future was in this woman's control. Or maybe it was all pointless, and I'd have to go through this with someone else a week from now. The emotional ups and downs were flattening me. What was she doing when she left the office? What was she checking? Who was she talking with? And in

I wouldn't learn until much later how important Habré's trial was; it was the first time an African court had prosecuted a former head of state for crimes against humanity. Human rights activists and prosecutors had spent years gathering evidence of the torture, mass murders and disappearances that occurred at Habré's direction. But while sexual violence was also widespread and committed by high-ranking government officials, including Habré, those crimes were at first not given the same attention. Finding victims willing to come forward would be challenging, it was thought—and then when victims did speak up, the crimes were dismissed as being too difficult to prosecute.

The initial indictment against Habré did not include any charges of rape, sexual enslavement or other forms of sexual violence. Later, when many victims of these crimes and their lawyers, supported by NGOs, exerted pressure, additional charges of sexual and gender-based violence were recognized as international crimes and added to the indictment: women had been forced to be sex slaves at Chadian military camps in the desert; others had been sexually assaulted and tortured in detention. One woman, Khadidja Hassan Zidane, courageously testified in court that Habré had raped her four times. In the end, Habré was found guilty of many of these crimes and sentenced to life imprisonment, though he was acquitted on a technicality on the charges related to Zidane's assaults. It was a trial and process that would later inspire Jammeh's victims to pursue justice as well.

As Topp and I moved through the crowd to the door, I had no way of knowing that two of the lawyers there that day, both working with Human Rights Watch, Marion Volkmann-Brandau and Reed Brody, would later become crucial supporters in the fight to bring Jammeh to justice. We passed each other without knowing our paths would converge just four years later.

Waiting. Hoping. Waiting. I had auditioned for parts before. Competed in the pageant. Waited for word about things I thought mattered. But never had waiting felt like this. My future literally depended on decisions others were making, in rooms I would never enter. And I had no way of knowing what they would decide.

During this time, Topp was my closest friend, my closest confidant. In my interactions with Jammeh, I had seen the worst of how a man could use his power: to degrade, to abuse, to harm. With Topp, I saw power used to help. He was under no obligation to listen to me; he didn't have to spend time with me, didn't have to care. Topp, the police chief, even Macky Sall, the president of Senegal at the time, all could have turned their backs on me and said, "Who cares, it's just some girl, let her figure it out." But they didn't. They helped me.

And then one day Topp arrived at my door. I'd asked him to get me some groceries on the way over. "Guess what?" he said as he entered the apartment.

"What? There are no chickens at the market?" I joked.

His smile was wide. "They've transferred your documents to the International Office of Migration. You are going to Canada!"

"Are you joking?"

The relief that washed over me felt like it filled every cell of my body. Topp handed me his phone and I called my aunt Marie in the U.K. so she could pass on the news to my mother, whose voice I hadn't heard since I'd left The Gambia. I was going to be safe. I was going to Canada.

The next day, Topp took me to the International Organization for Migration (IOM) in Dakar, where an immigration officer named Lamin greeted me. "How are you?" he asked, and then he answered his own question. "You are having a good day! You are going to Canada. Let's look at your file and see what we are going to do."

He gave me the details: I had qualified for an IM-1 visa, allowing me to enter Canada and become a permanent resident. But first I had to decide where I wanted to live.

Lamin brought out a map and put it on the table between us. "Where in Canada do you want to go?" he said. I didn't know where. I didn't know Canada. "So you hate the cold because you're from here and you're Black, so Manitoba and all those ones around it are off the list. You want somewhere that is really diverse, like New York vibes."

He circled Vancouver with his pen. "Vancouver is pretty cool. But it's expensive." Next he circled Toronto. "Toronto is diverse. And there are Caribbeans and Black people there and a great transit system and lots of industry, so you can find any kind of work. And it's close to New York," he said, pointing to the American city not far away on the map.

I put my finger on Toronto. "Toronto sounds great," I said.

5

AN UNSCHEDULED STOP

When I was growing up, I always knew when my mum was going someplace special and she wanted to look good: she would put on a wig. Now that I'm leaving Senegal to start a new life in Canada, I want to look good. I get dressed in my best clothes: an ash-coloured knit shirt, blue pants with fashionable tears at the knees, white boots and a wig, straight and long, pulled back into a ponytail. It's a big moment. A grown-up moment in a society where Black-girl hair isn't formal enough.

It's my first time on a flight. My first time in an airport. And because it's now safe, I'm finally able to call my mother on Topp's phone and tell her I'm leaving. I'm no longer afraid of Jammeh tracking calls. He can't get me because I'm almost gone.

"I'm heading to Canada today," I say when she answers the phone.

"What? When? With who? How?" Her questions fill my

ear. It is so wonderful to hear her voice, but the playfulness that is usually there is gone, replaced by a serious, worried tone. By myself, I tell her, now, soon, I'm at the airport.

"How long will it take you to get to Canada?"

I don't know, though I know I have to change planes partway. My siblings shout in the background. "Toufah's going to Canada! Toufah's going to Canada!" and then "Don't embarrass us—don't scream on the plane!"

I hear Mum starting to cry. My dad takes the phone from her. "Take care of yourself and when you reach there, call us." I can hear him say to my mother, "This is a good thing. Why are you crying?" and my mum replying, "My baby girl is going to Canada!"

The phone leaves his hand as my brothers and sisters take turns saying goodbye. "When are you coming back?" asks Nogoi, and though I don't know, I say, "Soon." My baby sister, Ida, is the last on the line. "Why did you leave?" she says. "You're going to Canada and you're leaving me here?"

Tears fill my eyes as I say my last goodbyes.

At the airport, we'd met Lamin from the IOM office to get my tickets, boarding passes and other documents. He'd also given me a blue and white bag with the IOM logo on it, telling me the bag would be how IOM agents in Brussels— my connecting airport—and Toronto would recognize me so they could help me through the official processes along the way. Topp had bought me a new brown suitcase to replace the one that had been passed secretly from hand to hand with my belongings in it, including the dress I'd been wearing that awful night.

We check the suitcase and now it is time for me to go.

I hand Topp the Nokia phone he'd given me when we first met, and I write his name and contact information in a little book I carry with me. Topp has been at my side for weeks, consulted on every decision I've made since I arrived in Senegal. "I've gotten used to your company," I say to him, emotion welling up inside me. I had left the safety of my family behind in The Gambia. And now I would have to leave the safety of my friend Topp behind in Senegal.

"I travel a lot," he replies. "Maybe I'll see you in Canada."

"Just follow the signs," Lamin had told me about navigating the airport, and so I do, making my way alone through security toward the boarding gate. A bus awaits passengers there, to carry us out to the middle of the tarmac where the jet sits. I climb the plane's steep stairs and find my seat as a trickle of other passengers come aboard as well. I buckle myself in quickly like the first-time flyer I am, anxious to be gone, not realizing it could easily be another hour before the plane finally takes off.

The takeoff isn't as terrifying as I thought it would be, though the roar of the engines is loud and my ears fill with air bubbles. And then we are in the air. I am on my way. Alone again. But out of Jammeh's reach.

The flight attendant's voice interrupted my thoughts.

"Ladies and gentlemen, due to logistical issues, our flight will be making an unscheduled stop in Banjul to pick up passengers before continuing on to Brussels." Banjul? Gambia?

The flight was supposed to have started in Banjul, then make the stop in Dakar, where I boarded, and then carry on to Brussels. Why were we backtracking to The Gambia?

I started to laugh. And to cry. I was laugh-crying. But it wasn't funny. Because all I could think was, *Did Jammeh arrange this? Are they going to take me off the plane in The Gambia?* Diverting a plane seemed well within what Jammeh could do, I thought. All my effort, all Topp's effort, everyone's effort, had been wasted: Jammeh was going to catch me and I was foolish to think I could escape. I didn't have a phone with me; I couldn't call Topp or Lamin to tell them what was happening. *I'm never going to make it to Canada.*

I waved to the attendant to get her attention. "When we get to The Gambia, do we get off the flight?" I asked.

"Oh no, no, no," she replied. "You stay on. The cleaners will come on and pick up garbage and then the other passengers are going to come on and we'll be back on our way."

My mind raced as she turned away from me. Would the cleaners recognize me? Would the other passengers? What if someone sat in the empty seat next to me and realized who I was? The Gambia is a small country, and I knew my face had been in the news under headlines about the missing beauty queen. My niqab was in my suitcase, stowed somewhere in the belly of the plane. I had no scarf to hide my head or my face.

Are you kidding me? I thought. I've spent all these weeks, done all of these things to get away, to get a visa to Canada. And now I'm never going to make it out alive.

All too soon we were landing in Banjul. As the plane rolled to a stop and the cleaners started to board, I got up and locked myself in the washroom. I sat on the toilet, my ears tuned to decipher what was going on in the cabin, dreading the possibility of an announcement calling my name. Soon, I could hear new passengers coming up the aisles and the sounds of bags being loaded into overhead compartments. Looking into the mirror, I removed the clip holding back the long, straight hair of my wig, and let the hair fall around my face, hiding my features. As the flight attendant's voice asked passengers to return to their seats and get ready for takeoff, I unlocked the door and made my way back to my spot, my head tilted down, my eyes not meeting anyone's. I was braced for someone to call out, *Hey Toufah! We heard you ran away! What are you doing on this flight?* or for some concerned grandmother to recognize me and pull me over, saying, *Let me call your mum. You should go home to your mother.*

No one looked up as I made my way to my seat. And no one had taken the empty seat next to me. I slid into place, fastened my seat belt, and silently begged the pilot to start the engine.

As the plane took flight again, relief flooded through me. But still I didn't trust I was safe, and I kept checking the flight-tracking screen to make sure the plane really was heading to Brussels. I felt like a coiled spring, tension contracting every muscle, so focused on what was behind me that I still couldn't imagine what might be ahead.

Finally, a few hours later, we landed in Brussels, an hour or more behind schedule because of the unanticipated reversal to Banjul. As Lamin had advised, I followed the signs through the Brussels airport, which stretched out in all directions, larger than I'd imagined any airport could be. I'd missed my connection, but the airline staff shifted me on to the next available departure. As I settled into my seat on the flight to Toronto, I was sure we'd be there in no time. I stared out the window at the clouds, trying not to let sleep take me, trying to take it all in. The meal, when it arrived, was flavourless in contrast to the cooking I'd grown up with: bland potatoes, soft carrots, spongy meatballs in a soggy sauce. And as the hours ticked past, I started to think the pilot was lost. Surely Toronto couldn't be this far away? I'd wanted to get on a plane my whole life; I'd imagined travelling to America to go to school or, closer to home, visiting Kenya, a country my mother had studied in and enjoyed for its beautiful country-side and vibrant cities. But at this point, my deepest wish was to get off the plane.

Finally, the pilot announced our descent into Toronto. I could see water stretching out below us, though I didn't know then that it was Lake Ontario, one of the Great Lakes. From the shore's edge, roads spread far into the distance and high-rise buildings reached into the sky, seeming almost to be trying to touch the aircraft itself. As soon as we landed, I was up out of my seat, a part of me still fearing a voice would announce that our flight was being sent back. The sooner I was off the plane and out of the airport the better.

Inside the airport, the lineup for customs and immigration shuffled slowly along. I had my IOM bag clearly visible at my side, following Lamin's advice, and looked for the person he said would pull me from the line to assist me once they saw it. Dotted through the line were others with the same blue and white bag, but no one seemed to be gathering us.

As I neared the front of the line, a woman in a veil approached me. "Are you Fatou?" she said, using my proper name. I nodded, and she brought me to the immigration officer, who greeted her as if he knew her. I handed over my passport, then had my fingerprints and photo taken, and he passed me a long form with my name, personal details and immigration status listed. The woman gave him a Canadian address for me, and he told me I could expect my permanent resident card in the mail in a few weeks.

"Welcome to Canada," he said, as the woman gestured for me to follow her.

"How long have you been in the refugee camp?" she asked as we made our way through the airport toward the taxi stand.

"I wasn't in one," I replied.

"Where are you from?" she asked.

"West Africa, The Gambia." My stomach tightened, as I realized the next logical question was Why are you here?

When she asked it, I pretended I didn't really understand. "I just came to Canada." She didn't ask more, perhaps thinking my English wasn't up to explaining the reasons for my journey.

She told the taxi driver the address I was to go to, and stood at the curb as the driver pulled away. In minutes, we merged into the traffic moving from the Toronto suburbs to the downtown core. The road had more lanes than I'd ever seen, with cars and trucks flying past us at great speeds on both sides. Beyond the highway's edge, I saw houses, apartment buildings, office towers, so many of them taller than any at home. Perhaps influenced by television, I'd always imagined the skylines of foreign cities at nighttime, their lights twinkling against the darkness, but now it was daylight. As my gaze shifted upwards, I was struck by the fact that above me was the same sun that shone in The Gambia, the same summer sky canopying me here and my family across the ocean.

The city's size was difficult to grasp, especially as the cab ride stretched past thirty minutes, forty-five minutes to almost an hour. Then we left the highway and drove along busy streets lined with shops and through residential neighbourhoods. Finally the driver pulled to a stop in front of a three-storey brick building. Heavy-looking columns stood on both sides of the front door, extending up to the second floor, a single balcony on each floor overhanging the entrance. A metal fence enclosed the brick-covered front yard, flanked by a school on one side and a playing field on the other. An Arabic family with two young children, one balancing on a small bicycle, sat out front, along with a few other people. I wasn't sure where I was or what this place was, though the people seemed friendly as they watched me drag my suitcase through the front door.

"We were expecting you earlier," said the man at the reception desk. I explained my delayed flight as I completed a registration form and he handed me a key card. "Room 205," he said. "You share the room with another girl. She's from Ethiopia, but I'm not sure if she's in the room right now. The empty bed is yours. You'll see a caseworker in the morning."

I carried my bag to the second floor, tapped the card on the electronic lock of room 205, and the door clicked open. A fine-boned Ethiopian woman, maybe twenty-four or twenty-five, looked up at me from the lower bunk bed and introduced herself. "My caseworker said you'd be here today," she said. She pointed to the top bunk—my new home in my new country—and showed me the closet where I could store my bag, then walked me down the hall to the shared women's washroom with two shower stalls, a sink and toilets. "You bring your own soap, your own body cloth," she said as she led me back to the room. "The papers they gave you at the desk tell you the meal times," she said, pointing them out to me. "If you miss the time, you miss the meal. You can't be out past midnight unless you register with the reception desk first."

The rules seemed simple but also overwhelming to take in. While I'd slept a little on the plane, I could feel fatigue seeping into my bones. As we came back to our shared room, she told me she was here with two brothers and two cousins, that she was a journalism intern in Ethiopia who had gotten into trouble because of some articles she was connected to and had to flee the country with her family. I said little, not ready to share my story, and soon she left me alone as she went to meet her brothers.

The room was so small. At home, while we weren't rich, space wasn't an issue because land was plentiful. Houses tended to be roomy. I'd never slept stacked above another person. I stared out the window at the football field where people strolled and played and children rode around on bicycles. Tears rolled down my cheeks. I felt so far away from everything I knew, from everyone I loved. I had no phone, no way to talk to anyone. The sun was dipping below the horizon, and while it was a hot summer's night by Canadian standards, to me, the air felt chilly, air-conditioned and so much cooler than at home. I showered to wash off the grit of my journey and pulled a long, thick dress out of my bag, one I would normally have worn for prayers, the warmest clothing I had. I climbed into the top bunk, pulled the blankets up over me and fell into a deep sleep.

"Hey, I tried to wake you," said my roommate as I crawled out of my bunk the next morning. "You better go get your breakfast!"

I quickly changed and washed my face, then headed downstairs to the dining area. At one end was a kitchen counter with an acrylic barrier shielding the food. Behind the counter, a cook in an apron and hairnet, an Eritrean lady, stood ready to place portions of food on a plate for me. People from around the world clustered at the dining tables: a Syrian family with a teenager and toddlers at one, a muscular Liberian man at another, an Ethiopian man at a third. The cook called out to me.

"Welcome! You're new! Where are you from?"

West Africa, I told her.

"Okay, good. Do you want eggs or do you want sausage?"

Eggs, I replied.

"If you say yes, you say 'please.' If you say no, you say 'thank you,'" she told me. "Now you say it."

I was embarrassed: I hadn't realized that in proper Canadian exchanges, this was the expected response. "Yes, eggs please," I replied.

It wasn't her job to teach newcomers how to be "Canadian," but as I would soon realize, almost everyone in the centre considered it part of their obligation to pass along clues to Canadian culture and behaviour. It was a way to become Canadian themselves. Okay, I thought, please and thank you: this is a serious thing that I'd better not forget.

Thanking her, I turned with my plate to find a spot at a table. There was an empty seat next to the young Ethiopian man, and so I set my plate down.

"Hello," he said. "Are you Nigerian?"

"No," I replied.

"You look like them."

"I'm Gambian."

"Gambian? I've never heard that one before."

Never heard of The Gambia? I thought. You're from Africa!

"Where are you from?" I asked in return. He was Ethiopian, but from Kenya, he said, as he pulled out his phone and pressed Google Maps, typing in Gambia. When the map popped onto the screen, he zoomed in on my country.

"Here?" he said. "This is a very tiny place! What do you guys do there?" His teasing was good-natured, and so I responded in kind.

"I don't talk to people with two citizenships, 'cause you're not proud of one or the other," I said, though of course we continued talking as I ate. His name was Solomon, he told me. I had just made my first friend in Canada.

—

"What we do here is help you settle," said the Asian man across from me. He'd introduced himself as my caseworker and was now explaining how the centre I was staying in worked and what the expectations were. "It's a resettlement program. We are here to give you the opportunity to stand on your feet."

He told me I could stay rent-free in the centre for up to one year, taking courses, improving my English, learning about my new home country. I would receive a stipend of $750 each month from the Canadian government. If I got paid work in which I earned more than a certain amount, I would lose the benefits. Today, they would give me $60 for immediate needs, as well as an additional $500 loan to help me manage until my first monthly stipend arrived. I would have to pay the $500 back, along with the $2,000 cost of my airplane ticket from Senegal, within two years. I had been in Canada less than twenty-four hours, and already I owed the government $2,500.

The next day another worker would take me to get my social insurance number and set up a bank account, both of which were necessary for me to receive my monthly stipend.

But what I needed most right now was a way to reach my family, a phone. The phone at the centre didn't allow long-distance calls outside of Canada, so the residents relied on their own cellphones to make calls to family and friends beyond Canada's borders. One of my roommate's brothers told me he could help, and we set out by streetcar and subway to the nearby Dufferin Mall. At every step, things were different from home. I'd never seen a streetcar or subway before, and even the buses I saw were nothing like the ones at home. Gambian buses were privately operated vans, with the passengers crammed onto bench seats and your fare collected by the driver's assistant before you got off.

On the Toronto streetcar, I was fascinated by the electrical wires overhead, the metal rod and other apparatus that connected the streetcar to the wires, and the tracks beneath us. Why did the vehicle need a driver, I wondered, since it looked like it should be self-driving? As we shifted to the subway, I was struck by the advertising on the platform walls and inside the cars: ads for colleges, online banking, immigration services. The face of a man I came to consider a Canadian celebrity was there too—the man who advertised on poster after poster that he would buy your gold. Did so many people here have gold to sell?

As I watched how people interacted on Toronto's transit, I was struck by how little they talked to each other. No Gambian bus was this quiet. The driver often had the radio on, and whatever came on—news, music, commentary—would inevitably prompt debate and discussion among the passengers. You couldn't avoid talking when you were sitting packed in as tightly as we often were. I was fascinated, too, by how people with obvious mental illnesses were able to travel on Toronto's public transit. At home the driver's assistant simply wouldn't allow someone who looked unpredictable or homeless to board, and they likely wouldn't have had the fare to pay anyway. But on Toronto buses, streetcars and subways, I often saw people who behaved erratically. The other passengers usually gave them a wide berth, but at least they were allowed on board.

I'd never been in a shopping centre like Dufferin Mall before, with so many stores and kiosks and food stalls under one roof. I followed my roommate's brother through the aisles to the booth he said had the cheapest options. I had no credit card, but for thirty dollars a month I could get a BLU phone, SIM card and a calling plan that gave me one hour of international calls a day. I handed over half of my sixty dollars and took the phone in return.

"Let's grab some food at the food court," my roommate's brother said. I'd only ever seen McDonald's in American movies. KFC and Chinese food were new to me. I searched the menus for something familiar, then spotted lamb on a Mediterranean menu. I'll get that, I thought. The cubes of meat tasted nothing like the lamb we prepared at home, but I swallowed them anyway, a full plate for less than ten dollars.

"Oh my God, everything is so cheap here," I said to my companion.

He looked at me strangely. "How much is a dollar in your country's money?" he asked. I had no idea; I hadn't even realized there was a conversion to make. He looked it up on his phone and translated it for me: one Canadian dollar equalled forty Gambian dalasis. Four hundred dalasis for a plate of poorly cooked lamb! I would never buy food that expensive at home. The meal I had thought was so cheap now seemed like a foolish waste of money, and the phone no bargain either.

But at least I could finally call home.

When I was back in my room, I dialed my mother's number. "I'm here, in Canada," I said when she answered.

"Oh thank God!" It had been two days since she had heard from me. I could hear her saying a few words of prayer. "Thank God you are there. Your siblings really, really miss you. I hope you are fine."

Yes, yes, I said. She asked me about where I was staying and what it was like. She didn't ask about what had happened to bring me here. She didn't know how to ask about it. I didn't know how to raise it. A part of me wished we could both forget it, that we could just pretend I'd applied for a visa like normal people do, and I had gone to the airport and ended up in Canada.

We carried on talking about the "whats": what Canada was like, what the food was like, what the money could buy. "It's sooo expensive," I told her, translating the costs of food to Gambian currency. "I could buy a car at home for what food costs here in a month!" I said.

My mother countered my claims. "Well, you're not going to eat if you think that way. You're comparing a Canadian dollar to some Third World currency. It's not the same thing."

And so instead of talking about the price I was paying for being raped, we talked about dollars and dalasis, as if the exchange rate were the most important topic we could find.

After hanging up, I wandered back to the first floor, where a group of residents had gathered in the television room. People were telling the stories of how they'd ended up here. Bombs going off that levelled the primary school they'd gone to as children, turning it to ashes. Journalists whose newspapers and TV stations had been shut down by dictators for telling stories the powerful didn't want told. There was a girl who had hoped to be a doctor but had to stop her studies in order to flee civil war. People who had futures and goals and dreams interrupted by forces beyond their control, futures and goals and dreams now on hold as they sat in a Canadian resettlement house, trying to figure out how to restart their lives somewhere new, in a language that for many was as foreign as the soil they now stood on.

As the conversation swirled around me, all I could think was, *How is it going to sound if I open my mouth and say I came here because I was raped by the president of my country?* I don't know if I thought my reason was more or less serious than bombings and other violence, just that I wasn't ready to tell others the truth of what had brought me here. My caseworker knew, but others didn't need to. And so when the conversation paused and faces turned toward me, I edited my past. "They wanted to marry me off to an older guy at a very early age, so I ran away." The conversation moved on. I pushed my past down a little deeper. I was starting a new life here. A new page. And maybe leaving the past silently in the past was the best way to do that.

Many of the employees of the centre were also immigrants: the Somali settlement worker who took me to get my SIN card and set up my bank account, the Eritrean cook, my Asian caseworker. And then there was the Filipina cleaner, the one we were all afraid of.

You know how there are some older ladies who are done with giving a fuck? She was one of them. She didn't feel the need to smile at you. She didn't feel the need to wait for you. She didn't feel the need to work around you. She had a job to do, and your job was to get out of her way. If you stepped on her freshly mopped floor, she would take a little turn and look at you with eyes that would get to your soul. She didn't say a word, but we all knew not to cross her. Behind her back, we called her "no-nonsense mama," but to her face, we made sure to get out of her way.

There were other characters at the resettlement centre as well: the Liberian man nicknamed "the Premier" because he had lived at the centre longer than anyone. We were supposed to leave after one year, but we could apply to stay longer if we hadn't yet gotten on our feet. Rumours swirled that he'd been there for five years, but I'm not sure any of us knew for certain. His good cheer and friendliness meant no one begrudged him his stay; we just greeted him as the Premier when he passed in the halls or dining area.

It wasn't long before my status as the newest resident at the resettlement centre was erased. A Liberian woman a little older than me arrived. She had the physique of a body builder. She not only looked tough, she also spoke plainly and strongly. It was my turn to be the person who helped show someone else how things worked here. I gave her the rundown on the centre's meals and schedule, who to ask for help, where to find your caseworker.

"Do you know how to do braids?" she asked me later. Someone had told her it cost thirty-five dollars in the salon for cornrows. Thirty-five dollars? Back home, almost everyone knew how to do cornrows—you don't go to a salon for that. Your sister or your cousin or someone in the neighbourhood would put three or four strands on your head and you were good to go. "Of course I can braid," I said. And so we spent time together, braiding hair and talking about food from home: hakko putteh, a dish of sweet potato leaves chopped and sautéed with onions and served with fish and rice; peanut butter stew; and fufu, a dumpling made with grated cassava and served with vegetable soup or goat meat. Maybe we could find a restaurant in Toronto that served familiar food, she suggested. We turned to Google to search and found an African restaurant a few blocks away with fufu on the menu. We went there and splurged on a taste of home, so much better than the lamb I'd had at the mall.

There were other happy moments. One came when I needed a new toothbrush and my roommate pointed me to a nearby Dollarama store. As I carried my basket around the store, I couldn't believe how inexpensive it all was: a whole bottle of shampoo for $1.50. Jewellery for $1. Soap. Nail polish. Underwear. Toys. Baby games. Puzzles. I told myself I would spend no more than $100 of my $500 advance as I filled the cart, feeling happier than I had since I'd arrived, piling treats for myself in along with gifts to send home to my brothers and sisters, especially for my baby sister, Ida.

Among my purchases was a bottle of what I thought was hair straightener. My hair had grown in the weeks since I'd left home, and the tight curls were hard to get a comb through. I'd never learned other ways of caring for natural hair. Later that day, as I applied the chemicals to the curls that framed my face, the colour of my hair started changing to blonde.

Oh my God, oh my God. I ran to the washroom, but no-nonsense mama was cleaning it. I turned back to my room to wait for her to finish: even blonde hair couldn't make me confront her. When she was finally done, I hurried into the bathroom and washed the cream out of my hair. There was no hiding it: the front section of my hair was blonde. Staring into the mirror, I grabbed my scissors and trimmed as much of the coloured mess as I could, though a short blonde patch remained. Until my hair grew out, the wig I had worn on my flight to Canada hid my failed DIY-straightening.

While others at the centre focused on learning English or searching for someplace to live, I felt like I was walking in place, moving but getting nowhere. I didn't need English lessons, but I wasn't sure exactly what I should do next. It was too late to enroll in school programs, and even so, I wasn't sure what I qualified for, what the options were in Canada, or even what I wanted to do. I wasn't supposed to work under the terms of my refugee support either. And so the days seemed to stretch out before me.

Another young woman arrived who had escaped an abusive relationship but had to leave her young child behind in Tanzania. She'd heard I, too, had escaped a forced marriage and sought me out as someone who might understand her experience. Together, we spent hours wandering through Toronto's malls: the Eaton Centre, Dufferin Mall, Fairview, Don Mills. It wasn't like either of us could buy anything, but it was a way to pass our hours in limbo. I'd never been too interested in clothing, so instead I spent my time looking at home decor, imagining how I would furnish a home of my own. Inexpensive jewellery caught my eye as well, and I would sometimes splurge on a cheap set of bracelets or earrings. There were certain stores we didn't enter at all because they seemed too fancy, too expensive. Instead, we gravitated to the ones that felt more like market shops at home: tiny stores crammed with goods from floor to ceiling, little decor items next to racks of sunglasses next to stacks of dishes and more.

And then one day, my shopping companion was gone, moved out of the refugee centre. I don't know where she went—if she returned to her country and her child, or found some other way to move forward. She didn't say goodbye. I never heard from her again.

I wouldn't realize it until much later, but I was slipping into a depression. I'd never had skin problems, but suddenly dark blemishes started to appear on my face. I tried to connect with other residents at the centre, but the untold truth of my past held me back from really getting close to anyone. While I shared a room, I didn't share my story, and that meant never really connecting honestly with my roommate. I would get on the Toronto transit and all around me I would see fancy people in fancy clothes and fancy shoes going to fancy places. I felt invisible.

I walked along College Street for kilometres, past dozens of restaurants, not seeing a single type of food that I recognized. In the evening, people would crowd the restaurant patios, laughing and talking, and I would walk along alone.

I'd see a group of young women my age, laughing, enjoying themselves, and I would think, *I used to be a girl who could laugh like that.*

One hot afternoon, I walked into a restaurant and asked for a cocktail—at home, the name for a non-alcoholic bottled drink. The waiter handed me an alcohol-filled glass. Having grown up in a Muslim household, I'd never had alcohol, but I knew as soon as the drink arrived that it wasn't what I was expecting. At home a cocktail was orange and fizzy, arriving in a tall-necked bottle. I pushed it away without trying it. *Even when the words are the same, it's not the same here*, I thought. I'd never in my life been so lonely, felt so misunderstood.

I was both embarrassed by not knowing what to do and so used to figuring things out on my own that I didn't ask for help—I wasn't even sure what questions to ask. On the subway, I saw an ad for CDI College and decided to visit their office downtown. I didn't realize it was a private college—I didn't even know what such a thing was. The counsellor was more like a salesperson, pushing me to sign up for courses, assuring me I could get a student loan, even setting up an Ontario Student Assistance Program account for me before I finally managed to leave, saying I'd think about it some more. I already owed Canada $2,500; I couldn't imagine taking on more debt to go to school.

I kept trying to make connections with others at the resettlement centre. I got to know Gabi, a blind man in his late twenties from Eritrea. He told me he'd lost his sight after being assaulted by security forces who had targeted his father, a journalist who had offended the government. In

The Gambia, people with handicaps rely on personal attendants or others for help because they don't have access to assistive technologies and devices. But Gabi, though blind, manoeuvred through Toronto on his own with the help of his cane and the GPS in his phone, using voice-activated Siri to search for information, send messages and more.

"Let's go for a coffee," he said to me one day as he headed down the street to College and Bathurst.

"Do you need my help?" I asked.

"Why? I'm a grown man," he said. "I can get myself to the coffee shop."

Gabi was smart and funny and wise. He also knew the story I had shared wasn't my whole story. "There is more to you than you are telling us," he said. No, no, I replied, sticking to my tale of a barely escaped forced marriage. Surprisingly, it was the man with no sight who came closest to seeing me. I felt guilty that I never told him the truth, my secret an ongoing barrier to connecting with the people around me.

Solomon and I spent time together as well, but now it looked like he was going to be moving out with two other young Ethiopian men he'd met. My first roommate had already gone. She and her brothers and cousins had found a three-bedroom apartment the five of them could afford to share, and a woman from Grenada took her place in our room. While the sensible thing for me would have been to spend my full year at the resettlement house, saving as much of my $750 monthly stipend as I could, I felt an urgency to move forward, especially as those around me seemed to be doing just that.

And always, just below the surface, was my discomfort with being in a place where everyone's story, everyone's history, everyone's reason for being here was part of the conversation. As long as I was a refugee in a refugee setting, the reasons for my status were going to be open for discussion. I didn't want to talk about it. I wanted to be somewhere where I could avoid the questions.

Even though I'd only been at the centre for two months, I started looking at ads for rooms to rent, spotting one nearby for just five hundred dollars. I met the landlady and she took me to the building: a three-storey brick house on a busy street, carved into single rented rooms. My room was at the back of the building, reached by walking down a narrow alley between the house and a chain-link fence and entering through a side door leading to the basement. The room was just big enough for a bed and a chair, with a small closet and a tiny ground-level window that peeked out under the back porch. The bathroom was shared, as was a stove that sat in the hallway between my room and the other rented basement room. The man who rented that room appeared while I was there, and he was so tall I couldn't imagine how he fit inside.

"He not talk to you," said the landlady. "He does not talk to anyone."

It was October, and already the basement was cold. Was the heat turned on? I asked. In winter, said the landlady. "It feels like winter now," I replied. They could turn on the heater for me, she said, but I shouldn't turn it too high or I'd have to pay more rent. From the street in front of the house,

I could see the back of the resettlement centre through a schoolyard that stretched between the two blocks. Close enough to be familiar. Far enough away to be on my own. I said I'd take it.

After paying my rent and my $120 transit pass, I'd have just $130 left over each month for all my other expenses, including food. But now maybe I could find a cash job, even if it meant working nights, because I didn't need to get anyone's permission to stay out past midnight. I tried to see it as a kind of freedom. But in truth, it was the most depressing, shittiest box of a room that you can imagine.

It wasn't good for my mental health. The apartment was so cramped and cold that each day, I would leave the house and get on a bus or climb on a streetcar just to escape its four walls. The 506. The 505. The 501. West to east. Back again. I'd watch people walking their dogs and imagine maybe someday I could have a dog of my own. At home few families had dogs, as they were considered unclean. Children often tormented the dogs that roamed the streets, throwing rocks or sticks at them, and it wasn't unusual for people to be even more cruel, sometimes cutting a dog's ears off or injuring them in other ways. But I had always had a soft spot for animals, from the donkeys that pulled the carts we could hire to carry heavy loads of groceries or building supplies home, to the dogs on the street. In the months before I'd left The Gambia, I'd befriended a street dog that had a litter of pups in an empty building near my mother's home. I snuck food to the dog, and before long, she started to hang around the gate to the house, waiting for whatever scraps I could save for her. My mother had told me the dog had disappeared after I escaped The Gambia. I couldn't help but wonder what had happened to her and think how different that dog's life was compared to the beloved pets I saw with Dog Moms and Dog Dads on Toronto's streets. While I'd noticed that people on transit didn't talk to each other, I'd also seen that dogs seemed to be conversation enablers, making it okay for people to talk to strangers. Still, except for those chatty dog owners, everybody seemed to be in a rush here. I was this slow, invisible person in the midst of a fast-moving stream of people.

I was trying to figure out the city, but everyone kept talking about northbound, southbound, east and west. I didn't have a compass in my head. The city is built on a grid with Lake Ontario to the south, but at the time, it didn't make sense to me. At home, if I wanted to visit your house, your directions might be, "Oh, walk all the way to the green—you see that tree there? Turn left, go three intersections down. There's a shop with a red door, and to the left is the house." But here in Toronto, it was, "Go southbound." Where is southbound? Many times, I ended up in the wrong place.

I used to think I was a smart person, but now I couldn't even process basic information. The negative thoughts swirled in my head. I was unworthy. I didn't deserve to have a life. What was I doing here?

I know this isn't the picture of immigration people want to hear: refugees are supposed to be happy to be here, grateful to find a way to integrate, to start over. But there is also this other immigrant story, of people who land in a new country all by themselves, carrying heavy secrets, the kind of secrets that hold them back.

I wanted to connect with people. Or at least I thought I did. But I now know I was retreating into myself. And maybe people saw that. As I seemed to reach out, I was also closing myself off. I distanced myself even from the people who were trying to be my friends, people like Solomon. *You don't really know me*, I would think. *I'm lying to you. This girl you like, this friend you want to be with, that's not the real me. If you knew the real me, you probably wouldn't want to be my friend.*

I felt like I wasn't a good refugee, a good migrant. And that made me not a good Canadian. I wasn't a good Gambian either. I'd fled that country and would never be able to return. And I didn't want to admit I was a rape survivor. I kept pushing those thoughts out of my head. It was as if I was denying everything I was, leaving me nothing to hang on to.

"Wow!" said Ahmad Gitteh as he stepped down from the streetcar at the corner near my apartment. "You've grown up! You look very much like your sister!" Gitteh was the one who had helped me in my escape from The Gambia by connecting me with Ebrima Chongan and, through him, Omar Topp. We hadn't seen each other in person since he had left The Gambia years earlier, but now he'd come from Ottawa, where he lived, to visit me. He was staying with another Gambian family in the Toronto suburbs, since my tiny basement apartment wasn't fit for guests. We spent the day wandering the city, making FaceTime calls together to my mum, as well as to Chongan, as we went. Gitteh suggested I join him the next day at a soccer match between two teams of Gambians taking place in a city not far away. There would be food from home and a chance to meet other Gambians, he said, and so, the next day, he and the family he was staying with picked me up in their car for the ride to Kitchener, a couple of hours outside of Toronto.

It was a crisp fall day as we stood on the sidelines of the playing field, and it felt like being home but not home. The jokes and stories were familiar. The people looked like people from home. Fula and Wolof words floated through the air. The Gambian community was small enough that people there knew Gitteh, and so it wasn't a surprise when they approached us. "Hey Gitteh, how are you? Who is this with you?" asked one after another. Because no gathering of Gambians happens without each person attempting to fit each new arrival into a map of connections, the questions that followed were familiar too: Who is your father? Where did you go to school? Who were your teachers? In a country as small as The Gambia, everyone knows someone who knows someone who knows you.

I could feel myself pulling back as each new person tried to fit me into their picture. Some knew I'd been a pageant winner. Others had no doubt heard the rumours flying about why I'd left, though I still hadn't spoken publicly about that. But even those who hadn't heard were asking me why I'd come to Canada, how I'd ended up here. I tried to "uh-huh" and "mm-hmm" my way through conversations, avoiding, looking away. I could see people giving me sideways glances and I was certain they were judging me as rude—or worse, if they believed the stories they'd heard about me on Gambian online radio and websites.

Instead of feeling closer to home, in that moment I felt further from it than ever. And my heart broke, because I knew I could not be part of this community, not now. This was something else Jammeh had taken from me.

At the edge of the field was a public washroom. As the others talked and laughed, I made my way to it and hid in a stall, hoping for the day to end. That evening, as Gitteh and the family he was staying with dropped me off, they invited me to join them for future gatherings, but I knew I couldn't accept. My discomfort at trying to hide my reasons for leaving The Gambia was too intense, and people's curiosity about my reasons for turning my back on my pageant success too great.

It was cold and icy a few weeks later as a bus dropped me off at 7 a.m. in the middle of a deserted industrial area. I'd answered an ad for a job packing medical supplies into first aid kits, no experience necessary. But as I stepped out of the bus and started to make my way toward the address I'd been given, my feet slid out from under me. Each time I tried to get up, I went down again. It might have been funny if it hadn't been so frustrating and humiliating. How was I supposed to get where I was going? How did people live in this icy, awful climate?

Finally, I gave up and scooted along on my bum, like a crab. I'm sure I looked ridiculous, and when I finally got to the door of the building, I was soaked through to my skin. I'd bought what I thought was a winter jacket and boots at a Toronto outdoor flea market, but the coat's cheap cotton and fake fur and the shoddy construction boots did little to keep me warm. (Every refugee arriving in Canada from a warm climate should get training in how to layer leggings, undershirts, T-shirts and more to stay warm.) I spent my eight-hour shift shivering, but at least by the time I finished, the ice had disappeared and I was able to make it safely back to the bus stop on my two feet.

I was miserable in this cold city.

Maybe I should have picked Vancouver when Lamin had rolled that map of Canada out in front of me in the IOM office in Dakar. Maybe things would be better there. The ad for Douglas College popped up as I typed "colleges Vancouver" into an online search one afternoon. I saw articles suggesting the Vancouver-based school was offering tuition reductions for new Canadian immigrants.

I contacted the college. I'd noticed they had a social work program, and its courses and the kinds of work it led to appealed to me. Yes, I was told, I qualified for the tuition break. Yes, I could start in January. I searched Kijiji for cheap accommodation and found a room for rent for seven hundred dollars. The only furniture I had was what the resettlement program had provided when I moved out. But if I left it behind, my budget wouldn't allow me to buy new furniture— could I find a way to ship it? I called one mover after another until I found a truck driver with room for my tiny load at a fair price. Then I booked the cheapest airline ticket I could find.

"I don't understand why you are going," Solomon said to me. We'd had this conversation many times already. When I had first hinted I might not stay in Toronto, he thought I was joking. Things hadn't gone perfectly for him either. When he had signed out of the resettlement centre to move in with the two other Ethiopian men he'd met, he'd shown up at the new apartment only to be told the others had cancelled the rental at the last minute. He'd had to scramble to find new accommodations, but it never occurred to him to leave the city. Now, as I talked about moving across the country, he tried to convince me we could rent something together. "Toronto is the place to be," he told me. "Vancouver is the wilderness. You won't like it there."

"I just don't feel it here," I told him.

"Not feeling it" wasn't a reason Solomon could wrap his head around. But I wouldn't budge, because of the stubbornness that was both my strength and—though I hated to admit it—sometimes my weakness. I'd made up my mind. I was going west.

December's chill enveloped us as Solomon helped me carry my bag to the taxi that would take me to the airport. "I don't get it, but okay," he said as he wished me well. We promised each other we'd stay in touch.

I had no money left. I was moving across the country. But maybe Vancouver would be the place where I could finally be happy.

6

THE INVISIBLE WOMAN

Rows of students fill the space between my seat near the back and the instructor at the front of my Canadian history class. I'm not used to this view of the backs of so many heads, of looking over shoulders, past laptop computers and other people's notebooks. At home in The Gambia, I'd always been the girl who chose a seat at the front and centre of the classroom, somewhere I could see the teacher well, somewhere that put me in the middle of whatever was going on in the room. But now, here in Vancouver at Douglas College, I stay tucked not completely out of sight, but not directly in the instructor's view either.

The lecture swirls around me, with other students putting up their hands to speak and contribute. I have so much to say. But by the time I'm ready to raise my hand, they've moved on. I never used to think twice about jumping in, but now I'm stopped by doubt. Who is looking at me? What if I sound stupid? Maybe what I'm about to say isn't right?

I'd entered the program confident I could keep up, given that the college had positively assessed my grade twelve results from The Gambia and I'd passed an English proficiency test. I was excited by the courses I'd chosen as part of the associate degree in social work program: an introduction to social work, a political science course, and the Canadian history class I am now struggling through.

In online assignments, where my contributions are written and I have time to choose my words, I participate more fully, adding my thoughts to discussion threads on topics ranging from building Canadian railways to the history of Indigenous people in Canada, happy to learn about my new country, happy to share my opinions. The difference between my online presence and my in-class silence is so noticeable my instructor asks to speak to me. "Are you doing okay?" she asks. "I notice you take part in the online discussions but not so much in class."

"I'm good, I'm good," I reassure her with a big smile. "It's fine."

She is reaching out to me but I slide away, not wanting to admit my fear of being seen, of being judged by the other students in the class. Part of me wants to tell her it isn't like me to sit silently at the back of the classroom. But the part of me that feels safer being invisible wins, and so instead I say, "It's fine. I'm good."

But it isn't. I'm not.

—

I was hot and sweaty under the zippered plastic suit that covered me from head to rain-booted feet, though not as wet as I would have been without them. I planted myself solidly on the cement floor and aimed the high-pressure hose at the carpet hanging over the line, pressing hard on the hose's lever. The force of the water was enough to rock me, but I stood strong as the jet of water forced the dirt from the carpet's fibres.

It was just over a year since I'd been crowned winner of the pageant. From evening gown to waterproof jumpsuit: how much my life had changed in twelve months.

I had arrived in Vancouver in December. As I waited for my luggage at the carousel that day, I watched other passengers being greeted by loved ones. There were no loved ones waiting for me, not even a stranger standing with my name written on a sign, ready to transport me to a conference or hotel. Instead, I grabbed the suitcase Topp had bought me and made my way to the SkyTrain station. An hour later, I was sitting outside the three-storey house in Burnaby where I'd rented a room, waiting for my new landlord to meet me with the keys. Another hour passed before he finally showed up and guided me through the dark main floor and up the stairs to a single small room on the third floor, with a shared bathroom down the hall and access to a main floor kitchen. My small load of furniture hadn't arrived yet, but there was a mattress on the floor and so I had somewhere to sleep. At least it wasn't a cold basement room, like the one I'd left in Toronto.

As I looked at the empty room, I tried not to think of how

I would make ends meet after I paid the seven-hundred-dollar rent each month.

The days that followed were filled with getting settled and started at school. I should have been excited as I found my way to the Douglas College New Westminster Campus, with its glass-ceilinged atrium and a sweeping wide circular staircase where students clustered in groups, chatting and drinking coffee from the Tim Hortons coffee shop and other fast-food outlets on the main floor.

I was nineteen, starting at a new school and surrounded by other young people. But looking back, I realize that I have flashes of clear memories from that time surrounded by long stretches of . . . nothing. I've heard people talk about how, when they're stressed out or preoccupied, they can drive from one place to another and not remember any part of the drive—just arriving where they were going. That's what so much of my time in Vancouver was like: a flash of a memory, a recollection of a place or a person. Physically my body was there, but mentally I was checked out.

I had classes just three days each week, but even with limited trips on public transit, getting back and forth to school was easily going to cost me a hundred dollars each month. That left me nothing for food, my phone and any other expenses. I needed paying work but had little experience to list on an application. The Student Centre at the college offered resumé assistance, but the young Sikh man, a student like me, assigned to help me was stumped: I'd held no real jobs in The Gambia.

"Let's talk about your skills. What skills do you have?" he asked me.

Ach. I couldn't come up with anything. He tried to be helpful, but his questions made me feel ashamed and stupid. Maybe I could apply at Winners or Tim Hortons, he suggested: they often hired people with little work experience.

I left the centre empty-handed, and later, on the mattress in my room, searched Google for examples of resumés and the kinds of skills you should list on them. My self-esteem was so low I couldn't remember the skills I had that caused me to volunteer to read the news each week at Gambia College and senior secondary school. And so instead, I put in words and phrases Google suggested: punctual, enjoys working with diverse groups of people and so on. I could have been writing about a stranger. I focused on trying to decode what an imaginary employer might want: What words did I have to put down to get someone to choose me? By the time I finished, I had two short paragraphs. But at least it was something. And a cashier or cleaning job was all I hoped to get, so surely it would do.

"Do you have experience cleaning?" asked the woman who called me from a carpet cleaning business.

"Yes," I said. "I clean my house."

"No, no, you need experience in carpet cleaning," said the woman.

"I can learn," I replied.

All right, said the woman, but we don't pay to train you, so you'll work for a week with no pay. That was fine, I said.

And so here I was: spraying high-pressure water at carpets.

At the end of my shift, I pulled back my plastic hood and peeled off my plastic suit, my muscles sore from counter-balancing the high-pressure hose. It was boring, hot and tiring. But after I completed my "training" week without pay, at least it paid me enough money for my food.

I'd moved 3,400 kilometres, but the Immigration Canada office I stepped into in Burnaby looked much the same as the one in Toronto: cubicles, computers, counsellors. While I'd managed to get enrolled in school and didn't require much assistance, my new counsellor was able to help in one important way: the rent on my room was too much for my limited budget to sustain. "There's a couple who might be able to help you," the counsellor told me, passing me the number for an older woman and her husband who had rental units. Though they weren't any closer to school than my current place, he said they gave a price break to newcomers to Canada. I dialed the landlady's number as I left the office.

No answer. I left a voicemail as I climbed the hilly street toward the bus stop. "Hello, my name is Toufah. I've been recommended by the immigration office. I'm looking for a place to stay. Please get back to me. I can come and see the place anytime during the week or weekend. Thank you."

Twenty minutes later, the landlady, whose name was Annameik, returned my call. Yes, she and her husband had two units they rented out, a whole house and a basement apartment in their own home. The basement was available if I wanted to see it.

Annameik's house sat close to the street, but I could see a large garden stretching out behind it. The woman who answered the door was older, her face framed by short blonde-grey hair, her smile greeting me. Her home seemed open and welcoming too: a light and airy entry and living room so different from the cramped and depressing main floor and dark hallways of the house I was staying in. I wasn't hoping for much more than someplace livable and cheap. But the basement apartment she showed me was a walkout with direct access to the backyard. It was bright and comfortable, with a bed in one corner complete with linens, a kitchen area with stove and fridge, a toaster and coffee maker, a small private washroom, a closet, and a washer and dryer I could access as well. Sunshine filled the space from windows looking out on the garden.

How much is the rent? I asked.

They usually rented it for $800, she replied, but they lowered the rate to $550 for refugees. They'd mostly rented to people fleeing from Syria or other war zones, not someplace like The Gambia, she added.

"The absence of war doesn't necessarily equal peace," I said. Looking back now, my response seems a bit embarrassing, but I was desperate. I didn't want her to refuse me because what I was running from wasn't bombs.

Annameik nodded, smiling. "Tell your counsellor to send your documents to my email and I'll let her know when you can move in."

Relief washed over me.

My furniture had finally shown up, but now I was moving into Annameik's furnished basement, I no longer needed it. Thinking perhaps I could generate some cash by selling what little I had, I posted the items for sale on Kijiji. No nibbles. I switched the listing from "for sale" to "free." Still no interest. I'd paid to move it across the country and now I couldn't give it away. Could I leave the furniture behind? I asked the landlord at the rooming house. Sure, he said. And so I donated my desk, chair and bed to his next tenant, and I moved into Annameik's basement with just my suitcase and some dishes and cutlery I bought from Dollarama.

Over the weeks that followed, Annameik and her husband did all they could to befriend me. "Come up for tea anytime," her husband told me. Both were very informed about international news and Canada's role in events around the globe, sharing their opinions freely with me on Canada's need to welcome more refugees and talking about the troubling situation in Syria. They were passionate about justice and global peace. Despite their kindness and their interest, I held back. I didn't want them to ask questions about my situation I wasn't prepared to answer.

When I wasn't at school or working, I slept, sometimes staying in bed for days at a stretch. Annameik would text me. "Are you all right? Haven't heard you make a noise down there for two days."

I slept until I felt sick from oversleeping, numb from the darkness. And then I'd watch a movie on my laptop or listen to the radio, and go to sleep again, waking up to eat, then sleeping some more. I blamed myself for the hours I spent unconscious, scolded myself for being lazy. It was like I was in a coma, where I would shake myself awake long enough to get to my classes and then return to my room to slide back into sleep.

When I was awake, my thoughts circled and spun, and at the centre, the question *Why am I even here?* kept floating through my head. I missed being surrounded by my siblings: baby Ida, who was now moving toward school age; Muhammed, in primary school, always talking about video games; Nogoi, almost a teenager, quiet but observant; Penda, who I had spent my teen years alternately ignoring and arguing with.

But when I spoke to my family by phone, I pretended happiness. "It's going great!" I told them. If I missed a call because I was sleeping, I didn't let them know that either, saying, "I was in class when you called, so I couldn't answer!"

I didn't know what was keeping me in this dark place, and I couldn't find my way out. Nothing felt good. But I had to admit the darkness wasn't completely unfamiliar. I'd been there before, after my brother Pa Mattar died.

This is what I remember. I am in grade ten and my parents are both away for work, my mother delivering school supplies to distant communities for a few days, my father upcountry with Peace Corps Gambia. Pa Mattar is almost two years younger than me, my first full sibling, my first baby brother.

He'd been so smart as a young child, so bright-eyed. But soon after he started school, his behaviour deteriorated and

the principal declared him unfit for the classroom. They have
no label for his condition. Some think he's mad because he's
obsessed with order, sensitive to noise, and sometimes tears
his clothing off or runs away for seemingly no reason. I've
helped look after him for most of my primary school, but as
I enter junior secondary school, I have fewer hours to spend
with him, and so my father hires a series of minders to keep
watch on him.

The day before he died, I'd taken Pa Mattar his tea in his
room, a few steps away from my mother's main part of the
compound on the other side of the outdoor kitchen, where the
boys in the family slept. He seemed pale, his skin lighter than
usual. Normally when I brought him food, he would jump
up, excited. But this time he didn't move, just smiled. I asked
the older man looking after him if Pa Mattar was all right.

"He's probably tired," he said.

That evening, Pa Mattar seemed like his usual self, peek-
ing around the gate, looking to see if Mum and Dad were on
their way home yet. He stayed up past his usual bedtime,
making noises, singing to himself, but I didn't think anything
of it. He was often full of energy.

This morning I bring him his tea, but he is still in bed.

"He's not up?" I say to his minder. "That's weird. He doesn't
sleep in this late."

"He's just tired," says the man and continues his ablutions,
getting ready for his morning prayers.

And so I go back to the main part of the house. My chore
that day is to scrub the floor tiles and wipe down the house,
something that always seems easier to do with loud music

to help me along. My younger siblings are at home as well, and I don't want them to venture outside, out of my view. So I close the front door and turn on Nicki Minaj's "Starships" as a soundtrack to my work.

I'm dancing and cleaning and cleaning and dancing as the children play on the floor around me.

Then one of my older half-siblings opens the door, and a youngster scoots outside to the common open part of the compound. When I go outside to pick him up, I see a neighbour girl across the way standing with the man who is Pa Mattar's minder. My dad's first wife, who is normally at the market at this time of day selling clothing at a stall she has there, is also with them.

I walk over to join them. "You are late to go to the market today," I say to her, but she won't meet my eyes.

"What's happening?" I ask.

The neighbour girl starts shouting, "Oh my God, oh my God." And my father's first wife hugs me and murmurs "Munyoo"—take heart—in my ear, the soothing words you say in our language to the loved ones of the deceased.

My first thought is that my mother is dead, that she has died in an accident on her way back from her village visits.

"Oh my God, what happened to her?" I cry. "What happened to her?"

But my dad's wife is crying so hard she can't speak. The children are about, and now other neighbours are there as well. Tears start to stream down my face, and the man who is supposed to be looking after my brother touches my arm and says, "It's okay. It's okay. We lost him. We lost him."

My thoughts jump to my father now. "Lost who? My dad?"

In a thousand years I wouldn't imagine it is Pa Mattar they're speaking of. And even when the man says my brother's name, I can't take it in. Pa Mattar had been named after my grandfather on my mom's side, so my brain tells me it must be my grandfather who is dead.

But then the man says, "Your brother is gone. Your brother is gone."

His words stop my tears. I don't know how I end up sitting down, but I look up from where I sit on the cement edge of the courtyard and everything around me just seems to be shadows moving, not people.

My brother is gone. He is just thirteen and a half years old. I can't make sense of it.

In my earliest memories of Pa Mattar, he was so much smarter than me and so handsome! He loved organizing, to put things in place: an orderly line of shoes, items arranged properly on a table. I was in my second year at nursery school when it was his turn to start, and so, each day, it was my job to walk with him to and from school, getting us both there and back safely. The principal made him the prefect of the class and he got to be the one who rang the bell to start and finish each day.

But then things started to change. When it was time to recite the ABCs together, if one or two children were out of sync, he would grow agitated. If the teacher spoke at too high a pitch, he would be out of his seat, shouting that his ears were hurting. If I changed our route home, it would upset him no end.

And then he began to pee himself in class. It wasn't completely unusual for a younger child to wet or soil themselves in school. When it happened, you would be sent to the cleaning lady, who would wash you off, rinse your clothes and send you back. But when Pa Mattar soiled himself, he would refuse to go get cleaned up. Exact routines were important to him, and the cleaning lady wouldn't re-iron his clothes before making him put them back on, which he couldn't tolerate. Physical punishment was common in our schools, and she would beat him for disobeying.

By his second year at school, he was screaming at teachers and tearing up his books. Soon the principal called my mother to tell her Pa Mattar was no longer welcome. I think now that perhaps he was autistic, but we had no proper diagnosis then. No other school would take him, and a specialized medical assessment would have required travelling to Senegal or Ghana or Nigeria, since The Gambia's medical facilities weren't advanced enough.

A foreign medical visit was financially out of reach for my parents, so Pa Mattar simply stayed home. At the time, we still lived in the compound with my father's other wives and families. My father was at work and my mother was both working and completing her university studies, so my brother was largely left on his own, even though there were adults and other children around. I spent more time with him than anyone, since I got home from school before my parents returned from work. Others saw his behaviour as naughtiness, but I could see that he was creating order: the shoes lined up perfectly, the containers arranged by colour, the fabric coverings on a chair rearranged neatly as soon as someone got up.

One day, as the two of us sat watching television, a woman appeared on the screen. She was completely covered in a black hijab, reciting the Qur'an in English. She had the most beautiful voice and her English was so clear. I remember being struck by the fact that she could be both religious and accomplished, fluent in English and appearing on television.

It gave me an idea. I'd been attending regular government-operated school, where the classes and after-school programs ran from mid-morning to late afternoon, and so I often wasn't home until 5 p.m. But the private Muslim school, what we called Arabic school, offered a tighter schedule, with classes finished by midday. Since Pa Mattar often stayed in his room until late, this would mean that I could spend most of his day with him and watch out for him. And maybe, too, I could become as accomplished as the woman with the beautiful voice.

My parents weren't enthusiastic about my plan. As the man and the head of the household, my father had the last word, though my mother was the person who would most often make the day-to-day decisions about what my siblings and I could or couldn't do. But on this question, neither seemed to want to make the decision. My father wasn't convinced it was a good idea but also said he didn't want to "step between" his daughter and God. I remember him saying, "I'm not going to be the one to stop you." He told me to ask my mother.

She wasn't fully in support of it either: she worried my education might not be to the standard of the English schools. But she also knew it would make life at home easier if someone who loved Pa Mattar was there with him for most of the day. Still, looking after Pa Mattar wasn't a problem my family asked me to take on: it was something I'd decided myself I could do.

"If your father says it's okay, it's okay," my mother finally said. In the absence of a clear no, permission wasn't so much granted as conceded.

A new Arabic school had just opened, and my father took me there to enroll. The man who ran it had studied in Saudi Arabia and was very strict in his observance. I remember how intimidating he looked. He prayed so much that he had a dark mark on his forehead from where his head touched the ground. He wore a skull cap and bragged that he dressed in the colours of the Prophet—green, black and white. His neatly trimmed grey and black beard added authority to his stern face, and as he talked, he would punctuate his words with expressive jabs of his long, thin fingers.

We'd been stopped before entering his office door by his male secretary. "You cannot go in and see the man with your head not covered!" he exclaimed, and sent us back to my father's Toyota pickup truck to get something to cover my head with. We improvised with a piece of fabric torn from a glove, but even so, the principal also disapproved of my bare arms. "You'll soon be getting rid of that clothing!" he declared, his long fingers flicking his disapproval at what I wore.

His school's uniform for girls was a long black skirt, a shapeless black long-sleeved shirt and a black head wrap. The only splash of colour came from the red dust that rose up from the road on the way to the school and coated the hems of the girls' skirts. Still, I was excited to go, picturing the woman on television with the beautiful voice and perfect English and happy to have time to spend with my brother.

For a time, it worked out. Pa Mattar and I spent our afternoons together, but after a while even I couldn't ignore that his behaviour continued to get worse. He would tear off his shirt in the heat and run around the compound and the street, not playing as a child, but out of control. In our community, the only explanation was that he must be mentally sick, and the stigma people attached to "madness" was extreme. There was no real help or treatment, just an expectation you would be sent away, that you had no future. And so it was unusual that my parents kept him close at home.

My mother worried constantly about what would become of Pa Mattar if his behaviour didn't improve. It seemed she was always smoothing over problems with my half-siblings and the other wives caused when my brother moved other people's belongings to suit his need for order and pattern, or became upset in response to their noise or behaviour. My father doted on him, and no one dared abuse Pa Mattar in his presence, but out of Dad's sight, it wasn't uncommon for them to punish him physically.

And it wasn't easy being the sister to the "mad" boy.

At school, my day's learning was focused on religion: studying the Hadith—the words, actions and teachings of the

Prophet—and memorizing the Qur'an. The girls and boys studied in separate groups and of course couldn't play with each other either. Play was limited for girls: skipping rope, for example, was sinful because it might cause our clothing to move and reveal some part of our bodies. And so our play was mostly watching the boys play. Even outside of school, we had to be careful, as the principal would drive around town looking for students who weren't properly covered. He would punish those he spotted when they returned to school the next day, strapping your hand or your bottom. In our small community, it was easy to imagine that word of any carelessness would make its way back to the principal's ears. While I began wearing the veil because I wanted to, I soon wore it because I was afraid of what the consequences would be if I removed it.

At home the questions I wasn't allowed to ask at school bubbled out of me, and I quizzed my father about the things I found puzzling. Why was God a he and not a she? Where is God? Is he in the sky? Can planes see him when they fly through the clouds? Why did God kill his prophet? If God could decide life and death, why wouldn't he just let his prophet live? Why didn't he send more prophets from my part of the world? Why weren't there women prophets, or prophets of other races? So many questions! Eventually my father brushed them away. "The mind has limits," he told me. "Especially when it comes to God. You can't think too much because then you will be committing the sin of questioning God himself."

But it didn't add up to me. And so instead of simply accepting the answers that Arabic school presented, I found myself filled with more and more questions, questions I felt the people around me were dodging. If I could memorize the whole Qur'an—like the lady on television—and still have so many questions, maybe this school wasn't the place to find answers.

And maybe my father wasn't the one to provide answers either. When I was little, I viewed my father as a kind of heroic figure: I was sure he knew everything. Mum and the other wives were so familiar to us that I think we didn't fully see them. They were our caregivers, the women who made us do our chores, help with meals, get to school—the managers of the thousand details that allow a home overflowing with children to function. When Mum or one of his other wives was mad or unhappy, they didn't hide their irritation— we heard the *get your chores done* sharpness in their voices. I saw my mother's fatigue at the end of a day of office work as she prepared supper, knowing she would be grading exam papers by candlelight late into the night.

But my dad seemed larger than life, somehow above daily concerns. While average in height and build, he filled a room when he entered it, his smile wide, his voice silky and loud and clear, his movements confident and sure. Adult conversation would stop and reorient in his direction, as others turned to seek his opinion. While Mum was too busy for long talks, Dad had time to answer my questions. Until they became too many even for him.

In the absence of answers that made sense to me, I developed the habit of watching, absorbing, thinking. My questions remained, though I mostly stopped sharing them with those around me.

I spent my spare time with Pa Mattar, watching him, caring for him. He would say random things, seemingly not connected to what I was doing or what was going on around him, but I would try to respond. His ability to look after himself diminished as he got older, and it wasn't long before I was bathing him, cleaning him in the most intimate ways after he went to the toilet. It was exhausting physically, especially as he got bigger; eventually he outweighed me. There were quiet times too, moments when he would rest with his head in my lap, and I would rub his head and sing quietly. At other times, he would catch my eyes—he had beautiful bright eyes—and he would smile. Small moments, lasting only a breath or two. And then he might be off again, all over the place, out of control.

When I could get Pa Mattar settled, we would watch television: programs from the U.K., America, Australia delivered through the satellite panel on the house's corrugated roof. He loved the purple dinosaur, Barney, and giggled wildly at the adventures of cartoon characters Tom and Jerry. I soaked up the English I heard, mimicking this British actor, that Australian presenter, or Oprah on American television. It's one of the reasons my accent today is hard for people to place: I speak satellite English. I was taught in Arabic, but I picked up my mother's textbooks and other English books in the house and taught myself to read English as well, often practising with Dad.

By the time I was ready to start junior secondary school, I knew I wanted to move from the Arabic school into the English school system. Normally, such a change is difficult: the marks from Arabic school weren't considered adequate to permit entry. Still, my parents tried school after school. No, no, no, said one after another, until finally, they heard of a new school being opened. Former college classmates of my mother's who were teaching there introduced her to the principal. Perhaps I could be on the wait list, he said. Then, perhaps I could enter if I could pass the English and math exams.

I was certain I could pass English, but math? There had been no math programs on television for me to learn from, and I was not taught much on the subject at my previous school. Still, I knew I had only to get a passing score, and so I found the math exam papers from past years and compared them to see what the most common questions were. I studied those questions, figuring that all I had to get was half of them correct—which is what I did, scoring a bare pass on math and a solid 85 percent on my English exam. I was able to enter regular junior secondary school after all.

While I was happy about that, I still felt guilty about not being able to help as much with Pa Mattar. My parents had had what little assessment our hospitals could offer done for him, though they turned up no obvious injury or illness. As his behaviour continued to decline, they soon needed to hire a minder to help watch him.

Herbal remedies were so common in our country that our president promoted his own versions, and faith healers weren't unusual either, with their roots in both tribal and Muslim religious traditions. Family, friends and my mother's work colleagues all suggested treatments designed to combat the supernatural forces they suggested might be causing Pa Mattar's behaviour. It sounds strange to me now, but at the time, with no medical explanation for why my brother was as he was, spirits seemed as likely a cause as any. It also didn't seem impossible that herbal concoctions might cure whatever ailed my brother.

There were many interactions with traditional healers, but one stands out. My mother arranged for me to take Pa Mattar to a healer's home for a series of treatments. The room we entered was dim, the walls filled with shelves of bottles with various medicines and ingredients, the windows darkened by a coating of soot from the fire. The healer came from Foni, a region known for strong supernatural powers. His hair was matted, as if he were starting dreadlocks. His teeth were stained yellow by the nicotine of the cigarettes he smoked constantly. Over a burner, he had a pot of herbs and roots cooking, the scent of it like vegetation left rotting in water for days or weeks. He would bring the pot to a boil, drape a big blanket over it, and make Pa Mattar sit under the blanket, breathing it all in. Of course, my brother didn't want to be under the material, but the man would get other grown men to hold him there, struggling under the blanket.

"He's going to choke in there!" I yelled at them the first time they did it. But the man said no, the jinn in him was fighting back, trying not to be drawn out. Of course, the more my brother fought, the more the healer said it proved that the jinn was strong.

Pa Mattar stayed there for a week. Each morning I would make the journey from home to the healer's place, bringing my brother his food for the day. I still feel guilt over his excitement at seeing me, followed by his incomprehension as to why I left him behind again. At the end of the week, the man gave us bottles filled with yellow water and green water that we were to use to bathe Pa Mattar and rub on his face. The bottles were to be stored outside, and when it was time for his morning bath, they were cold and especially unpleasant. When my brother continued to fight against having these chilly foul fluids poured over him, that was more proof the jinn was strong and he needed more of this awful medicine.

At home the series of minders hired by my parents were also harsh in their treatment of Pa Mattar. Sometimes they would tie him up to stop him from roaming. I often helped Pa Mattar bathe, and when I saw bruises and marks on his body, I told the minder to stop beating him.

"You think you can care for him better?" he said. "You take him. And when he runs away from you, you go find him on your own!"

One minder encouraged the rest of us children to sit on his lap, where he let us play with his phone, but this physical contact made me uncomfortable. As my awareness of sexuality grew, I worried Pa Mattar might be at risk for abuse, since he didn't have the words to tell us if something was wrong, and I tried to keep close watch. I would also tell his minders what it meant when he made this sound or that sound, trying to get them to treat him gently, with kindness.

While I worried they didn't care enough for him, part of me also didn't want to take back the responsibility for Pa Mattar's care. I was at school all day, finally enjoying my classes, making friends, doing things I wanted to do: joining the debate club, taking part in drama competitions. Sometimes I wouldn't see Pa Mattar for two or three days at a time and then, when I did see him, I would just say hi, give him a quick smile and be gone.

And then he died.

I'm still stunned and unsure of what's happening around me. They don't call an ambulance. They don't call a doctor. They call the Imam, and the Imam declares Pa Mattar dead and calls for those who are responsible for taking care of the dead body.

Hours later, cars arrive. And I can hear screaming inside one of the cars. And then the screaming is outside of the car. It is my mum and she is here with my dad. Her eyes are red. Her body is limp. Someone is holding her up. They bring her into the house and sit her on the couch, but she slides off the edge onto the ground and sits crying with her hands in her hair.

I can't cry. I haven't cried since I realized it is my brother who is dead. All around me people are screaming and wailing: my father's other wives and family, people who didn't lift a finger to care for him, the ones who hit him. My parents' tears are genuine, I know, but the others I judge harshly. *Why are you crying? You didn't care when he was alive, and now you are crying because he is dead?*

And as crazy as it might sound, part of me is relieved that he doesn't have to suffer any longer and selfishly relieved for me as well. Because I don't have to try to watch over him anymore, I won't fail at watching over him, won't feel the guilt of that failure. I won't see the suffering in his beautiful eyes anymore, and that suffering won't be my responsibility.

The next twenty-four hours pass in a blur. According to our religious and social beliefs, Pa Mattar needs to be buried by sundown. But those beliefs also push the women who loved him away: If you are female, you aren't encouraged to help prepare or see the body unless it is your job. You aren't permitted to accompany the body to the graveyard. We are just supposed to cry, cook for those coming to mourn, and wait at home.

I can't. After he is buried, I persuade one of my younger half-brothers to take me to where he is buried. When we get there, I send him off to play, telling him to come back for me later.

The soil over Pa Mattar's grave is freshly turned. The tears I have blocked since realizing my brother has died are released. For an hour, I cry and howl and pound the sand under which he is buried. I ask for a sign that he is all right, that he is happier now, that he isn't just dead and buried. No sign appears. And the sadness of Pa Mattar's death stays with me, knits itself into my bones, buries itself deep in my heart.

My brother will always be thirteen. And as close as I hold him inside me, the distance between us will grow.

Now I am almost twice his age. Someday I will be three times as old, and then four. I still imagine what it would have been like if he had had a proper diagnosis, if I had known then what I know now about the autism I suspect he had, and had been able to bring him to Canada. Being with him shaped my beliefs about being of service to others, trying to be kind and patient. I wish he had been able to wait for us to understand. But we didn't understand. And he couldn't hang on.

There was no investigation of the cause of his death. He was mad. He went to sleep. He died. It wasn't unusual in The Gambia for no further reason to be sought. And so my brother's death will always be a mystery to me.

And whenever sadness visits me, my grief about Pa Mattar visits me too.

"You're a young person," Annameik said to me when I emerged from the basement after a few days of darkness and sleeping. "Go hiking! You should be active!"

Not long after, she knocked on my door and pointed to a turquoise bicycle and grey helmet. They were for me, she said, to make it easier for me to get around. "I don't need a helmet," I said—we'd hardly used them for bikes at home. But Annameik insisted: it was illegal to ride without a helmet here.

I'd ridden a bicycle every day when I attended Arabic school, but now, peddling this bike through Vancouver's hilly streets seemed almost impossible. Even the hills didn't seem enough of an explanation for my difficulty. "I think this bicycle has a problem," I said to Annameik.

"What gear do you have it in?" she asked.

Gear? I didn't know bicycles had gears, or that you shifted them depending on whether the terrain was hilly or flat. She showed me how the gears worked and gave me advice on when to gear up and gear down. One more thing I didn't know.

But Annameik was right: getting active did help. I used the bicycle to fetch groceries and navigate the neighbourhood, saving the transit money that I so desperately needed for other essentials. I also used the bike to cruise the area's thrift shops. I loved to look at the decor items, to imagine what I might buy for my own home someday. I liked the idea that things someone had discarded might find a second life somewhere else, their beauty and usefulness rediscovered.

And no matter my mood, I still pushed myself to go to class: the psych class where the instructor tried to hypnotize us, the introduction to social work class filled with students from so many backgrounds, the Canadian history class that was introducing me to my new country. When our history teacher announced we were to research the story of someone who had been involved in the First World War, I chose a nurse from Sarnia who had served in battlefield hospitals. At the library, I dug into online databases, learning all I could from her records of service and other publicly available information. I pulled what I'd gathered into a slide presentation and wrote a script for what I would say. And then at the last minute, I lost my nerve. I quickly recorded a voiceover track, and when it was my turn to present, I loaded my presentation up and just hit play. I'd been sure I would be able to tell the nurse's story to my classmates, but instead I sat silently to the side as my prerecorded voice did the job. Visible, but invisible.

All around me, the other students seemed to connect and talk so easily. Maybe I just needed more to talk *about* with them. At home in The Gambia, it was easy: we had family and culture in common. Perhaps learning more about Canada would help, I thought. Maybe my passion for the past was a way to step forward. And so I spent hours in the library, reading about prime ministers, even Canada's first one, who seemed to always be drunk. I read about the construction of the railways in Canada, and how the Chinese immigrants who did most of the work weren't allowed to bring their families here. I read about Canada's treaties with Indigenous people, and about the abuses of residential schools and reserves, how unfairly they were treated—and still are. I learned so much. But when I tried to strike up conversations with Canadian students in class, it turned out my history studies weren't much help: they knew little about Indigenous history or long-dead prime ministers, even the drunk one. Instead, they talked about hockey, a sport I didn't understand and wasn't all that interested in. I'd thought Canadians would know their country's story inside and out, but it was soon clear to me that I knew more than the Canadian-born youngsters in my classes. And I realized that when you're born here, you get to be Canadian without understanding how Canada came to be.

Eventually I did manage to share notes and homework with one or two other students, and I became friends with Zaira, a Middle Eastern girl from Italy in my psychology class. Her broad smile was infectious, and we shared meals at my apartment—fish stew and spicy seafood I loved to prepare—but we drifted apart. With most people, when talk turned to our families or our pasts, I shut down. I wasn't ready to talk about why I'd ended up here and had no petty home squabbles to share, which meant much of my life was off-limits—and that reluctance cut me off from a potential relationship.

It was easier to lose myself in my new country's past than to consider my own. And so, with hours between classes to fill, I retreated to the library and buried myself in books about things that had happened decades before I'd been born.

It was February. I'd been at the library for hours. The room was filled with windows, but I liked a corner where two solid walls met and I could tuck myself into a chair and be almost unseen. When I'd first started visiting the library, I'd had to ask the librarians for help in navigating the shelving system: the library in my high school had been small enough that it was easy to find what you were looking for. Here, though, there were hundreds and hundreds of books, organized by a number and letter system that I needed to understand.

I can't remember now what book I was looking for, but as I stood at the shelf, I lifted one book to move it out of the way and that's when the slim man next to me spoke up. "I've read that book five times," he said. "It's really, really good." I don't know what I said back to him: probably not very much, since it wasn't my habit to make small talk with strange men.

"I'm going to get coffee," he said. "Do you want one?"

"I'm more of a tea person," I said.

"I'll grab you a tea, then," he replied.

"And how am I supposed to trust that tea?"

"My bad," he said. "You're right. You can come with me if you like."

I'm not sure why I did. His name was Anderson, and he was slightly built with long brown hair and an easy smile, just a few years older than me. The conversation was unexpected and random, but he was so friendly and non-aggressive, his voice low and not intimidating at all, that I let my guard down a bit.

"Hey, do you play darts?" he asked as we stood drinking our hot beverages in the building's atrium.

Darts? One more thing I didn't know.

"I can teach you—you can come out with my brother and me."

He wasn't a student at Douglas, but he had a cousin's library card that gave him access. Later, I learned he wasn't checking out the books for himself that day; he rented his small flat on Airbnb and he'd stock it with books he thought might appeal to his visitors. Then he'd spend the nights

A childhood photo of me taken around 2000 with Mum and two of my father's wives. L to R: Awa Bah (Penda's mom); my mother Awa Saho; me; my father's first wife Jariatou; and Pa Mattar with his back to the camera. Behind us is my half-brother Cherno and further in the background are Dad and other siblings.

After I spoke out publicly, my grandfather offered these words of comfort: "May you be content, and may that man be punished by God."

Me with my dad in 2013 at the main family compound. With us are my half-siblings Binta and Isatou.

About half of our big family! Front centre: Dad with my half-sibling Abdoulie and sister Ida. Second row: My sister Nogoi, me, brother Muhammed, half-siblings Isatou and Binta, father's wife Nenegalleh holding her granddaughter, and half-sibling Jarrie Bobo. Back: Nenegalleh's daughter, my oldest half-sister Hajakaddy, a cousin, father's wife Kadijatou, my mother, and half-sister Aminata.

Me with my amazing mum, Awa, in 2019, just after the Human Rights Watch press conference. I am inspired by her strength.

At my mum's compound in 2020. Me in foreground, Mum in the middle, and my grandmother in the back.

Waiting to board the ferry to return to The Gambia in 2019 for the Human Rights Watch press conference publicly naming Jammeh as a rapist. In the foreground with their backs to the camera are Fatoumatta Sandeng and Reed Brody.

In 2020, we re-enacted my escape from The Gambia for a documentary about sexual violence survivors.

When Jammeh was deposed in 2017, I was able to go home and see my family for the first time since my escape. Left to right, outside at my mother's compound: a cousin, my father's wife Kadijatou, an aunt with a baby, my father's wife Nenegelleh, me with back to camera. (Yes, I'm wearing socks!)

Learning to box was part of the emotional and physical training I did to prepare myself for speaking publicly about being raped by Jammeh.

Surrounded by allies and speaking to the crowd at the end of our first protest march in The Gambia in 2019. I never imagined that my testimony would spark a movement! In the background on the left is Retsam Chambai, one of the organizers of The Toufah Foundation.

In June 2019, over 200 of us protested along the main road of Serrekunda in the first march of its kind in The Gambia, raising our voices together to speak out for victims of sexual violence.

After the Truth, Reconciliation and Reparations hearings in 2019, I was able to meet in person with some of the girls from the mentoring group.

At the UN after speaking at a youth panel for Human Rights Day, 2019. Left to right: Feliciana Herrera Ceto from Guatemala, me, Secretary-General António Guterres, Alexus Lawrence from New York and Carl Smith from the Yupiaq tribe in Alaska.

Behind the scenes as we filmed the "reverse reality" video in the streets of Serrekunda in 2020, to demonstrate the absurdity of everyday sexism.

After we debuted the reverse reality videos in Dakar, I took selfies with women who attended the viewing.

sleeping in his car or at his brother's place. Like me, he was an immigrant, though he came from Ireland. And like me, he was doing what he had to do to get by.

The way he said my name in his accent made me laugh: Tow-fah.

"Do you like jazz?" Anderson asked me after we'd gone out and played darts.

It was something else I'd never heard of, but with Anderson, I didn't feel embarrassment, just curiosity. And so he took me out to a local bar with live music. I loved it: the music, watching the other people listening to the music, some dancing, all of us getting lost in the sound. At the end of a day at school, I'd text Anderson: "Can we go see some jazz tonight?" Often, he'd be working until late and I'd go on my own—he'd show up when he could. Sometimes we'd go back to his flat and watch videos of old musicians. I fell in love with "Sleep Walk" by Santo & Johnny, mesmerized by the dreamy twang of the steel guitar, the measured beat of the rhythm guitar and the gentle thrum of the drummer's brushes against the snare drum.

We were friends. Anderson had a girlfriend in the U.K.— I'd even spoken to her on the phone a few times. But I'd been so lonely, so friendless, that having one friend felt like a long drink of water after months in a desert. He was so easy to talk to, so good at just listening. I didn't feel judged, didn't worry about not measuring up. With Anderson, I could just be.

—

"How did you get your permanent resident status in less than a year?"

Anderson and I were driving from Burnaby into downtown Vancouver to help his brother move. He navigated his second-hand Nissan through the city's side streets in the grey light of a steady afternoon rain, preferring the slower route to the highways. With Anderson, the route was always slower: if a speed limit said forty kilometres, he wouldn't drive forty-one. A stop sign meant a complete stop, not a slow roll past the sign. I didn't have my driver's licence, but I had plenty of driving advice to offer, which Anderson put up with, simply shrugging my comments off and driving as he always did: cautiously. "You're such a rule follower!" I teased him.

He had been in Canada much longer than me but was only now applying for his permanent residency and wanted to know how I got my status so quickly.

"It's because I came to Canada as a protected person," I said. And when he followed up with the inevitable "Why?" I gave him the answer I'd given the people at the refugee placement centre when I'd arrived. In my country, I said, young women were often married off to much older men, and I had come to Canada to escape a forced marriage. The conversation drifted away from my reason for coming to Canada to more general questions about men's and women's roles and expectations in The Gambia. Did parents expect girls to get married young? Were male children more valued than female children? And then the questions drifted back to me: Did my parents value my brother more than me?

"I didn't have that dynamic with my brother," I said, "and it doesn't exist now because he passed away." I hadn't expected to tell Anderson about Pa Mattar, but as we drove through the rainy streets, the story of my brother's life and death spilled from me. It felt good to talk about him, good to bring him back to life by sharing his story here.

Over the weeks that followed, Pa Mattar would come up in conversation again, sometimes when I shared a thought of him, sometimes when Anderson brought him up. When I told Anderson I had received a good mark on my history project about the First World War nurse, his words were simple: "Pa Mattar would be proud of you." The sharing wasn't just about Pa Mattar. Anderson told me details of his life and his family too. It helped to have someone who acknowledged the brother I carried in my heart. I felt safe. And I felt seen.

I never thought I would tell Anderson about being raped. But then one afternoon, it just happened. We were at his apartment, and he was cleaning in preparation for another Airbnb guest. As he wiped his leather couch, I watched him from the chair across the room. And I just started talking.

"I was raped," I said. "By the president of my country."

Anderson kept cleaning as the details tumbled out of me. The pageant. Jimbee. The house they offered me. My refusal of his proposal. His anger. The injection. My begging. His rage. My pain. His contempt. Going home. My secret. Jimbee's order that I return to see him. My fear. My escape.

I didn't cry. I told him what had happened, matter-of-factly, calmly. And Anderson let me. He didn't ask questions, didn't interrupt, didn't offer advice or suggestions, didn't look at me with pity. He just let me talk as he continued tidying, his quiet acceptance of what I was saying making it easier for me to continue to speak.

When I stopped talking, he said, "That's really shitty. But I know you've got this."

The room was quiet. No drama. No tears. No big emotions. But no real relief for me either. I didn't feel like I'd unburdened myself or that something significant had shifted or changed. I'd just talked. He'd listened. That was that. I headed home not long afterwards, and as I unlocked the door to my apartment in Annameik's basement, my phone pinged.

"I hope you got home okay," said the text from Anderson.

I didn't respond. I turned off my phone. And eventually ghosted him.

I didn't intend to avoid Anderson. But hours turned into days, days into weeks.

When I'd told Anderson about Pa Mattar, I'd felt relief and connection. Telling him about being raped had also felt right in the moment, but afterwards insecurity flooded through me. Would knowing about the rape change what he thought of me? Would I still be the same person in his eyes? And rather than let myself find out for certain whether things had changed, I avoided him.

It seemed like he was avoiding me too. I received no calls or texts from him after the message checking about whether I had got home okay.

Finally he called. "What's up?" he said.

"I was thinking you'd decided you didn't want to reach out," I told him.

"But I did reach out. I sent you that text, and you didn't reply."

"Well, I thought you would reach out after that," I replied.

"Look, I think we should meet and talk," he said.

And so we did.

"I was afraid you'd feel differently about me, see me differently," I told him as we sat in the same living room where I'd shared my secret weeks earlier.

Anderson said, "I thought I should let you share what you wanted to share, to tell me what you want to tell me. I didn't think it was my place to ask more. And it doesn't change what I think about you, other than making me respect you even more." For the first time, I considered the possibility someone would respect me for surviving rather than blame or shame me for having been raped.

In the days that followed, we settled back into our routine of conversation and jazz and darts. About a month later, we were playing darts when one of Anderson's friends approached. "Hey, we should go out for a drink," he said to me after we'd chatted for a bit. I don't remember now exactly what I said, but I shot him down and the man drifted away.

After we finished playing, Anderson drove me home through the dark city streets. I don't remember what we were talking about, but there was a moment where we were both silent. And then Anderson spoke. "I'm very angry about what happened to you," he said.

I started to cry. "Sometimes I feel like he's winning," I said. "Like, if his goal was to break me, to make it so that I can't connect to people, that maybe he's achieved that."

Anderson reached out, put his hand on my hand. "It's okay," he said. "It's going to be okay."

I don't know why, but I believed him.

Over the weeks that followed, Anderson and I continued to spend time together. Though we didn't talk at length again about what had happened to me, he found ways to help me see Jammeh not as a larger-than-life monster but as small and pathetic. "Look, you can see the outline of a bulletproof vest there," he said as we looked at a photo of Jammeh. "If he's so powerful, why is he afraid of being shot?" He made fun of Jammeh's proclaimed cures for HIV and AIDS, claims that were obviously absurd once you were outside of Jammeh's information bubble. (Later, I would learn an estimated nine thousand Gambians received Jammeh's useless herbal treatments in what a study in *Health and Human Rights Journal* called "cruel, inhuman, and degrading treatment." No one knows how many people died as a result.) Anderson pointed out the theatrical aspects of Jammeh's formal costumes, public prayers and supposed acts of Islamic devotion. They were things that probably seemed obvious to someone who hadn't grown up under Jammeh's regime, but I'd never known a president other than Jammeh, and many in my country literally worshipped the man. Anderson joked about castrating Jammeh, and the two of us made up unusual ways to torture him. One of Anderson's more novel suggestions was that he should be pinched ten million times, in agony one tiny twist after another.

It might sound foolish, small. But I'd never laughed at Jammeh before. And with each crazy suggested punishment, with each time Anderson pointed out another of the man's insecure posturings, the ballooning presence Jammeh had in my imagination deflated just a little bit more. Maybe that's why dictators fear comedians, cartoonists and satirists: laughter loosens fear's grip, diminishes its ability to control. Each time Anderson and I poked fun at Jammeh, it made it easier to see he wasn't all-powerful, all-seeing. He was pathetic. He was laughable. And I was laughing at him.

I felt lucky to have Anderson as my friend, but eventually our lives began moving in different directions. He and his brother were making plans to move to Australia. Trying to survive in Vancouver while working poorly paid jobs had become too difficult, and someone they knew in Australia had offered them construction jobs.

I was nearing the end of my second term at Douglas College and didn't have the money for the next term's tuition. Soon my refugee income support payments would end and I'd have to start repaying the $2,500 I owed the government. While Vancouver wasn't exactly the wilderness Solomon had declared it to be when I told him I was moving there, it also hadn't turned out to be the solution I had hoped for. Yes, things had improved for me since I'd been here, but without Anderson or Zaira or school, there was nothing keeping me in the city. And so I made plans to move back to Toronto.

I'm sure anyone looking at my situation from the outside would have thought I was mad. Though I did everything to keep the costs low, two cross-Canada moves in less than a year wasn't exactly financially sensible. But moving back felt right. I felt stronger, a bit more sure of myself. Maybe Toronto was where I should be.

Now that I knew the city—or at least knew it better than when I'd first arrived—I realized I didn't need to live right downtown. I searched for more economical accommodations and found a room for rent in a house in Scarborough owned by a Caribbean family, arranging the rental from Vancouver. My trip back was exhausting. The cheap airfare routed me through two other cities, and then I had to take a train ride from the airport to Union Station. I splurged on an express GO bus from downtown to Scarborough. The first time I'd arrived in Toronto, I hadn't known what to expect. This time, along with my suitcases, I had packed determination: I was going to restart my life here, in this city.

Over the weeks that followed, I patched together minimum-wage jobs, washing dishes in a restaurant and getting shifts at a Tim Hortons. After paying my bills, I used what I had left to pay for classes in social work at Seneca College, a CPR course, and a food-handling certificate to qualify me to work in better restaurants. I discovered Broadway shows I could watch online and started searching out dance and other performances as well. And I continued to research things that seemed uniquely Canadian to me. At home in The Gambia, people didn't take out mortgages to buy a home: they more often paid cash for a plot of land and then either built a home bit by bit, paying as they went as my mother had, or saved the money to hire a contractor to do it all at once. Only the most wealthy people purchased ready-built homes. I'd never heard of mortgages, and so I looked up online how they worked and researched other financial products, like retirement savings plans and tax-free savings accounts.

As September approached, so did Eid al-Adha. The Islamic "festival of the sacrifice" commemorates the willingness of the Prophet Ibrahim to sacrifice his son as a demonstration of his loyalty to God. The dates shift each year. The previous year, Eid had fallen in July, not long after I'd arrived in Senegal, and had passed in a blur as I struggled to find safety. But now, alone in Toronto, the distance between my family and me seemed greater than ever. Unlike in the West, we didn't pay much attention to birthdays unless you were wealthy, in which case they might be a chance to show off your wealth with a party and expensive gifts. Me missing family birthdays and them missing mine wasn't notable. But missing Eid? Eid was always our family's biggest celebration of the year. It was the one day Mum didn't have to struggle to get us out of bed: we would all be up at 5 or 6 a.m., she and the other mothers up even earlier to begin the day's cooking. As they prepared breakfast, my father and brothers would wash the ram each family purchased for their feast, ensuring it was clean and well fed and tied securely in the courtyard.

After fresh porridge, we would dress in our best clothes, often wearing a new item or outfit, and by 8 a.m. or so, all of us children would pile into my father's truck, the girls sitting on each other's laps in the cab with Dad, my brothers climbing into the open bed at the back. Together we would drive to the religious ceremony, often held outdoors because so many attended that we could not fit inside the mosque. As people gathered, you could smell the newness of their clothing, freshly laundered and ironed, and hear the crisp slap of the cloth of the men's robes as they moved. If you were lucky, you got to hold Dad's hand, but with so many children, more often you were holding the hand of the sister holding the hand of the sister holding on to the back of Dad's robe. Photographers set up shop as families stopped to get a group photo.

Following the formal prayers, the Imam would slaughter his ram in view of the congregation, the head of each household there to witness it, ensuring that he did not slaughter his own family's ram before the Imam had done his. Then it was time to go home, though the socializing that happened as the ceremony ended could stretch our time there, as my father greeted people he knew.

When we got back to the compound, my father and brothers would slaughter our ram. As the women prepared the meat for our meal, we would visit poorer families around us, bringing them gifts of bags of rice and sugar. And then we would gather for the meal. The best of the food would be given to my father, as head of the household, though he always let the youngest children have bites from his plate—not something every father did.

After we ate, we would change clothing again, putting on another new outfit. While earlier in the day, we wore traditional clothing—robes for the men and boys, long skirts and blouses with head scarves for the women and girls—our afternoon outfits were more likely to be Western. And then the visits would begin, to family, friends and neighbours. At each stop, the children would be given a salibo, a gift of a small amount of money. On the following day, the visits would continue.

While Eid is marked by Muslims around the world, the festivities vary widely from culture to culture. In Toronto, the distance from my Gambian family was starker than ever. It still seemed too complicated for me to join the Gambian community. And so, as my family gathered almost seven thousand kilometres away, I attended the ceremony at a nearby Lebanese mosque. Back in my room afterwards, I spent the rest of the day on my phone, using WhatsApp to talk to my family, asking for photos of what they were doing and wearing and eating. And longing to be with them.

As autumn turned to winter, my days were packed. I was taking college classes three mornings a week, working afternoon shifts at Tim Hortons, and then heading to a T-shirt factory where I worked a shift that finished at 2 a.m. I should have been exhausted—and sometimes I was. Some of my overscheduling was avoidance: if I filled my hours, I didn't have to think about what had happened to me, didn't have to notice how much I missed my family. But some of it was more positive, focused on enrichment rather than escape. As much as I was tired, I was energized. On my evenings off, I found free poetry open mic nights, where I struck up conversations with others in the audience. I wasn't ready to get on the stage again myself, but I worked to find other creative outlets. In my room, I watched guitar lessons on YouTube, trying to teach myself to play. Solomon and I reconnected as well, and though he too was busy with school and work, we found time to get together. I was recreating myself, reimagining myself back to life as I tried to awaken the Toufah I'd been before everything had changed, not realizing that a different Toufah might emerge.

I belong here, I thought. *I'm not going anywhere. He's not going to win. I'm not going to be invisible anymore.*

7

A DICTATOR FALLS

"**A**re you there, caller? Are you there?"

The voices in my ears are plotting to depose a dictator. I, on the other hand, am loading T-shirts, one at a time, into a printing press: pick one up, put it in, print; pick one up, put it in, print; pick one up, put it in, print. The scent of the heated plasticized decals adhering to the cotton fabric fills the air. To fight the boredom of eight hours of repetition, I tune in to Gambian diaspora radio stations on my phone, listening to the familiar accents and languages as people discuss conditions back home and share the latest news of the government's failures and corruption. They aren't subtle. One program's motto is "How to Oust a Dictator," and guests and hosts strategize about how the Gambian community worldwide can support opposition parties at home in an effort to finally depose President Jammeh. Gambians from around the globe call in, and before long, I join the queue, punching in the number between T-shirts, and then waiting on hold for my own turn on air. When the call-in host announces the name I've given them, asking "Are you there, caller?" I run to the washroom or sneak outside for a few minutes so I can speak. Other workers take smoke breaks; I take call-in show breaks.

"Our people are suffering!" I declare, as I argue that we have a responsibility to do all we can to push Jammeh out of power. I am, of course, preaching to the converted—many of the other listeners have left The Gambia under threat from Jammeh's regime. "My sister, it is true!" declares the host as I finish my impassioned plea for action.

One host in particular regularly catches my attention, someone who is more radical and progressive than the rest. Where others simply say people need to get out and vote, Babou Abdoulie asks questions that point to the structural deficiencies in The Gambia's government and society. Where are the women in parliament? he asks. Our parties use women to mobilize voters but don't put them forward as candidates—why not? What about minimum wages and workers' rights? And the Cadi Courts—the Islamic civil justice system that has jurisdiction over Gambian Muslims on matters related to civil status, marriage, guardianship and more—should be reformed as well, he argues, since they are led by men and mostly favour men.

These are opinions I rarely hear put forward in the Gambian community—and if they are made, never by a man. When I call in, he listens to what I have to say, and we often end up having long discussions on air about everything from how theatre could be used to get progressive political messages into communities to imagining what The Gambia could be like fifty years from now.

"Would you like to host a program?" he eventually asks me. I haven't told him the specifics of why I left The Gambia— he simply knows I am passionate about what we could do to create a better country. And so I start hosting my own call-in program on Saturday afternoons called "Community Sense." I book guests on topics ranging from tourism, mental health and prostitution to the need for educational reform, then open up the lines to callers who share their own stories and ideas. I don't hint at what happened to me, don't share anything personal about myself on the program at all. But then I decide to do a session on the lack of mental health support systems in The Gambia.

On the program, I open up the conversation by sharing the story of Pa Mattar with my guest, a psychiatric doctor from The Gambia. I've told my mother I'll be doing the program, and she calls in anonymously to share her thoughts about being the parent of someone who was ill, her experiences in seeing how Gambian society stigmatized her son and, by extension, his family. Callers queue up to join the conversation, one unlike any we would ever hear at home.

Behind the microphone, I am both visible and invisible: sharing my opinions but not having to deal with the in-person reactions of people who know about my pageant win and the fact that I fled the country. I also continue to call in to other Gambian radio shows as a listener rather than a host, and I start to slowly lift the lid on the secret I've been carrying. I am a victim of sexual violence, I say, anonymously to begin with but later using my first name. I don't say who or how—I am not ready for that step—but yes, I say, this is part of my experience. "I was raped," I say. "I'm a survivor."

The doorbell chimed inside the house as I pressed the button. I was standing on the steps of a home in a wealthy Toronto suburb. I'd left the T-shirt printing factory and gotten a job with a telecom company, going door to door to convert customers from one of the other carriers to ours. Every other door I'd knocked on that evening had been answered by an older white person, so when a Black woman in her forties answered this door, my first thought was, *She must be the maid.* I started my pitch, wondering when she would interrupt me to go get her boss. "You know what," she said, "I'm just going to get my husband and see if he wants the package you're selling."

Husband? I was embarrassed by my assumption that a Black person wouldn't own this house, in this neighbourhood, startled by the internalized stereotypes we carry even about our own skin colour. As the man came toward the door, I overheard him use a Nigerian slang term to his wife.

"Oh my brother!" I said as I greeted him. "You are Nigerian!"

He smiled in return. "Where are you from?"

Gambia, I replied.

"Ah! I couldn't pinpoint your accent—you don't sound Nigerian, but you don't sound Gambian either," he replied as he invited me in.

"I learned my English from TV first. My accent is a bit messed up," I said, as we both laughed.

I was there to pitch him on phone, cable and internet combos, but our conversation ranged widely from there. I should have been getting his signature and closing the sale, but I welcomed the warmth of their living room and a conversation with someone who had a thread of connection back to Africa.

"You know, I'm Black, I'm Nigerian and people here assume that I must do bad things to make my money," he said. He had come from a poor family and used his brains to get a scholarship to Oxford University, eventually becoming a surgeon, the skill that had brought him to Canada. "I live here in this house, but people still think I don't belong."

I admitted I, too, had assumed his wife must have been the house help for a white homeowner. He nodded as we talked about how deeply embedded stereotypes about race were. "Yes, even me," he said. "We all make assumptions."

Before long, he was advising me to return to school. "I think you are too smart for this job that you are doing," he said. "I think you could do better." As he signed up for the internet bundle I was offering, he gave me his phone number and took mine in return. We stayed in touch in the months that followed, as he invited me to seminars for Black entrepreneurs and panels on racism. Our lives couldn't have been more different, and yet we shared a common thread of experience as Black African immigrants in a country where white was still the baseline, the norm.

I made other connections too.

The boy on the balcony looked like he was maybe fourteen years old. I called up to ask if his parents were at home. He didn't answer directly and instead asked me over and over what my employee ID number was. I repeated the number back to him again and again as he laughed, his unexpected question and repetition reminding me of Pa Mattar. We played this way for a few minutes before his father finally appeared.

"Who are you?" he asked.

I told him the company I was working for, but he seemed more interested in my willingness to talk to his son for so long. "Not too many people can hold him in conversation," he said. "He doesn't usually like to talk to strangers."

He reminds me of my brother, I said, and told him a little about Pa Mattar.

"Did he have autism?" he eventually asked me.

"I'm not sure."

My answer puzzled him. "How can you not know?" he asked.

As we talked, he shared with me some of the details of his son's diagnosis: the things he was good at, the things he had trouble with. "There's a video on YouTube you should watch," he said. "A very famous autistic guy, a Black guy from the U.K., who can look at a building and then sit down and draw it in perfect detail." It was the first time I'd heard that word: autism. It sounded better than "mad."

While I'd spent days in the library in Vancouver trying to understand Canada's history, my door-to-door time in Toronto was another kind of education in what Canada was. There were people who turned me away—and some who seemed to hate my employer with a passion I didn't take personally—but people, too, who gave me an umbrella on a rainy night or a towel to dry myself off with. I saw people of so many races and backgrounds: white, Black, mixed race, Indian, Arab, Asian. More often than not it was the immigrants who invited me in to talk. And as I knocked on one door after another, there were people who judged me and those I judged, or misjudged, as well, both our judgments sometimes literally skin-deep. But there were so many more who just saw me, a woman named Toufah, someone they defined by her actions, not her skin colour or some unknown past. It felt good.

Solomon and I sometimes met downtown in Little Italy, not far from the resettlement centre where we'd lived when we first arrived in Canada. We teased each other constantly. I made fun of Solomon for being loud, telling him he was an uncivilized refugee. He poked fun at my feminism.

As we walked down College Street one busy evening, the sidewalks overflowed with people and we were pushed into the street to get around the crowds. "You better watch out for the streetcar," said Solomon as I stepped close to the tracks.

"Ah, they better not touch me!" I joked.

"Oh, you think as a woman you have the right not to be hit?" Solomon shot back, punning on the connection between being hit by a streetcar and being hit by a person. I laughed at his foolishness.

"All you do is play football," I said. "You know nothing about women's rights!"

Later as we waited in line at a Starbucks, the teasing continued. "The refugee is now ordering a pumpkin latte," Solomon commented as we moved up the line.

"You do need to integrate," I told him. "Perhaps the pumpkin will feed your brain."

"You're such an asshole," he shot back, as we laughed at each other and ourselves.

At home in The Gambia, preparations were underway for the presidential election, which occurred every five years. The likelihood of a shift in government seemed slim. President Jammeh had won every election since his coup in 1994, and the president before him, Dawda Jawara, had been in power ever since The Gambia's independence had been declared in 1965—just two presidents in fifty years. Jammeh's ascension had come with a gun in hand, and certainly his continued hold on power was aided by his control of the armed forces and other national power structures. But the country's political system also helped keep him there. The president was elected by a plurality of votes, not a majority. The proliferation of opposition parties in the country could have been seen as a sign of a healthy democracy, but Jammeh routinely imprisoned opposing leaders. Having so many small opposition parties also worked to his advantage, since no single opposition leader was able to garner enough votes to defeat him.

Then, in the lead-up to the 2016 campaign, Jammeh's forces arrested Solo Sandeng, a senior member of one of the main opposition parties, and murdered him while he was in custody. Outrage grew over Sandeng's death and the opposition parties made a surprise move. Seven parties united under the banner Coalition 2016, fielding a single candidate, Adama Barrow, for the top post. Only one other party stood outside the coalition, supporting its own candidate. There would be just three men vying for the presidency.

The two weeks of official campaigning in November were peaceful, but at times, Jammeh's government blocked access to mobile messaging apps such as WhatsApp and Viber. During the election itself, internet access and international phone calls were limited as well. Beyond Gambia's borders, expats organized to support Barrow, the underdog, a businessman who had never run for public office before. People in the Gambian diaspora sent donations to the opposition coalition and broadcasted support for Barrow's campaign via internet and social media channels. Donations poured in to print T-shirts, posters and more with Barrow's image and coalition colours. In addition to hosting my online show, I continued to tune in to other online broadcasts, calling in to programs on more prominent sites. Soon I was being asked to represent the point of view of young people, like me, who had never known a national leader other than Jammeh but were nevertheless hungry for change. As election day approached, I found it harder to sleep, and I was awake the whole night of December 1 to 2 as I waited for the results.

The Gambia's voting system is unique, simple and accurate, designed for a country with many languages and low literacy rates. Marbles, not paper ballots, are used to vote. Polling stations feature a sealed drum for each candidate, painted in the colour of the candidate's party. The candidate's picture also appears on the drum. Each voter receives a marble, which they drop into the drum of the candidate they wish to vote for. On December 1, 2016, over 525,000 marbles were dropped as almost 60 percent of Gambia's registered voters showed up at the polls.

Yahya Jammeh lost by just under 20,000 votes.

"Gambia's Jammeh loses presidential election to Adama Barrow in shock election result" read the headline on the BBC News on December 2. As the results were announced, Jammeh conceded defeat, congratulating Barrow on his victory and wishing him "all the best." People in Banjul and elsewhere took to the streets in celebration at the prospect of a change in the country's leadership.

At home in Toronto, I couldn't believe what I was hearing. The underdog had won!

As excited as I was for my country, my heart also lifted at the prospect that maybe I would be able to go home. With Jammeh no longer in power, perhaps it would be safe to see my family. But even as I heard that Jammeh accepted the results, I thought, no, this was too easy. The man I know wasn't accepting these results.

"Are you okay?" I asked my mother when I was able to get through on the phone lines.

Yes, yes, she told me, but things were uneasy. Troops were patrolling the streets, and though there had been celebrations, there were also rallies of Jammeh supporters. Things didn't seem settled at all.

And then on December 9, Jammeh appeared on state television to say he was rejecting the election results because of "serious and unacceptable abnormalities" in the election process. He wasn't leaving office, he said, as he called for a new election.

Then he closed the borders, holding the whole country captive.

There he is, I thought. *There he is. That's the real him.*

But Gambians didn't back down. Older women showed up with brooms, quietly sweeping the street in front of the presidential palace. Others took to the streets carrying calabash gourd ladles, called kalama in Mandinka, chanting, *We need change, enough is enough,* in what came to be called the Kalama Revolution. Demonstrations continued even as protestors were arrested and detained. That January most of the world was watching another president, who had taken the world by surprise in an upset victory over Hillary Clinton. But as Americans and others focused on Donald Trump taking his oath of office, Gambians exiled abroad watched instead for news from home as negotiators laid out terms for an orderly transition of power. Jammeh refused to budge. Other African heads of state weighed in, encouraging Jammeh to depart. He ignored them. The Gambia bar association, teachers' union, press union, medical association and the University of Gambia condemned his actions. Jammeh took no notice. The United Nations Security Council, Economic Community of West African States and African Union denounced him. Jammeh held firm.

As the days ticked by, I stayed at home with my headphones on, tuning in to one Gambian online news program after another, searching for the most current insights.

"People are stocking up on food," my mother told me when I was able to get through to her. "Everybody is closing their doors."

Doubts washed over me: Had those of us outside the country made things worse by working to overthrow Jammeh? Would he be even more dangerous now? My anxiety climbed as I worried about my family. What would happen if Jammeh fought to stay in power?

And then, on January 19, Adama Barrow was sworn in as president in the Gambian embassy in Dakar, Senegal. At the same time, armed forces from Senegal, Ghana and Nigeria took joint action, entering The Gambia and enforcing a naval blockade. Two days later, Jammeh and his wife, Zineb, left for exile in Equatorial Guinea. (It would later be reported that Jimbee joined them there as well.) In his last week in power, Jammeh used a cargo plane to ship his luxury vehicles out of the country and drained US$11.4 million from the state treasury. In the weeks that followed, the reports of his thefts while in office would continue to grow: US$50 million stolen from The Gambia's ports, social security and national telecom company; US$4.5 million of pension funds used to purchase his private jet while Gambian pensioners had seen their benefits shrink to just US$5 a month or had been denied them completely; funds from the Jammeh Foundation for Peace diverted for his personal use. In all, the Gambian Ministry of Justice would eventually conclude that Jammeh "wasted, misappropriated, diverted or simply stole" the equivalent of more than US$300 million from the country's coffers.

Still, a dictator had fallen. And his exile meant I and other Gambians like me could end ours.

I can go home, I thought when I heard the news. It had been almost eighteen months since I'd fled. *I can go home.*

8

HOMECOMING

The bat-shaped concrete-and-glass structure of the terminal building at the Banjul International Airport gleams in the late-November sunlight as my flight touches down on the runway. It has taken me almost a year to save the money for the trip. The last time I was here, I'd been hiding in the airplane's washroom, desperate to depart again. I'd never stepped inside the terminal, never seen the towering white columns of the passenger atrium. Now as I wait for my two suitcases—one of them filled with Dollarama gifts for my family—local languages tumble in the air around me: Wolof, Fula, Mandinka, Jola and more. My ears are so thirsty for their sounds.

A friend picks me up and drives me to my mother's home. I haven't told any of my family I am on my way, wanting to surprise them. Caution is part of the reason as well: though Jammeh is no longer in power, he still has his supporters; the fewer people who know I am coming, the safer I feel.

I come around into the courtyard, where I see Ida, Nogoi and Muhammed. They look so tall! We hug and cry. And then I shush them before I open the door to my mother's house. Inside, Mum is sitting with two ladies. As I walk into the room, she falls to her knees and starts to cry.

"Who are you?" she says.

"I don't know," I reply through my own tears as she stands and hugs me tight. She holds my face in her hands and squeezes.

"Don't you ever do that," she says. "Don't you ever do that." She gazes into my eyes, her brow furrowing a bit when she notices my eye colour. Through her tears she says, "What? Canada is so cold it has turned your eyes blue?"

"I'm wearing coloured contact lenses, Mum," I say.

"They won't hurt your eyes?" she asks. I shake my head.

And then she is in full mother mode. "Have you eaten?" she asks as the children gather around.

Eight-year-old Muhammed's interest goes quickly from "How's Canada?" to "Did you bring video games for me?"

"What? You think your sister is some rich Canadian mogul?" I tease him.

"Why are you talking like that?" Nogoi asks, picking up a subtle shift—a Canadianizing—of my accent. Ida climbs close to me in the chair, and I peel off my socks. "Why are you wearing those?" asks my littlest sister. It is uncommon to wear socks at the house—it is too hot.

Later, I pull my bags down the hallway to my old bedroom. On the door, the sign I'd put up as a teenager is still there: "If you come into this room, what you see, what you

hear, what you know stays here." Inside, it is as if I'd never
left: pages from magazines I'd glued to the wall are still there,
pictures of the pageant competition, of me wearing my
crown, me shaking Jammeh's hand. The box from the laptop
I'd been given as a prize sits on the dresser, and the dresses I'd
worn to the events still hang in my wardrobe. I've been gone
more than two years, and they could have used the space. But
my mother had simply shut the door, awaiting my return.

The children crowd in behind me, and soon we are all
piled onto my bed, laughing and talking. My father appears
at the door: he had been saying his evening prayers when I
arrived and now he's come to welcome me home.

"You had a good journey?" he asks, his smile wide as I stand
to greet him. "It's good you are home."

Before long, we all gather to eat.

"If you had told me you were coming, I could have cooked!"
Mum says, having pulled together a simple dinner of salad
and fried fish, a meal that to her mind is not a full meal at all,
but to me, tastes better than anything I've eaten since I'd last
been at her table. When I ask for a fork, she gives me a strange
look. "You need a fork?" she asks. I realize I've forgotten how
much we eat with our hands at home, and I laugh. "I forgot!"
I say and use the leaves of the salad to wrap up the fish to
bring it to my mouth.

The evening stretches into the night and we all laugh and
talk. I keep catching her watching me as if I might dissolve
before her eyes. "You're too thin," she says at one point.

"I go to the gym now," I tell her, an explanation she rejects
as she worries that I am not eating enough.

Though we don't get to bed until 3 a.m. that first night, Mum rises early the next morning to prepare a full breakfast for me of gorom soup, a meal made of deboned bonga fish mixed with cucumbers, onions, peppers, tomatoes, lemon juice and Maggi seasoning, served with bread and mayonnaise. It is her favourite dish and had been Pa Mattar's as well.

As she sets the bowl in front of me, I know I can't finish it all, and it feels as if I've barely taken my last bite when lunch appears. Putting more flesh on my Canadianized bones seems like her top priority—that and trying to get me to go on visits to every family member, no matter how distantly related. But I don't want to see them or the friends I'd once had here. Yes, I don't want to answer their inevitable questions, but I also want to fill my hours with my siblings, making up the time we've lost. Though I don't drive, I rent a car and get a friend to take us to the beach each day, filling the trunk with towels and food to cook on the sandy Atlantic shore.

My mother's boss lets her leave work early for the three weeks I am here—*Your Canadian daughter is home!* But though we spend hours together, we don't talk about why I had left. Even when she discovers me tearing some of the pageant pictures down from my bedroom walls, peeling the paint off with them as the glue refuses to let go—something she'd normally be unhappy about—she laughs it off. "You put them up, nobody's going to take them down for you." If she notices the ones I remove are those featuring Jammeh, she doesn't remark on it.

My father doesn't ask me why I'd fled either. It is a conversation none of us knows how to begin.

But other things are remarked upon.

"We don't pray now?" Mum says one afternoon, as the time for daily prayers slides past without me pausing to observe them.

"Oh I talk to my God," I say. "He hears me."

Though I can tell she wants to know more—what I am thinking, what I believe, and perhaps what had happened—she can't find a way to ask, and I can't find a way to answer questions that remain unspoken.

Mum and I talk about the possibility of me adopting Ida so she can join me in Canada, something we'd spoken of over the phone. It would give Ida a chance at a life far different than the one she would have in The Gambia. But it isn't a realistic option yet. As I stitch one low-paid job after another together in Toronto, I am in no position to take on raising my sister.

And then it is time for me to go . . . home? That word no longer feels the same in my mouth, no longer has just one flavour. The Gambia *is* home—but it also is no longer my *only* home, as Canada has edged in under that heading as well.

It still isn't clear whether Jammeh will stay out of the country. The party he'd headed is still active and continues to challenge the new president. I've been at home in The Gambia for three weeks, but remaining here still seems unsafe.

This time, my journey out of the country is a normal one: a simple drive to the airport with my siblings and Mum. As I hug them at the security gate, Ida looks up at me. "Did you finish all your money?" she asks. I laugh and open my purse, spilling the dalasi coins I can't spend in Canada into her little fingers. As I walk away, about to disappear through the gate, she begins to cry. "Take me with you," she shouts.

"I'm going to take you someday," I promise, as I wave through my tears, and hers.

Back in Toronto I was job-hunting again. Though I'd been a top sales performer at the telecom company and had even been promoted to a team leader, when I'd asked for time off to go back to The Gambia, I'd been told that when I came back, I'd have to start on the bottom rung again and work my way back up the commission and pay scale. I'd gone any-way—nothing was going to stop me from seeing my family. Soon I found work soliciting donations for a children's hospi-tal. At least people didn't dislike hospitals as much as some of them hated phone companies.

I took on some unpaid work too, volunteering at a retire-ment home in the evenings, spending time with seniors who didn't have visitors. Sometimes I would read aloud from a book of their choosing, or if they weren't able to tell me what they'd like, I'd pick something myself. One evening, bored with the book I had been reading from, I started to tell one of the folk stories my grandmother had told us when we were children. The stories featured the animals from home: lions and hyenas, alligators and snakes, elephants and rabbits.

"This is the story of the rabbit and the hyena," I began as I sat with a small group of seniors in the lounge—two ani-mals who seemed at first to be simply victim and prey, one relying on its strength, the other forced to survive by its wits.

"The rabbit had gathered some food for herself," I began, "and set up her pot and fire to cook it."

As the residents listened, I told them that the rabbit knew the scent might attract others, so she surrounded herself and the pot with barbed wire. Before long, the hyena appeared, following his nose.

"Can I have some?" he asked from the other side of the wire.

"No, you cannot," said the rabbit. "If I give you some, you will want it all."

But the hyena persisted, trying to negotiate, and as he did, he circled the rabbit's enclosure, slowly pulling up the barbed wire.

The rabbit could see what he was doing and decided to make a concession. "Here," she said, as she pulled wide an opening in her fence, "why don't you come in and we can share the food?"

The hyena smiled wickedly, licking his lips, as he stepped inside.

"Wait, wait!" said the rabbit. "We must wait for it to be cooked. After all, that's how our human bosses do it—they don't eat raw food, they cook it well!"

The hyena considered for a moment. "All right," he said, "you cook the meal."

And so the rabbit made a show of stoking the fire and stirring the pot. But each time she went to the wood pile for more wood for the fire, she ate some of the raw vegetables. They were animals, not humans, after all, and it wasn't really necessary for them to cook their food before eating it.

After some time, the hyena started to get impatient. "What is taking so long?"

"You know," said the rabbit, "we should do what the humans do while they are waiting for the food to cook. We should braid each other's hair. By the time we are finished, the food will be done!"

The hyena was hungry, but also vain and proud, and he wanted so much to be like the humans. "Yes, that's a fine idea," he said to the rabbit. "Let's braid each other's hair. We'll go up in the tree together, where we can watch the pot from above."

And so they climbed the tree together.

"Let me start," said the hyena.

"Oh no, no, no—let me be the one to begin," said the rabbit.

"No, I'll begin," said the hyena, more sure that he wanted to be the one to braid first with every objection the rabbit made.

Eventually the rabbit agreed, and the hyena started to braid the rabbit's fine hair. He put a lot of effort into it, and when he was finished, the rabbit's braids were very nicely done.

Now it was the rabbit's turn to return the favour, and the hyena relaxed, secure that he was in charge since he had convinced the rabbit to let him braid first.

The rabbit began weaving strands of the hyena's fur into an artful braid—and with each braid, tying a knot of hair into the tree bark. Another braid, another knot. Another braid, another knot. The hyena, relaxed and thinking of the stew he would soon eat, paid no attention as the rabbit worked away. Finally, the rabbit was done.

"We will count to three and jump from the tree," said the rabbit, "and whoever gets to the pot first will get to eat all the food."

The hyena smiled, certain that, since he was bigger and stronger and had longer legs, he would beat the rabbit to the pot.

"One, two, three!"

"Away leapt the rabbit," I finished, "while the hyena hung suspended by a thousand knots, tied to the trunk of the tree. The hyena howled, calling his mates to help him, as the rabbit grabbed what was left of the food and scampered away into hiding, a refugee in the jungle who the hyena would search for, once he was freed."

As I'd told my tale, my love of theatre came through: my voice rose and fell with the action and I stood up and gestured to mimic the animals. The story became my own Broadway show, my audience a handful of seniors in a sitting room. I'd made a promise to myself that when I returned to Toronto, I'd give my best no matter what space I found myself in. Here, now, in the nursing home, I felt I was honouring that promise. And like the stories my grandmothers had told us, this tale would continue on another night, for each time the rabbit escaped, the hyena would pursue her and the tale would take another twist.

When I was done, an elderly Asian man said, "Hmm. Hyena's hair isn't long enough to braid!"

The others in the group shushed him. "Stop spoiling the story," said Katarine, a Russian woman I often spent time with.

From the time I saw her in her "F$$k the misogyny" T-shirt, Katarine was one of my favourites. She wasn't a permanent resident but was staying for a short time while the daughter she lived with travelled for work. Unlike many of the other residents, she avoided watching television and preferred to read, often sitting in the cafeteria with a coffee and her book. As we struck up conversations, I learned two things: her swearing wasn't limited to her T-shirts, and she loved to talk about politics and feminism.

"You don't have to have a PhD to be an activist," she said as we talked one evening, after I'd shared my worries about not having been able to move forward with my education as quickly as I wanted to. Katarine didn't discourage me from pursuing my school goals, but she also told me I didn't need to wait for a piece of paper to give me permission to try to make a difference in the world. "I know lots of PhDs that are shitty, shitty human beings," she said. "Concentrate on the work. Figure out what change needs to happen and how you can help make that change."

One afternoon she told me about a protest coming up, a march for Indigenous rights in a fight against a pipeline development. "You should go," she said. "I'll tell you what to put on your signs!" Of course, the options she suggested were profanity-laced.

"I'm not sure I want to carry a sign saying that," I said with a laugh.

"You young people are too polite," she shot back. But I did follow her suggestion to go and ended up at my first political rally. After her daughter returned from her travels and Katarine left the residence, we stayed in touch.

During that time, I'd also started seeing a therapist, trying to unravel the complicated legacy of my family, sexuality and the impact of Jammeh's crime on my life. The sessions weren't always easy, but as they progressed, I could feel myself coming to terms with what had happened. As my shame diminished, I was able to place the blame squarely where it belonged: with Jammeh and his enablers, Jimbee in particular. I couldn't help but think that every victim of sexual assault should have access to this kind of help, and I wondered what kind of services were available back home in The Gambia.

I pulled out my computer and typed in the search terms Gambia, rape, survivor, support, gender. All that came up was data from the United Nations. Numbers and numbers and numbers. But no women's stories. No support services. No faces. No help. No actual human beings.

Maybe I'm not looking in the right place, I thought. I switched to Facebook to see if there were Gambian support groups using the social media platform to connect with survivors. Nothing.

Maybe I wasn't using the right search terms. I tried new combinations, other words.

Nothing.

What would happen if I typed in these search terms linked to "Canada" instead? I wondered. Thousands of results appeared, page after page of links. The same thing happened when I swapped "India" for "Canada": women's stories appeared. But when I put "Gambia" back into the search bar, nothing but statistics came up.

I knew there were women like me behind those numbers. But their stories weren't there. And that made them—made us all—invisible.

When I had first escaped The Gambia, Senegalese-based human rights organizations had been among the agencies Topp and I had reached out to for help. Some had said they would investigate my claims, but nothing had come of it.

Maybe I should reach out again, I thought. Maybe it was time for a woman to step out from behind the numbers.

9

"I WANT TO USE MY NAME"

"I don't want to be a number."

My therapist sits across from me. A tall, slender blonde, she is a woman whose roots are in Australia and South Africa and whose husband is Eritrean, so she has an understanding of my African culture and background. While my physical exile from The Gambia has ended in a way, I feel I am still in emotional exile, a condition almost as daunting as being physically barred from re-entering the country of my birth. I still haven't been able to share my secret with my parents or most of the other people in my life.

I know from the research I've done online that other Gambian victims of sexual assault are as invisible as I am, all of us exiled to the land of statistics. The only evidence of our existence is estimated numbers in reports by NGOs and UN agencies, reports that don't reveal the details of the crimes committed against us or the human costs we carry as a result. It is the difference between saying, "Two people were killed in a car accident," and reading the story of two mothers who are killed, and the hole left in their families, workplaces and communities. Without those details, their stories don't seem real.

My therapist asks if I am prepared for what might happen if I speak out publicly.

I'm not sure what I want to do, I tell her. I am only certain that being invisible, being a statistic, isn't an option anymore.

She looks at me as if I've just told her I want to climb a mountain, and she is tallying the supplies and training we'll need to survive the trip. "Let's talk this through," she says. And so our work begins.

Can I visualize someone who has done what I am planning to do? she asks me.

There are no Gambian examples I can think of, and few African women I'm aware of beyond The Gambia's borders have named themselves as sexual assault survivors. But as I consider it, I think of Oprah and the biography I borrowed years earlier from my mother's bookshelf. More than a decade before I was born, in December 1985, Oprah had done an episode of her television show on sexual abuse. In the middle of interviewing other women about their childhood experiences, she shared that she too had been assaulted as a child. Eventually she disclosed she had been raped by a cousin, molested by another cousin's boyfriend and then her uncle as well, assaults that had happened from the time she was nine to fourteen, assaults she'd told no one about until she shared them on live television.

While many applauded her disclosure, she'd also faced criticism. People said she'd done it for the ratings, and family members disputed her claims. Some accused her of making it all up as a way of building hype for her soon-to-be-released movie, *The Color Purple*. But Oprah didn't sling mud back at those who threw it at her. She'd spoken her truth. And she responded with grace, dignity and strength when others disputed it. This is the role model I imagine I want to be.

I know that if I tell my story, I'm not simply taking a risk for myself. In The Gambia, no woman I know of has publicly claimed that she was raped. I worry that any misstep will make it harder for women who come after me. I know I will be judged unstable if I appear too emotional, too angry, and that I might also be deemed untruthful if I am too calm or don't seem emotional enough. My behaviour, either way, could be used to discredit all victims who come forward. I don't want to mess this up and make things worse for other women who might also walk this path.

As my therapist and I work together over the months that follow, I feel as if I am building emotional muscles to carry whatever burdens might come. When we consider the backlash I might need to deal with, the online trolls who may come after me, we decide it could be helpful to desensitize myself to the names I might be called. I had already seen and heard some of them when I first fled The Gambia. I write down the words: *Liar. Gold digger. Whore.* They are just collections of letters shaped into sounds intended to hurt me. But they can't wound me if I handle them enough to wear their sharp edges off. And so each morning, I look at those words, repeat them in my head until they become nonsense sounds, until I can bat them away like pesky mosquitoes whose power to draw blood has been eliminated.

In their place, I focus on other words. *Grace*, I think. *Dignity*. And *strength* as well.

The sleek, single-storey, black glass building at Bloor and Dovercourt looked like it could have been an upscale furniture store, with the stylized UBC logo on the exterior wall. The words underneath the logo told another story: United Boxing Club. Inside, boxing gloves hung on the wall, and black Everlast punching bags were suspended in a row from the ceiling with smaller red, black and white speed bags nearby. In the ring, a student sparred, jabbing at the curved punch mitts a trainer held. The thud of gloves on bags, the twang of speed bag springs, and the grunts and huffs of perspiring boxers filled the room. The air felt supercharged with sweat and strength and exertion.

Earlier in the week, my therapist had asked me whether I liked sports. I told her I felt too short for some, too heavy for others.

Would I consider boxing? she asked. It might be a good way to burn off some anxiety, focus my energy.

I'd never considered it. Women boxing wasn't something I'd seen growing up. To the headmaster at the Arabic school I'd gone to, a woman in boxing gear would have been completely outrageous, unimaginable. Later, as I watched videos online, I thought maybe I would give it a try, and I called a friend who was on a women's basketball team to ask if she knew a boxing gym I could check out.

Now I stood in the entryway, mesmerized by the energy, the power, the focus on the faces I saw around me. On the wall nearby, a sign outlined the club rules. Near the top was the word "respect": "Respect the coaches, the facility, the equipment, the members and yourself."

As I talked to the attendant at the front desk, he advised starting with a one-on-one session with a trainer. I told him I wasn't ready to make that kind of investment. I just wanted to hit the punching bag. Eventually he relented, helping me lace up a pair of rental gloves so I could give it a try.

From the first punch, confidence filled me. I was balanced between being relaxed and being tense, focused not on how my body looked to others, but on how my body *felt* to me. I wasn't judging my body, I was simply *in* my body. A passing trainer offered advice, and with each visit, I learned more. Eventually I took classes and some personalized sessions as well, even boxing with a female trainer who demonstrated escape manoeuvres. I loved it! And with each workout, I grew stronger.

The months passed as I trained at the gym. My therapist and I continued my emotional strength-training as well, talking through the implications of telling my story.

As we worked, it became clear I needed to unpack some of the baggage I carried with me from my family and the culture I had grown up in. I considered myself a feminist, and considered my mother a feminist too. But we were embedded in a family and a culture that depended on women's contributions but viewed them as inferior. From the outside it looked like men were the ones in control, though I also knew from my lived experience that the women around me exerted control where they could, like Aunt Marie fighting back against her brother, like my mother choosing to leave my father's family compound so we could live in our own separate house, like my grandmother doing all she could to ensure that my mother had more choices than she'd had—even while making the choice of husband on Mum's behalf. That legacy stretched even further back: my great-grandmother had sold her jewellery to build a mud house and raise her daughter on her own after her husband left her.

And there were battles to face in my own generation. In mid-2018, I received a worrying phone call from my mother.

"I want to discuss something with you," she said. "Your father's brother wants to arrange a marriage between Penda and his son." Penda was seventeen, still a year from finishing her senior secondary school studies, and her proposed husband was in his late twenties. In our culture, marriages between cousins were common enough that they had their own label: family marriages. Because of polygamous relationships, such cousins might not be as closely related by blood as they would be in monogamous situations, and the marriages were viewed as a way of further strengthening family bonds. But still, they posed particular—and often unacknowledged—risks for the women. Should the relationships prove unhappy or abusive, the pressures on the wife to remain

lived with her for a time. It had been early in my parents' marriage, before my brother was born. My mother was trying to complete her college education, but with a toddler at home and a husband to look after, her classes were proving impossible. Finally, in desperation, she packed a bag for me and told my father he needed to send me to stay with his mother until she finished school. I think it may have been one of the first independent decisions she made as a young wife, prompted by the desperate knowledge that neither she nor I, her daughter, would have much of a future if she couldn't complete her education.

My father took me to the small island where my elderly grandmother had lived on her own since her husband had passed away. Her name was Fatou, which is my formal name as well. Her home was a traditional mud hut. Inside were two bedrooms; outside, she kept a few goats and sheep in a wooden pen. My earliest memories are of that place, of my old grandma milking the goats and sheep early in the morning, filling the calabash gourd bowl she used. People tell me they remember me as always having what we called a "cow horn" on my face: the milk residue from the drinking bowl forming a semi-circle from my lips up both sides of my cheeks.

It seems like a stereotype: an old African woman living in a mud hut with a half-dressed child and some livestock. To some it would look like poverty. But for an African woman, owning livestock was a source of both nourishment and income, a way to control one's own destiny.

It is easy, too, to imagine that picture of an old woman in a hut is all there was to my grandmother. But it wasn't. She had been born in Guinea and married at fourteen to a prominent chief there, with whom she quickly had two girls. When her much older husband died, she was married off to one of her cousins and moved with him to Senegal, where she had a boy, my father. When the second husband decided she was not obedient enough, he told her he was going to return her to her parents, where she knew she would be married off again. When they got to the border of Senegal, she escaped, telling the immigration officers she wished to stay in Senegal. She must have made an impassioned and persuasive case, because unusually for the time, the officers took her word over her husband's.

Free of her husband and parents, she eventually travelled with her son, my father, to The Gambia, where she had a distant cousin, and settled in the town of MacCarthy where her daughters eventually joined her. There, she was a single mother, raising hens and cattle to sell at the market. During her time there, she became a spokesperson for a group representing other women exiled from Guinea, speaking out for the rights of women who had left that country for political reasons or to escape abusive relationships. Eventually, she married a man of her own choosing and had more children with him. As a child, when I refused to back down on something or tried to get my own way, my father would call me "Mum," comparing me to his own mother, whose formal name I shared. It was a nickname I carried with pride.

I know there are Western feminists who view African Muslim women such as my aunt, my mother and my two grandmothers as victims. And yes, they existed within a system that tried to place all of the power in men's hands. The poverty they faced complicated their choices as well. There were no government supports. Many women could not read or write. Leaving an abusive marriage could mean a woman would be homeless or without income, unable to feed her children. But the women in my family, and in other families too, subverted men's power where they could; made choices in their own interests where they could; and where they could created a world in which their daughters had a little bit more power, more choice. Social and religious circumstances pushed them down. Their strength and will pushed them forward—and perhaps in these ways they were more similar to the mothers and grandmothers of Western feminists than is often acknowledged.

Still, I struggled with the legacy of men's choices in my family's history and with my father's role. He hadn't been open with my mother and grandmother about his existing wives and children when he married Mum. Within our family, he remained firmly at the head of the combined households, the ultimate decision-maker, though he could be influenced by the persuasion of the women around him. As a child, I'd looked up to him—we all had. But I had seen my mother's frustration too.

One episode, from my early teens, stands out in my memory. Pa Mattar was still alive, and Mum was telling Dad why she needed—*we* needed—to live in a home separate from the other wives and children. "My child is sick," she told him. "He keeps touching the belongings of the others, and they get angry and punish him for it, but he cannot help it—and

I cannot stop him from doing it. I need to get out of here."

My father tried to calm her, promised her he would make things right, but Mum stormed out of the compound, slamming the gate as she left. Dad noticed me sitting under a tree in the courtyard, as I pretended not to hear, though my ears had grabbed every word from the angry air around them. "You know, your mum is impatient," he said, and he told me he was building a house in town for us. "It's a surprise for your mum—you mustn't tell her about it."

Over the days that followed, I could see how sad my mother was, how worn down by the burden of trying to keep the peace as the children and women in the extended family continued to complain about Pa Mattar's behaviour. And while I had promised my father I would keep his secret about his surprise for Mum, I couldn't watch her be this miserable when I knew happiness was on the horizon. One evening I went into her room and crawled into bed with her.

"Let me tell you something," I began, "but please don't tell Dad I told you, don't tell anybody. It's a huge secret, but if you promise me you're not going to tell anybody, I'll tell you."

She looked at me with a mixture of puzzlement and concern.

"Okay," she said.

The words tumbled out of me: all the details of the house in town Dad had told me, that it was halfway done, that she would have a car there, that soon we would move. I could see by the look on her face she didn't believe me. "I swear to you, it's true," I said. "Dad didn't tell you because it's a surprise. Dad wouldn't trick me."

I'd expected her to be happy, but there was no joy in her eyes. Looking back, I can see she didn't want to disappoint me. She sucked a breath through her teeth and gave her head a small shake. "Oh child. Okay, okay," she said. "Let's wait for the house."

I left her room happy I had shared this good news with her, sure now she would be happy too.

But the move didn't come. My father never spoke of it again, and I never had the courage to ask him. Did he build a house and rent it to someone for the income? Did the house ever exist at all? Did he mean to lie, or was he sharing a plan he hoped would come true? I never knew—I still don't know.

When Pa Mattar died, my mother took matters into her own hands, buying the small plot, scavenging concrete blocks for its walls, directing us, her children, to help clear the bush from the land, hiring a mason to build the structure, an electrician and plumber to wire and plumb it. The work took years, but eventually, it was ready.

My father promised a home. My mother made one.

Yet . . . I have memories as well of my father debating with me, listening to my ideas, respecting me enough to hear me out and talk things through. And I learned things from him, like how to hook the television up to the car battery we used to power it before we had electricity at the house. When we children played games with him, he explained them with the seriousness of an Olympic coach—the rules, the strategy, the goals—before launching into the foolishness of playing with an enthusiasm that matched our own.

He entertained us with magic tricks, twists of his fingers that shifted objects from one hand to another, making things appear and disappear.

And while other fathers around us hit their children and beat their wives, my father never did.

As a child, I studied him, watching what he did and how. I was fascinated by the way he signed his name—he had the most intricate signature I'd ever seen. My siblings and I would try to copy it, with its fancy swirls and complex whirls.

When I was thirteen, he noticed me attempting to match his script. "You know, you should make your own signature," he said. I wrote one version. He shook his head. I tried another. On the third, he said, "I think you should stick with this one," and he handed me three sheets of blank paper to practise on. I scribbled my name for the rest of the afternoon, perfecting my own swirls and whirls, creating my own muscle memory for the signature I still use today.

It is hard to hold these two images together: the father who teaches, the man who disappoints. The father proud of a daughter's accomplishments, the man who accepts that society tips in his favour and compounds it with choices that put him on top and push the women in his life down.

I don't know that my Gambian culture is all that different from any other when it comes to navigating these gaps between parent and person. How do I shift the burden of his actions, his decisions from my shoulders? Would a conversation in which I interrogated my father's life choices make things better or worse between us? Is there an explanation my father could give me—would give me, as a man now seventy who has lived his life as he has lived it—that would bring closure? And what do I do if I am disappointed with his answers? I don't think these are questions I am alone in asking. I think maybe other feminist daughters ask them too.

As I contemplated telling the world about Jammeh's crimes, I knew there were people I needed to share the secret with first. Still, I struggled with finding the right time, the right place.

One afternoon, as Solomon and I watched TV at his apartment, my phone rang. I checked the call display: someone I really didn't want to talk to. "Ach, I'm not talking to you right now," I said as I silenced the call.

"Did you do that to my call yesterday?" Solomon teased me.

"No, actually I was at therapy when you called."

Solomon knew I had seen a therapist in the past but seemed surprised I saw one still.

"How long is this therapy?" he asked, still joking a bit but also with some seriousness in his tone. "Do you need to go forever? What do you need to talk about?"

"Do you know why I came to Canada?" I asked.

"You told me it was because of a forced marriage," he replied.

"It was actually because I was raped," I said. "By the president."

I could see the surprise on his face as he took in what I said. "What happened?" he asked.

As I told him the details, he listened without meeting my eyes, his head bent as he focused on my words. When I finished, he looked up. "Are you serious?" he asked. "How do I know you all this time and I don't know this?"

Because I needed time to process it all, I said, and I didn't want to talk about it.

"But it's me," he said. "You could have told me." He paused. "Does anybody else know?"

A friend in Vancouver, I told him. I could tell it stung that I'd told someone before him.

"I never suspected," he said. "You've handled it so well."

"Actually not," I told him. "That's why I go to therapy, because I need help to handle it."

I shared with him my plan to go public with what had happened to me, my intention to name Jammeh publicly, though I wasn't sure yet how or when.

I could see him trying to absorb it all: the rape, the dictator, my intention to speak publicly about it. He called me brave, told me he'd support me in whatever ways I needed him to. "Please, though, never ever hide something as important as that from me again. Don't think I can't handle it," he said.

"It wasn't a judgment of you," I told him. "I needed to wait until I was ready. It was a decision about me. Not every decision is about you." I was part serious, part teasing.

He nodded, then got up to go to the washroom. As he passed by me, he said, "You really are an asshole."

I laughed. From anyone else, the words wouldn't have been right, but with Solomon, the teasing told me we were okay. The space inside our friendship was a place where we could laugh at anything, even the worst things that had happened to us. Our laughter was part of my healing.

The office tower at Toronto's Yonge and Eglinton corner was Saturday-morning quiet as I made my way to the Human Rights Watch office on the sixth floor. I'd told my story to an investigator from another group, TRIAL International, months earlier. Today I was meeting with Marion Volkmann-Brandau, a lawyer working with Human Rights Watch in Senegal, another HRW lawyer named Reed Brody, and Farida Deif, the organization's Canadian coordinator.

Marion had reached out to me when I'd first returned to The Gambia in 2017, but I hadn't responded to her then. Inspired by the successful prosecution of Chad's former dictator Hissène Habré, a woman named Nana-Jo Ndow had approached Human Rights Watch. Her father, a critic of Jammeh, had been murdered while Jammeh was in power, and she and other families of murder victims wondered if pursuing charges against him was now possible, eventually launching a campaign called #Jammeh2Justice.

Marion was investigating Jammeh's crimes, including sexual violence, and had heard rumours that something had happened involving me. At the time, I hadn't been sure how much I wanted to share. Still, she'd stayed in touch.

Now in March 2019, more than two years had passed since Jammeh had been voted out of office and forced to flee The Gambia, and a little more than a year since I had decided I wanted to go public with what Jammeh had done to me.

But my path to this weekend meeting hadn't been straight or simple. I knew I had the option of remaining anonymous, my identity shielded by Human Rights Watch while my accusations were made public. But I also knew faceless accusations would be easier for Jammeh to dodge. Without a woman willing to step forward and say publicly that Jammeh had raped her, the former dictator had a better chance of brushing the claims aside.

Reed Brody, Human Rights Watch's counsel and spokesperson, had earned the nickname "The Dictator Hunter" for his involvement in cases against Augusto Pinochet of Chile and Jean-Claude "Baby Doc" Duvalier of Haiti. In Africa both he and Marion had been in the courthouse for Hissène Habré's trial in Senegal on the day Topp and I had met with the Senegalese lawyer there. I'd watched videos of Reed on YouTube as he spoke about Human Rights Watch's work. In one about Habré, the interviewer asked what made the difference in cases like these. The victims, Reed said. The strength of victims' testimony—widows, orphans, poor people, other marginalized people—was critical to holding these criminals accountable for what they had done.

Marion wasn't as high-profile as Reed, but I knew she was a committed human rights defender, her research the ammunition the agency used to fight criminals like Jammeh. I could tell she operated from a deep concern for those who had been traumatized by the crimes of dictators like him. She was a quieter but always thoughtful presence. I wasn't the only woman Marion had spoken with. I knew two other women were willing to come forward to say they had been assaulted by Jammeh, and a third that she had been confined in a hotel at Jammeh's direction but had escaped. I could tell Marion was being mindful of my needs, trying to avoid scaring me off, while Reed sometimes took over the room. And while I hadn't met Farida before, she too seemed concerned for me and my safety.

Reed left not long after I arrived. Marion and Farida and I spent most of the day going over the details of my accusations. They didn't just accept what I said. They compared it to what I'd told the TRIAL investigator and to other evidence Marion had gathered. She had tracked down video recordings of the pageant, talked to others who had been in Jammeh's circle to corroborate what I'd said, cross-checked dates of who was where when. Of course, only two people could say what had happened behind closed doors at Jammeh's residence that night. But all of the details around it could be confirmed, and Marion had worked tirelessly to do that.

The other women's stories bore similarities to mine. The woman who had escaped Jammeh's advances was Fatoumatta Sandeng, and she was willing for her name to be used. A well-known singer in The Gambia, she had been summoned to a hotel by Jimbee, the president's cousin and fixer. Once at the hotel, Fatoumatta had been held against her will for four days, but she was eventually released after promising Jimbee she would return. She didn't. A year later Fatoumatta's father, the Gambian opposition leader Solo Sandeng, was tortured to death after being arrested at a protest march, and Fatoumatta eventually became the spokesperson for the #Jammeh2Justice campaign, calling for Jammeh's prosecution.

Fatoumatta had been a few years ahead of me in senior secondary school, a small but powerful girl who walked with so much confidence that I liked her from the first time I saw her. She was active in debate, drama and the press club, and had spoken to our class about these activities. I was following her example when I signed up for the clubs that had given me so much enjoyment through those school years, sparking my love of performing arts. We had often been together at competitions and events, and I remembered being struck by her political insights and awareness. It was through conversation with her that I first considered the idea of whether The Gambia could truly consider itself a democracy, when one man had held power for twenty years and controlled the state television and other media. Her opinions were more informed than my own, in part because of her father's role in the opposition United Democratic Party.

The other two accusers had both been hired as protocol officers, the same job Jammeh had once offered me. Both had been coerced into having sex with him, and Jimbee had given them or their families cash and other gifts to secure their cooperation and silence. "When I tried to stop him, he said to me to remember that he was supporting my family and that he could end it at any time," said one. "[We] had to come in for sex whenever he wanted," said the other. Both women had chosen to be shielded by pseudonyms: in the HRW report, they would be called Anta and Bintu.

And there was my story. The TRIAL researcher who had first interviewed me shielded me under the name Francine in her report. And while the facts of my story that she had gathered were accurate, when I read them with that name attached to them, it felt wrong.

Later that afternoon Reed rejoined us. "So let's talk about strategy, how we bring this report out," he said. "What protective measures can we take?" As he spoke I felt as if his words were sliding through me, past me, in my ears and out again without lodging in my brain.

When he stopped speaking, I said, "I'm not going with 'Francine.' I want to use my name."

The others looked at me across the office table.

"If you make that choice, we can't go back," said Marion.

"We won't be able to protect you completely," said Reed. "We can hire security in The Gambia, but once you're back here in Canada . . ." He knew I was worried about the Gambian community in Canada, some of whom still supported the dictator. There were Gambian dissidents who had died under suspicious circumstances while in exile, and it was risky for even one Gambian to know where I lived in Canada.

"What do you mean by using your name?" asked Farida. "Your whole name? Your first name?"

I understood why the other women didn't want to come forward, I said, and I respected their decisions. But my story would be stronger if my face was attached to it, if my identity could be shared as well. "I'm speaking out because I don't want to be a number," I said. "If I use a false name, it just makes me an invisible person again: raped invisibly, healed invisibly and now fighting invisibly. I refuse to be invisible.

When I was growing up, I didn't know what rape was; I had never heard anyone even speak of it." I wanted to give rape a face in The Gambia, to be a visible survivor, I continued; I was tired of the pretense that it didn't exist. I wanted girls like me to know that someone who looked like them had survived this—and that if they had been raped, they could survive too.

"Let's consider what the consequences of going public would be," said Marion, and she started listing them. The media might follow me. People in my community and beyond would know what had happened and attach the incident to me forever. Jammeh's followers would attack me online—and possibly in real life as well. Every online search for my name would bring up stories about me being raped.

"There's no going back," said Reed. "Once your name is out there, it's out there."

It would haunt me. That's what they seemed to be saying. But it already haunted me.

"Whether other people know it, whether the media asks me about it or not, it is always with me," I said. "It is with me 24/7. And I am carrying it by myself."

I tried to explain what it meant *to me* to go public. "If I tell people what happened, then it isn't just my burden anymore. I'm sharing the burden of knowing with everyone else. And if it bothers people to know what happened to me, that's fine: I don't need to protect people from the uncomfortable feeling of knowing this happened. Why am I protecting people from what happened?" The shame of it wasn't mine to carry, for me, for society and for him.

I knew attaching my real name would ensure the story was more widely covered by news media around the world, resulting in less room for Jammeh to hide and more likelihood that the girls and women I wanted to reach would hear my message. I knew Marion, Reed and Farida knew that too, and I could feel the excitement of it in the room, even as all three worked to make sure I was really willing to do this and talked through the logistics of making it happen safely. I had one more thing I needed to be clear about, though. Human Rights Watch wanted to do the news conference for the announcement in their main office in London, England.

"I'm not doing it in London," I said. "There has never been a press conference about rape in The Gambia. I want to be the one who does that. I want all of the girls like me to know they are not alone." I wanted to tell my story in Africa, in The Gambia. In the place where it had happened.

In the weeks that followed, Marion and Reed stayed in close contact with me. Because Dakar, Senegal, was a larger centre than any city in The Gambia, with more international media stationed there, we decided to do two press conferences. The international one would happen in Dakar in June, followed a few days later by another in The Gambia, to ensure the story would be heard by those I most wanted to hear it: the women and girls of The Gambia and the region at large. Reed started speaking with reporters at major media outlets, all on the condition the story would be embargoed until the day the report was released.

The *New York Times* committed first and negotiated to be able to publish online twenty minutes in advance of any other news media on the day the report came out. The *Guardian* would be second to post. I did interviews with their reporters, repeating the specific details of the crime Jammeh had committed against me. A photographer from the *Times* arrived to take photos of me in the backyard of my Toronto rental.

I hadn't seen Solomon in weeks, and I knew I needed to let him know what was happening so he didn't find out by reading something online. I called him to share the details. "I'm scared for you," he said after I told him what was planned. "Why do you have to go back home?"

"I don't want to hide anymore," I said. "I've faced bigger risks in the past than what I face now and I made it through those. I'll make it through this."

Solomon wasn't the only friend I needed to tell. I slowly shared the news with others close to me. Then I needed to tell both my parents what was about to occur.

I called Mum first. "So this is serious," I told her, and shared the plans for the press conferences, the news reports. "I'm putting myself out there, which means I'm putting you out there too," I said. "But I don't want this to be a secret anymore."

There was a moment of silence on the other end of the phone line. "Do you really, really need to do this?" she asked.

"Yes, I need to do this," I said.

We still hadn't spoken of the details of what had happened to me, but now she pushed that door ever so slightly open.

"He hurt you, right?" she asked.

"Yeah, he did," I replied. Even now, we avoided the word "rape," though we both knew what she meant by "he hurt you."

There was a longer pause, Mum's breath gentle over the phone line. "I never wanted to confirm that," she said quietly.

"But it happened, you know?" I said. "Not confirming it is not going to take it away. And I want to hold him accountable for this."

"Are you able to do this?" she asked. Yes, I replied.

"I'm so sorry," she said. "I just . . . I'm sorry that happened. I'm your mother and it hurts as a mother not to be able to protect her daughter." Was I prepared for the consequences of speaking out, she asked again. "Because I can't protect you from those either."

"You don't have to protect me," I said. "You can just support me."

"If this means I can have my daughter back again, then yes, go ahead," she said. I knew in that moment what she meant: there had been a distance between us because of this unspoken, unnamed abyss we had been navigating around. Its presence had made it hard for us to be easy with each other, natural with each other, open with each other. Now, maybe, once this secret was out in the open, we could find a way back to each other again.

"Okay," she said. "Explain to me what's going to happen."

I told her the plans: the press conference in Dakar, a second one in The Gambia. It would be in the papers, on TV and radio, online. "I'm going to need to tell your grandma and grandpa," she said. I was grateful—and a little guilty—that would be her conversation, not mine.

My talk with my father was shorter, simpler. I was going to speak publicly about what had happened to me, I told him, because I wanted to fight for myself and for other women.

"Was it Yahya Jammeh?" he asked.

"Yes," I replied.

"Have you told your mum?"

Yes, I said.

"I just hope it will not affect your job and your life."

Well, I replied, it will probably affect my life, but I hoped in a positive way.

"I will talk to your mum," he said. "You know, she is very emotional. I will just try to talk her through it."

And that was the end of the conversation. The people who needed to know now knew.

But this wasn't my last conversation with my father before my trip. My departure date was nearing when my mother called me, asking whether I'd received an email about Penda. What email? I replied. I thought the family marriage idea had been dropped. But now that she had graduated from senior secondary school, my father had sent a WhatsApp message to some family members announcing she would soon marry our cousin. I was so angry, I thought my head might explode.

In the flurry of phone calls that followed, my father defended the marriage: Penda had agreed to it, he insisted. When I called Penda, she did tell me she'd said yes. Though she didn't really want to get married, she said, she felt she had little choice if Dad wanted her to go ahead with it.

"But what do *you* want?" I asked her. "You need to stand up for yourself! This is a lifetime decision!"

I kept losing the phone signal and had to keep reconnecting. Finally, I got my father on the phone again. "Penda said yes," he argued.

"She doesn't know what she's saying yes to," I yelled. "You tell her she's too young to go out, too young to have her own phone, but she's not too young to get married?" The phone link dropped again. Frustrated, I used WhatsApp to record a long, loud and clear voice message to him: How could he suggest this? Was he marrying her off simply because she had no mother to defend her? The whole idea was ridiculous. If I had to, I would get on an earlier flight and physically stop the arrangement. I can't believe you are doing this in the middle of all I am fighting against, I said. I swore. I threatened. And then I hit send.

Before long, my father called me back. It's fine, don't worry, he said. If Penda doesn't want it, we won't go through with it. It's nothing to get so angry about. The marriage was off.

In the days that followed, I got ready to travel, telling my landlord I was going to Africa for two weeks.

"Ah," he said. "Have a nice vacation—don't forget to go to the beach!"

10

#IAMTOUFAH

My hands are shaking so hard I can't hold my phone. It's June 25, 2019. Fifteen minutes to go, the *New York Times* reporter who had interviewed me said when she called. In fifteen minutes the world will know I am the woman accusing a president of rape.

I keep hitting refresh on my phone's browser, waiting for the story to appear.

Next to me, Marion and Reed sit with their laptops open, hitting refresh as well. I'm not the only woman accusing Jammeh of rape. But I am the only woman using my real name, the only woman whose photo will appear along with her accusations.

Around us, the wait staff on the terrace at Dakar's Hotel Sokhamon move between the tables overlooking the mirrored blue surface of the Atlantic Ocean, refilling a glass here, taking an order there. I stare into my reflection on my phone screen.

Refresh. Refresh. Refresh.

A few hundred kilometres away, in Serrekunda, my mother sits in her living room, waiting for my message to tell her the story is out. Every few minutes she calls. "Is it out yet?" I can hear the shakiness in her voice. Soon we will travel to The Gambia to repeat my accusations in the country where the crimes were committed. But for now, we sit here in Senegal, waiting for someone on the other side of the Atlantic to publish my story online.

Then the headline appears: "A Beauty Queen Accuses Former Gambian President of Rape: 'I Literally Stumbled Out of There.'"

Marion holds my hand. "I'm so proud of you," she says.

I'm going to faint, I think.

Then the *Guardian* piece comes out: "Gambian Pageant Winner Accuses Ex-president Yahya Jammeh of Rape."

I push back from the table, bring my knees up to my chest, trying to make myself as small as possible.

"It's okay," Reed says. "It's going to be okay."

I'm not sure it will be. I'm not sure at all.

"When we started working with the victims of Yahya Jammeh, one of the first things we heard . . . was that Yahya Jammeh was abusing girls and women," Reed said in French, facing a room full of reporters in Dakar. Those rumours, he continued, prompted Human Rights Watch to focus their efforts on those charges. Marion, Reed and I sat at a table alongside Fatoumatta Sandeng, Alioune Tine, former director of

Amnesty International West Africa, and activist Baba Hydara, whose journalist father, Deyda Hydara, had been killed by Jammeh's military personnel.

Then Marion too spoke in French, outlining the investigation she had carried out to support the charges Human Rights Watch was levelling against Jammeh, describing how she had contacted almost fifty people in her work to verify the testimony that I, Fatoumatta and the other two women who had been raped by Jammeh had given to the organization. Reed talked of how Human Rights Watch had also decided to focus on the accusations of sexual violence because in other cases, such as those against Chad's Hissène Habré, allegations of sexual violence had been ignored until late in the prosecution of perpetrators.

Though Fatoumatta had escaped being assaulted, she said she believed what I and the other two women had shared. "The people who came . . . to bring them to Jammeh, these are the same people who came to get me. Our cases are similar, so if these girls say they have been raped while I escaped, I can only believe them and support them," she told the reporters, speaking in Wolof, her head covered in a blue hijab. "A rape victim is very frowned upon in our society," she added, offering understanding to the two women who chose not to be named in the report for fear of being shunned by their communities.

It seemed especially brazen that in Fatoumatta, Jammeh had targeted the daughter of a political opponent. Perhaps he thought if he assaulted her, she would be too ashamed to tell her family—or if she did, there would be nothing they could do. Or perhaps he imagined his power would be so enticing to her she would be unable to resist him. Who knows what delusions propel predators like Jammeh? A year later, in April 2016, her father had been tortured to death. Now, in 2019, Fatoumatta and I sat together, accusing the man we held responsible for so much harm in our lives and the lives of others.

Most of the reporters filling the press conference room in Dakar were men, and many of the questions they asked focused on the specific details of my accusations, what Jammeh had done to me, to my body. While I had talked about this both privately and to other reporters in the lead-up to the press conference, until now I had been speaking to just one or two people at a time. As I faced a room of report-ers and cameras, I steeled myself to answer their questions, responding in Wolof, allowing my tears to fall as I tried to keep my voice strong. What I was saying was difficult, but I wanted people in West Africa, especially in The Gambia and especially women, to hear *my* voice, a *woman's* voice, and understand my words in a language familiar to their ears. I didn't want to hide my tears, because to me those tears were a sign of strength as well: an acknowledgement of the harm done, the loss and pain caused, but an unwillingness to let that loss and pain stop me from speaking the truth. The work I had done in preparing for this moment, focusing on responding with grace and dignity, helped, but the experi-ence was still daunting as reporters asked for more details.

"My fight now is that we can talk about rape . . . so that victims of rape can go to the police and talk openly," I said, using the English word for rape. Later, Amnesty's Alioune Tine would repeat for reporters one of my remarks: "It is very important what Toufah Jallow says; she says, 'I asked my sister how is the word rape [said] in Wolof, in Fulani, in Mandinka.' Her sister says she has no answer. When you do not have a word to describe a thing, to make it a crime, a reality . . .'" Speaking out, even in the absence of precise words in our languages, would make a difference, he said.

Finally the questions were finished, and Marion, Reed, Fatoumatta, Baba and I left the room. That evening after I returned to my hotel, Topp visited me and we went for a drive. We'd stayed in touch via WhatsApp messages throughout my time in Canada, but this was the first time we'd seen each other since I'd left four years earlier. "There has always been fire in your tone and your eyes," he told me. "I'm not surprised you're speaking out."

"No one's talking about it," Mum said over the phone later that night as I spoke to her from my hotel room. "That's good, right?"

Earlier Marion, Reed and I had watched online as the stories appeared. A BBC camera crew had driven with me through Dakar to get footage to accompany their report, interviewing me at the hotel about what Jammeh had done to me. "Anything that he could have done in that moment to degrade me, to put me to the lowest of my moments, he did that," I told the reporter. "He rubbed his genitals in my face, then pushed me down on my knees, pulled my dress up, sodomized me." I couldn't hold back the tears as I spoke.

The BBC report, like the newspaper stories, noted that Jammeh had not responded to my accusations publicly, but a political party spokesperson had denied the charges made by me and Jammeh's other accusers.

"I fled my country for safety," I said. "And now I want to start a conversation about sexual violence. I want him to know that I am here right now, in this moment, taking back the narrative and telling my truth as it is." I looked at the BBC reporter's camera, hoping Jammeh would hear my words. "I hope he has the courage also to answer to this, or to face this, or to share a room with me again—but this time around, in a courtroom."

But while our press conference in Dakar had been underway, the region's attention was focused on a different hearing room. The Gambia's Truth, Reconciliation and Reparations Commission had been holding hearings since January. That day, at the hearing hall in Serrekunda, Yankuba Touray, a soldier who had stood alongside Jammeh during the coup that put him in power and became one of Jammeh's closest allies and later a government minister in his regime, had been summoned to testify about his own role in the murder of The Gambia's former finance minister Ousman Koro Ceesay, in 1995. Other witnesses had testified that Koro Ceesay had been beaten to death by a number of men outside Touray's home, with Touray delivering blows with "a pestle-like object and other dangerous weapons." The minister's bloodied body, it was testified, was disposed of by setting him on fire inside his car.

Touray stood accused of other murders and assaults as well, and he was also connected to someone who had been instrumental in my escape. Ebrima Chongan, the man who had helped connect me with Topp when I first arrived in Senegal, had been one of the first witnesses at the TRRC hearings. Chongan had been among those who tried to stop Jammeh's 1994 coup, and he spoke at the commission hearings of the torture he had been subjected to while being held in The Gambia's Mile Two Central Prison after Jammeh took power. During one questioning session at the prison, Chongan testified that Captain Yankuba Touray shoved a 9-millimetre pistol in Chongan's mouth, a terrifying show of power and intimidation.

When Touray appeared before the TRRC, he was contemptuous of the commissioners, first refusing to answer their questions about his role in Koro Ceesay's murder or other crimes, then storming off the witness stand. One commentator would later describe it as "a moment of national jaw-dropping." Touray's defiance of the TRRC dominated the region's headlines. And so, it seemed, though my accusations against Jammeh were heard around the world, closer to home they were drowned out by a murderer's bravado.

To my mother, who was worried about the backlash I might face after speaking publicly, the silence seemed a good thing. For her, "no one is talking about it" meant no one was threatening me and no one was lying about me. I felt a bit of relief as well, but the silence in The Gambia about my accusations also carried a hint of failure. Had all of this been for nothing? Mum and I said our goodnights and I tried to sleep. But my mind wouldn't settle. Had I come this far, worked so hard to speak out about sexual violence, only to be silenced again in my home country? What if the women I most wanted to reach didn't hear my message?

When I woke up the next morning, it was like my world was on fire. Every Gambian I know had messaged me on Facebook or WhatsApp.

Is it really you?

Toufah, where are you?

Toufah, are you okay?

People I hadn't heard from in years were reaching out to me. I even got a message of support from the man who ran the second-hand clothing store where I'd bought my first pageant dress. On their Facebook pages, some shared the *New York Times* story. "Have you seen this report?" they asked their friends.

Soon, Marion was at my door. "You should turn off your phone and your laptop," she said, trying to shield me from the crueller responses she'd already seen online. But I didn't. I went to the comments to see what was being said. *Oh here we have another lying bitch . . . Who is she? . . . She's making it up . . . She's a gold digger . . . She's a western puppet . . .* I had known these comments would come, had tried to prepare for them. But the reality is you're never really ready for it, even when you think you are, because they drip like acid and burn into your memory.

Our plan had been to head to The Gambia three days after the Dakar press conference, but now we decided to leave Senegal immediately and move the Gambian press conference to the following day. I was wrung out. The ups and downs of the last few days—the exhilaration of speaking out and knowing Jammeh would stand publicly accused, the gut-churning impact of having to repeatedly describe in detail what he had done to me, and the mixed responses online were taking a toll that, even with all of my preparation, threatened to grind me into dust.

"I can do the press conference in The Gambia, but that's it," I said. No meetings with officials, no public appearances. After that second press conference in what had once been Jammeh's domain, I was going to spend the rest of my time with my family. Marion hired a van and driver for the eight-hour trip to Banjul, and we set out: Marion, Reed and his son, Baba Hydara, Fatoumatta and her young daughter, and a journalist from The Gambia. We didn't yet have bodyguards, as we didn't think we would need them until we arrived in The Gambia.

As we travelled through Senegal, Marion balanced her computer on her lap, tapping out adjustments to the press releases and documents that would be shared with the Gambian news media, making calls to coordinate the shift in the timing of the press conference. As we neared the border, I could feel my anxiety rising. This time I wasn't coming back to The Gambia simply as Toufah Jallow. This time I was coming back as Toufah Jallow, survivor of rape and Jammeh accuser.

The border crossing was the same one I'd snuck across almost exactly four years earlier, wedged into the cramped cab of a cattle truck between the driver and his apprentice. Unlike that journey, though, we weren't waved through. Instead we were pulled to the side to have our passports inspected and our entrance to the country registered. As we piled out of the van, I picked up Fatoumatta's daughter and held her close, as much to calm and distract me as to do so for her. Baba gathered our passports to bring them into the small customs office for processing, mine bearing my formal name, Fatou, rather than the nickname I'm known by, Toufah, a small difference that offered me the possibility of passing unnoticed. I ducked back into the van to wait. In a few minutes Baba was back and we passed into The Gambia, heading toward the ferry terminal.

We arrived just in time to see the ferry depart. The van driver announced he would not wait for another ferry to take us across, and so we would have to take the ferry on foot and get transportation on the other side. I pulled the cap I was wearing lower over my face and picked up Fatoumatta's daughter again. As we waited with the other passengers, Fatoumatta, well known as a musician, soon became the centre of attention as people came up to greet her. I was happy for their distraction as I stood off to the side, gazing out to the water, watching for the ferry's return.

"Hey, are you Toufah?" A man stood next to me, tapping my arm to get my attention. My heart skipped.

"Yeah, I am," I said, trying to gauge his intentions. Was he one of the online haters, stepping forward to confront me in real life?

"I am so proud of you!" he said. "You're so brave. I don't know how you do this, but keep it up. You are coming to The Gambia, right?"

I could feel my stance relax. "Yes, yes, we are," I told him. It turned out he worked for one of the television stations at home.

"How are you?" he asked.

"I don't know," I said, answering honestly. When he asked what I would be doing in The Gambia, I told him about the press conference, and he said he would attend, then headed back to his car. I could see him talking to another man in the car and pointing in my direction. As friendly as he had been, it was still unsettling to think he might be telling a stranger about what had happened to me, that they might be talking about my assault as they looked across the waiting area at me. *They're talking about me for sure,* I thought.

Along the still-empty ferry dock, a group of young boys were diving into the water, then climbing back up to dive in again. One of them approached me. "Oh, you are Toufah," he said.

"Yes, I am," I replied.

"My sister likes you," he told me, before running back to the other boys. I could see him sharing the news of who I was as the other boys looked my way, could hear the daring that now began as they laughed and talked. "Go and talk to her!" I could hear them say to one another as they tried to work up the courage to approach me. I watched as adults leaned in to ask what was going on, and the boys pointed in my direction.

I turned around, searching for Marion and Reed in the crowd and making my way toward them.

"I need to get into some sort of car or hiding place," I said. "People are recognizing me and it feels like . . ." I trailed off, paranoia and panic working their way into my throat. "I'm just in the middle of unknown territory right now."

The journalist who had approached me earlier came over to us. He said, "If you need somewhere to sit, you can get into my car." Reed asked for his name and some ID to ensure he was who he said he was, and then I took refuge in his vehicle, leaning low into the back seat and tugging my cap down so those passing outside the windows couldn't see my face. When the ferry arrived, we drove on board. I stayed hidden as we crossed the river into Banjul.

Marion had called ahead to arrange to have Mum meet me at the ferry terminal, a family friend driving her to collect me. The journalist helped me find her in the crowd and transferred my bags to her vehicle. Then he handed me his number. "Contact me if you're having any events and want coverage for them," he said, and I thanked him for his unexpected and welcomed kindness.

"That must have been a long trip," said Mum, hugging me. "Where are the others?" I told her they'd gone on to their hotel. As we climbed into the car, Mum turned to me in the back seat. "Are you all right?" she asked. "It was so quiet when the story came out, but now everybody is sharing it all over the place. My phone hasn't stopped ringing." I had turned my phone off, but my mother wasn't of a generation that felt comfortable ignoring a phone call. She'd picked up every one she received, answering questions from callers who were genuinely concerned as well as those who were just nosy.

"You don't have to talk to them all," I told her. As we spoke further, though, I realized the burden of the calls she was receiving was even greater than I had imagined. While the people who called me focused on my bravery in speaking out, the family and friends calling Mum were of an older generation that never spoke openly about sexual violence and viewed it as shameful for the victim to acknowledge. Their calls emphasized my victimization more than my survival. They were calls that gave my mother the kind of condolences expressed after a death. My mother's friends had no model for how to react to a situation where someone had survived a sexual assault but was now in a place of strength rather than pity. It brought home to me again how limited we were in our ability to talk openly about these crimes.

As we pulled up to Mum's house, the kids came out to greet us, the younger ones oblivious to the news that now swirled around us. To them, I was just making another visit home, and we hugged and laughed our way into the house.

The next day the online chatter was focused on the press conference scheduled for midday at the Princess Hotel. Local media had been reaching out since the session in Dakar, but rather than do individual interviews, we had pointed them all to the press conference. As Baba led me through the lobby, I could feel people watching us cross to the meeting room where Marion, Fatoumatta and Reed were already seated at a table. The room was full, cameras set up across the back. A women's group that worked to prevent gender-based violence—Gambia Against Rape and Molestation, an organization until then unknown to me—had shown up to support me. Members of the country's Truth, Reconciliation and Reparations Commission sat in the audience too, next to other public officials, journalists and activists. Some faces were people I'd only ever seen on television or the internet.

As I seated myself next to Marion, I saw a girl named Mariatou, who like me had participated in the July 22 pageant, sitting at the back of the room. She now worked for a Gambian media outlet. My stomach tightened. I had no idea what she thought of me. We had competed alongside each other, but because I had come late to the competition from a social circle outside that of many of the other contestants, we had only the thinnest of connections. All of us had wanted the scholarship promised to the winner—and then I had disappeared, casting a shadow over the event. I hadn't stayed in touch with any of the girls, but I was sure Jimbee would have done all she could to poison them against me, casting me as the villain, and Jammeh himself would have done likewise, discrediting me so if I did speak out about the assault, I would be less likely to be believed.

I knew some of the other contestants had swallowed the poisonous rumours spread about me after I left. In the comments on the news stories that had been published, some had even spoken up against me, defending Jammeh, arguing they had never seen the president touch me, that he had been like a father to us. It reminded me of the backlash against the women who had accused movie mogul Harvey Weinstein and other powerful men in the United States, as if saying "he didn't rape me" meant he had never raped anyone. One of the other contestants had contacted me on Messenger in the months after I fled to Canada, calling me out for the self-ishness of my disappearance, threatening me with God's judgment for walking away from the blessings the pageant and president had offered to me. Another had written to criticize me for turning my back on my country. At the time I had been astounded, unable to process what they might have been thinking. They didn't know I had been raped, but did they imagine I had simply left out of spite, flying off to a magical life in Canada?

And yet at the same time, their letters had made me feel that somehow I had robbed them of the benefits the pageant should have given them, that my disappearance had tainted what should have been their chance to shine. I'd heard that Jammeh had turned some of his anger at me onto the pag-eant more generally, so that the remaining winners had fewer opportunities. The next year the pageant was cancelled, though it was later reinstituted. But after Jammeh's down-fall, it ended for good.

Then I saw some of the pageant girls' recent responses to the news I had been sexually assaulted: denials. And in that moment, I realized I didn't owe them anything.

When I saw Mariatou at the back of the room, a chaotic mix of emotions washed through me. She had been one of the senior secondary school winners, from the outskirts of Banjul, like me, and I had felt closer to her than to the others. But I hadn't spoken to her since I had run away four years earlier. In that moment, all I could think was, *Just explain it clearly enough that Mariatou gets it, so she doesn't hate you like some of the others do.* I had started out wanting to tell a nation what had happened, but now in that room, I simply wanted Mariatou to understand.

Looking back, I think maybe I found it safer to focus on Mariatou because Mum was in the room that day too, along with Penda. They had read the stories online, but we still hadn't had a detailed conversation about it. Now for the first time, they would hear me say what had happened. I knew, too, that Dad was watching the press conference on television at home.

As we had in Dakar, we took turns talking, this time in English: Marion outlining how the report had been verified, Reed speaking about the importance of holding Jammeh accountable, Fatoumatta sharing the details of her near miss. Then it was my turn.

I knew what I had to say, knew who I had to say it to, but I needed to distance myself from my self, pull my *self* outside of the body that had been subjected to Jammeh's crime, sit outside the body others now stared at as I told my story.

I described the work we contestants had all put into the pageant, the other brilliant young women who had competed, all of us hoping for a scholarship to allow us to improve our lives. "Winning that day was the proudest moment of my life," I said. I shared with them my naïveté in thinking I could avoid directives from Jammeh's office, from that day on the movie set when I tried to make excuses to stay and film my small part, to my more dangerous refusal of Jammeh's marriage proposal and Jimbee's tour of the home that could have been mine. I described how Jimbee left me to wait for the president that awful night, and how Jammeh entered the room full of "anger, rage, frustration at the fact that maybe I had said no too many times."

I described what he had said to me then: "Who do you think you are?"

"For the past four years, I have been trying to answer that question," I said. "Who do I think I am? And today, I am here speaking to him and to Gambians, because I want to tell him who I am. I am the survivor who has come back to haunt him and men like him. That's who I am. I hope he hears that answer, that answer that I never gave on that night. That's who I am."

As I shared the details of the night I was raped, I knew I was doing something shocking, something Gambians had not seen on their televisions or heard on their radios before. I paused in my telling. "To people who are wondering why I am saying this so vividly and so loud, it is because it's time that we hear this," I said. "It's time that we are uncomfortable, because comfort has been disastrous." I tried to explain that in silencing women to preserve our own comfort, to protect our families from shame in a misguided effort to protect our family dignity, we were condemning our sisters, our mothers, our cousins to being forever broken, forever hidden, forever traumatized. "I speak because I have to," I said. "The conversation has to start somewhere."

I knew Gambians had been transfixed by the broadcasts of the Truth, Reconciliation and Reparations Commission, watching men give testimony about the torture they had undergone at the hands of Jammeh's security forces and his death squad. We believed those men who said they were tortured, I said, and rarely did we ask, Did the torture really happen? But when women come forward to say they have been raped, "we want CCTV camera footage, we want DNA, Lord, we want God to come down and tell us. We really do invest a lot in evidence when women speak out." But perhaps that desire for evidence was unsurprising, when in our languages we had no clear words for rape, no words to differentiate between consensual and non-consensual sex. "It is time to start finding words for it, language for it," I said.

I was lucky, I continued, because for the past four years, I'd had opportunities most Gambian women do not have. I had gone to therapy. I had found ways to express my anger. I had learned to centre and calm myself, even in the moments when my trauma threatened to knock me over again. "To heal so that I can say my ordeal in pride and not shame," I said. "But so many other women do not have that. There is no safe place for them to say it." The Gambia needed police stations set up to allow private conversations, with police officers trained to hear and act upon rape complaints. Gambian women needed access to therapy. "Our bodies are our bodies. Our stories are our stories. And I hope Gambian women start to take back their power, their narrative, their stories."

There were moments where I struggled, when Marion rubbed my back to comfort me or wrapped an arm around my shoulders to help me continue. And as I spoke, I could see Mum crying and Mariatou crying too. Soon Marion called Mum forward to sit with us at the head table so we could offer comfort to each other.

When it came time for questions, a representative from the women's group stood to thank me. As she finished, Mariatou raised her hand from the back of the room.

"Come forward, come here," I said to her, motioning to the front of the room. She stepped to the front, taking a seat beside me as we hugged tight. Then she turned to the room and took the microphone.

She had participated with me in the pageant, she said. To her, everything looked fine. But one day I disappeared. She hadn't been sure what was going on and had heard all of these bad things about me. But something told her there was more to this story. Mariatou looked at me as she continued. She said she was glad I was telling my story now and was sorry she hadn't reached out to me, sorry it had happened to me.

I had spoken out because I wanted Gambians to know what had happened to me. But in that moment, it mattered that Mariatou and those closest to me now knew—and believed me.

As we wrapped up the final questions, I asked others to share their stories too, using #IAmToufah. Later people would ask why I wanted women to use my name. My intention wasn't to take their stories as my own. Rather it was a way of saying, "I am willing to use my name, and if it isn't safe for you to use your name, if you aren't ready, you can use my name too." My hope was perhaps now, we could all find a way to speak, to be visible, to claim our stories, our lives, our strength.

Then we were finished. The stories in the *New York Times*, the *Guardian*, the BBC; the press conference in Dakar—all of them had been building to this, to telling the truth in the place where this had all begun.

When I had escaped The Gambia in 2015, my intention had been never to speak of what had happened to me. My partners would never know. If I had children someday, I hoped they would never know. My parents would never know. I was going to lock what had happened away inside me, a secret I would never share, never tell. And yet here I was, having made the journey from a place of shamed silence—a journey that had taken me halfway around the world and back—to a place where I sat, my dreadlocks piled atop my head in a brown and gold wrap, speaking to a country that had never had an open conversation about sexual violence, telling my people about the power dynamics of sexual assaults, using what had happened to me as an opportunity to tell women young and old their stories mattered, telling them I knew what it was like to try to push what had happened away only to discover that you were pushing parts of yourself away too. And it didn't matter if it took you four years, ten years or forty years: you could tell your story when you were ready to tell your story.

I imagined Jammeh in exile, watching the press conference, knowing he hadn't been able to silence me. He wasn't in control anymore. And I wasn't invisible.

—

"That did not happen. That did not just happen."

In the aftermath of the press conference, I had escaped to Marion's hotel room with Penda. The door was barely closed when I let myself crumple into a chair. "That did not just happen," I repeated as I took a deep breath of relief at making it through telling my story in the place where it had all happened. Penda's eyes were red from the tears she had shed while I was speaking, but now that we were in the privacy of a closed room, she teased me about how the pin I'd used to secure the gap at the top of my blouse was crooked, how my belt wasn't straight and how I'd ugly-cried.

Our relationship hadn't always been this comfortable. The day I left for the market to escape The Gambia, Penda had seen me go and had sensed something was wrong. When Jammeh's security forces had come to question the family about my disappearance, it had been Mum and Penda who were most strenuously interrogated. But Penda had stood firm, refusing to say anything that would get anyone in trouble. Later, when I called home from Canada, she was always excited to hear from me. In the time since Jammeh's downfall and my return trips to The Gambia, Penda and I had grown even closer. Taller and more slender than me, she had taken to joking I was her "little sister." She was always the first to share positive news about me, posting news stories about me on social media, especially on her WhatsApp status. She didn't judge me, simply accepted me, and had become my closest confidant within the family.

"Give me your phone," Penda said, wanting to take some selfies as we let ourselves unwind from the tension of the event. As I handed it to her, it pinged. "Can't I take a photo in peace?" she said, so I switched it to flight mode, cutting us off from the digital world.

I watched, exhausted, as she snapped photo after photo. It was as if I had finished a marathon. At each stage, I had simply focused on what needed to be done next: Do the HRW report. Do the interviews. Do the Dakar press conference. Do the Gambia press conference. Now there was no "need to do" left to do. I would spend three days with my family and then fly back to Toronto. I was done.

When Penda finished taking photos, I turned my phone back on again. Email after email downloaded into my inbox, WhatsApp messages and Facebook notifications pinging one after another as well.

The messages overflowed. Women sharing their stories with #IAmToufah on Facebook, each one heartbreakingly unique and horribly familiar. Those too ashamed or afraid to attach their name to their story emailed me instead: women and girls I knew and those I'd never met. Links to news stories flowed into my inbox as well, as reports were posted from the news conference.

Not all of it was supportive.

Lying we are not that stupid. The west is behind this.

Don't let this fool you, you didn't know this girl she is capable she and her greedy mother . . .

This girl is a gold digger.

Others said I wasn't really Gambian, that my behaviour wasn't truly Gambian.

Jammeh still had many followers, though even among those who didn't support him, the impulse asserted itself to disbelieve a woman, to give a powerful man "the benefit of the doubt." Reading the messages was like taking a master class in rape culture: I learned more in those hours than I could have learned in a classroom in months.

Some called my press conference a performance, suggesting whatever dramatic skills I had were being put to use with fake accusations and an actress's tears. I was too strong to have been raped. I was too ugly to have been raped. I was beautiful and so he couldn't resist me. I had gone to the State House too late at night. (I hadn't realized there was a time of day that made you deserve to be raped.) If I wasn't to blame, Mum was. Where had she been—shouldn't she have stopped me from going to the State House that night? (I saw no messages blaming my father.) Others claimed to have dated me, to have had sex with me (as if that mattered, even if true). It was a real-time demonstration of misogyny and rape myths.

Back at my mother's home that evening, I continued to read online. Against the backdrop of the angry shouts of denial were the voices of survivors filling my inbox, confiding in me, wanting me to continue the conversation I had started. A former teacher contacted me: Would I consider meeting with some of his students who now considered me a role model? Teenagers reached out to me directly, wanting to talk to me, meet me. In the days that followed, I would hear too from a family friend, a woman my mother's age, who had lived on her own her whole life, locking herself into her home every night, barricaded, alone. She had hoped to marry and have children one day but had been assaulted by her father, she told me, and had instead lived her life in fear and isolation, trapped by her secret shame.

I wanted women to speak up, to step out from behind the statistics, and they had. But along with their stories was a backlash from rape apologists. Faced with this ugliness, could I in good conscience encourage any other woman to risk telling her story?

I can't talk to every woman individually, I thought. It isn't safe for every woman to step forward. But maybe we could show our strength in a way that didn't require participants to label themselves as victims. I thought back to the collective power of the Indigenous protest I had attended in Toronto, where supporters had marched alongside those directly affected. I thought about the Gambian women of the Kalama Revolution demonstrating against Jammeh in 2016, carrying brooms and calabash ladles. We'll march, I thought.

The morning after the Gambian press conference, I called Marion at the hotel. Reed had already departed. "So my vacation with my family is over," I said. "I want to organize a march."

"Tell me what you need," she said.

The next two days were a blur of activity. Friends from school, family members and activists joined us as we scrambled to get police permission to march, posters printed,

T-shirts made, bottled water donated, a sound system rented. Marion was at the centre of it all, helping manage logistics and more, though she wasn't able to stay for the march itself as she had obligations in Dakar she couldn't dismiss.

As the crowd gathered on the day of the march, I was still helping with T-shirts. My phone rang. "Where are you?" asked a friend who was at the rallying point. "You need to get here—leave the T-shirts to the others."

I rushed out, grabbing rolls of black and red tape we'd purchased to help make our statement. Once at the rallying point, we passed out signs printed with "No Means No" along with our white T-shirts. "#IAmToufah" said the front. "Our silence is their protection. Speak Up" and "The Next Victim Could Be YOU" said the back. At the leading edge of the march, half a dozen people held a banner that fell from their waists to the ground, a stack of slogans printed on it:

No to Sexual Violence
Rape Destroys Human Dignity
No Woman Deserves Rape
No Society Deserves Rapists. Expose Them.
Speak Out Today for the Next Victim Could Be You

Before starting the march, a number of us taped black and red X's across our mouths, a symbol of the silence demanded of victims. For me, the tape served a second purpose: I knew journalists would be walking with us, wanting to interview me. While I had organized the march, I did not want it to be solely about me. My taped mouth would force them to speak to women in the crowd, to make room for their voices and their reasons for marching.

Over two hundred of us set out down Kairaba Avenue, one of the main thoroughfares through Serrekunda, a street of banks, shops and offices. It was the first march of its kind ever in The Gambia, a white T-shirted wave of women and men united in a belief in our combined power to create change. Under Jammeh it had been unsafe to march. But with Jammeh gone, we could make ourselves heard. Mum was at work and then at home with the younger children, but Nogoi and Penda marched beside me. It filled me with pride to know they were being exposed to ideas of women's rights and autonomy, about the right to control their own bodies, messages I had never heard at their age. As we approached the march's destination, we pulled the tape away from our mouths, signifying a new era of speaking up, and our chants lifted up and over the sound of the traffic around us: *Stop rape now! No means no! Our silence is their protection! No more rape!* And to the men who raped, a direct message: *We are coming for you!*

I looked out at the crowd and saw both strangers and faces I knew: lecturers from my school days, friends, family, people I had been in drama groups and theatre productions with, schoolmates from primary through to college—even the daughter of my Arabic school headmaster. All of the threads of my life gathered to form a rope of support, stronger together than any one of us alone.

My voice was hoarse from shouting slogans as a group of journalists gathered around me. Like the reporters at the press conferences, they peppered me with questions. *Should you have gone back to the State House that night? Why did you take so long to speak out?* I have to look back with generosity; for most of them, it was the first time they had ever interviewed a rape survivor.

"Are you going to do anything to help other victims?" one asked.

Yes, I was making plans for ways to help other victims, I said. I was starting a foundation to do just that, with plans for counselling, public education and more. The idea for the foundation, only a day old, had emerged as women continued to share their #IAmToufah stories online. Many of the women were seeking support, and some therapists had offered to provide free sessions during our protest week. But more was clearly necessary. And we needed a way to capture and share the stories being voiced. "A hashtag alone won't sustain what you're trying to do," said one friend when we discussed it. "You need something more formal." Retsam Chambai, another friend who would work closely with me on the foundation, added, "There is an opportunity here, a chance to make a difference for Gambian women that goes beyond simply starting a conversation. It's a chance to transform that conversation into concrete action and change lives."

As the crowd dispersed, Nogoi, Penda and I made our way back to my mother's home. That evening, as I packed my bags for the return trip to Canada, I could hear Dad in the living room. "Toufah's march is on television again!" he shouted every time a news report featured us, calling the other children in to watch it again and again. He said, "I didn't know my daughter had the ability to call this many people and they would answer."

Later, Mum entered my room with food for me to tuck into my bags: canned pepper sauce and smoked fish and chereh, a cereal mixture used in side dishes, so I could taste home once I was back in Canada. As I packed we spoke about the foundation. There was paperwork to be finalized and other tasks connected to getting it set up that I wouldn't be able to manage from Toronto.

"I'll do whatever you need me to do," she said. "I am with you one hundred percent on this." There was a pause as she considered her next words. "I know what you are doing is really great," she said, "and I am so very, very proud of you." I could hear the "but" before she said it: "But what I really want for you is for you to go back to school." It was a refrain familiar to every African child. Later, I would joke that if I won a Nobel Peace Prize, my mum would say, "That's a nice prize, but where is that degree you promised me?"

I knew, though, her words were heartfelt. She was the daughter of a smart but illiterate mother. Mum had fought hard to complete her own college and university education, and she knew from experience education had lifted her up, provided her opportunities, saved her in many ways from the conditions less educated women faced. "I feel like whatever you do, you will be stronger, more secure if you have an education," she said. "I need you to do that for me."

I told her I would. I knew that to have a happy African mother, it helped to have a degree with your name on it.

We talked too of the security arrangements for her house. I'd paid to have extra cinder blocks added to the wall around her property so that it was higher and fully enclosed; it had been topped with barbed wire as well. Baba Hydara and Reed Brody had arranged for an NGO to pay for private security for a few months too, and Marion had arranged for her boxing teacher to stay with the family for a few days until the private security detail was in place.

The next day, I scrambled to renew my Gambian passport, due to expire in the weeks ahead. Normally, it would take ages for the paperwork to wind its way through the Gambian bureaucracy, but at the passport office, a friendly official had expedited my file. "Don't I know you?" he asked when I came to pick up my documents, which like all official papers, carried my proper name, Fatou Jallow. "I know you," he repeated, as recognition dawned in his eyes. "You are Toufah!"

He looked at me again. "You are so beautiful. I can see why he raped you."

I didn't know what to say. I think he thought it was a compliment, that I was beautiful enough to rape. And I knew the work to change attitudes, to make a difference, was only beginning.

11

A COUNTRY LISTENS

"Is this you?"

I'd ignored the text from my call centre boss when it pinged onto my phone just after the *New York Times* story appeared, but now that I'm back in Toronto, I can't ignore his question. I'd told him I was going to The Gambia "on vacation." At work I just . . . worked. I haven't shared any of what I am going through with colleagues or my supervisors. Hired through a temp agency, like many of my co-workers, I am a one-step-removed not-quite-employee of a telecom company again, and while I go to the same call centre for shift after shift, my assignment there can also be terminated with no notice or justification. The physical set-up of the centre discourages employees from forming friendships at work. There are no "permanent" workstations—you move from desk to desk depending on what time you arrive and are rarely seated next to the same co-workers. To be honest, I like the anonymity. I go to work. I do my job. I go home.

But now, my boss knows more about me than I would otherwise have shared, so when I arrive on my first day back, I stop to talk to him. Yes, that was me in the paper, I tell him. He seems supportive, even congratulates me on my activism, and when I ask that he not share the information with other people in the office, he readily agrees.

And so I settle back into Toronto, in a place where I'm not Toufah, the woman who accused a president, but just another face in the crowd. In The Gambia, after the press conferences, I'd been recognized wherever I went. And while I'd wanted to be seen, there is relief in just being an ordinary woman again. Here I am Toufah, the woman taking calls from customers about their billing issues. It feels safe, even liberating.

In The Gambia, debate continued about whether my claims were true or not, and my "performance" at the press conferences and march continued to be dissected. My tears were crocodile tears. My dreadlock hairstyle meant I was lower class, uncultured. I was unreligious. I was manipulated by foreign powers, the United Nations and Gambian political parties opposed to Jammeh.

I had gained some distance from it all by returning to Canada, but my family continued to live with the impact. My mother received threatening phone calls, prompting police to investigate. While the aid agency kept paying for private security guards to keep watch on my mother's home, guilt at putting my family in harm's way weighed on me. People who didn't believe me posted online that I must be making money from these accusations somehow—being paid off by I don't know who—but back in Toronto, I was scrambling to earn the money to pay my rent.

So much of what was said and posted was hurtful. And ironically, the most hurtful reaction of it all was the publication of a cartoon its creator said was intended to support me.

The image appeared in one of The Gambia's national newspapers: a black and white drawing under the heading "NKO beauty queen accuses Babili of having carnal knowledge of her . . ." The headline referenced a Mandinka honorific used for Jammeh: Babili Mansa, meaning "king bridge builder" or "conqueror of rivers." The image depicted Jammeh in his presidential garb, a Qur'an in one hand, a ceremonial sceptre in the other. He stood above a naked woman, whose lower half was covered by a blanket, but whose legs were spread, her naked breasts showing above the blanket's edge. Next to her, a syringe lay on the ground. "Done! You can go home!!" read the speech bubble above his head. "Mr. President you rape me?" read the bubble over the woman's head.

It made me sick. Jammeh was depicted in all his power: presidential looking, clothed, the trappings of his religion and position in his hands. The drawing of me tapped my deepest fears: that in speaking out about being raped, all anyone would see when they looked at me was me naked, me being raped. And in this particular image, with arms and legs spread wide, breasts on show, the woman looked like she was welcoming her assaulter—asking to be raped—and even respecting him by calling him "Mr. President" as she accused him. The cartoonist didn't imagine Jammeh naked.

Later I would see cartoons of other women, some intended to "support," some intended to degrade, like the one depicting Christine Blasey Ford as a blindfolded Lady Justice who is being assaulted, after she'd accused U.S. Supreme Court nominee Brett Kavanaugh of raping her; a cartoon bumper sticker of a girl being grabbed by the ponytails and assaulted from behind, the name "Greta" printed across her back to indicate she was meant to be teenaged climate activist Greta Thunberg. All drawn from a man's perspective showing the worst moment in a woman's life. The cartoon that claimed to support me actually ridiculed me, rendering me naked, diminished, open to assault. I knew there would be those who would call me a whore, and I had worked to desensitize myself to that word. But the image, as crudely drawn as it was, stung so much more than any words.

Each day after work, I released my frustration and anger at the boxing club. The thud of my gloves against the heavy bag, the rhythmic movement of my fists on the speed bag, the sparring in the ring: when I boxed, I was focused in the moment—no grappling with the past or worrying about the future, my attention fully absorbed by how I moved, what it felt like to fully inhabit my bones and muscles and ligaments and sinew.

I spent the few hours every day that were left after my call centre job and the boxing club online and on the phone, as Marion and I worked together long-distance to get what we'd named The Toufah Foundation set up. We recruited an advisory board and slowly got the official structures in place.

The Gambia's Truth, Reconciliation and Reparations Commission was also in contact with me asking whether I would testify about what had happened. I was willing to do so, though the organizers weren't clear about when my appearance would happen. I needed enough notice to arrange to be away from work and to travel to The Gambia again, I told them, and my boss at the call centre had told me October and November would be busy, so it would be harder to get time off from work then. Marion and I had become friends, and I also wanted her to be able to attend the hearings, as a person who could support me through what I knew would be another emotionally draining experience. She was available anytime except the last week of October, when her husband had planned a vacation for the two of them to celebrate their anniversary. When the TRRC asked about my schedule, I told them I would come anytime except late October.

At the beginning of October, I got a call from the TRRC telling me that my testimony was scheduled for the last week of that month. My heart sank. But as difficult as the timing was for me, there was no way I could back out. In The Gambia, not testifying would be interpreted as proof that I was unwilling to offer my testimony under oath. In other words, that I had lied.

"I can't cancel this trip," Marion told me when we spoke. Her work often took her away from her family, and this anniversary journey was one her husband had been planning for some time. I understood. Anyone involved in this work needs time to recharge. Still, my relief was real when she called back a few days later to tell me that her husband had

Gambian therapist who had trained in Nova Scotia, Canada. She was, in many ways, the perfect person for me to speak with: someone who understood what it was like to live across two cultures, but most importantly someone who understood in her bones what it meant as a Gambian woman to speak up about rape.

She handed me paper and coloured markers. "I'd like you to draw a map of where you are and where you'd like to be at the end of all of this," she said. As I started to draw, she gave me more instruction: What did I want my testimony to result in? The beginning of a conversation about sexualized violence? Ten women inspired? A hundred women seeing their story reflected in mine? Whatever my goals were, I was to write them down, to draw them as the destination of my map.

"Along the way," she asked, "what might distract you?"

Facebook comments, hurtful emails, news reports, Jammeh supporters.

I listed them and then drew them as other vehicles on the road or distracting sights along the route. It sounds simple, but visualizing it in this way was helpful and even calming. At the end of the exercise, I could imagine myself navigating around the distractions; I could see where I wanted to go.

Later, I met with Horejah Balla Gaye, the commission's deputy lead counsel, who walked me through the hearing process: the introduction of me as a witness, the structure of the questioning by the commission counsel, the opportunity for other commissioners to ask questions, my chance at the end to give a final statement. I was permitted to bring notes to remind myself of what happened when, so I could be as precise as possible about dates and times. It wouldn't be like a movie courtroom, though. There would be no lawyer at my side, whispering advice in my ear. I would be alone at a table, facing the commissioners and my country.

Many rape victims never get the chance to be heard. Few are heard by an international audience. Fewer still have the chance to be heard more than once. I had told my story to the world in June and said I hoped for the opportunity to confront Yahya Jammeh in a courtroom. Now, four months later, I had the chance to tell my story again, and while it wasn't in a courtroom, it would be under oath, before counsel and commissioners empowered by the Gambian government to uncover the truth. Jammeh wouldn't be in the room, but I was certain he would be watching.

The threats against my family and the steady stream of hatred directed at me online worried the commission, and so they arranged for me to stay in a series of hotels, shifting me each night. I was told to hide my dreadlocks under a head wrap, to take off my glasses, and to avoid wearing the jewellery on my nose that I had been photographed with at earlier press appearances—anything to reduce the likelihood I would be recognized.

I'd been in touch with Marion: she was arranging for drivers to bring my family to the hearing and would be there herself. I'd wanted to be with my family the night before my testimony, but the TRRC officials said it was too dangerous, and so I was alone in a hotel room. I didn't sleep. I'd watched the testimony of other victims before me: Binta Manneh had been raped as a teenager, almost twenty years earlier; her assault had helped trigger the student protests of April 2000, when Jammeh's troops fired on the crowds and sixteen people died. Afterwards, to preserve their "honour," her family had forced her into an arranged marriage with a much older man, and so she was subjected to legalized rape within a marriage she didn't want. One of the other women who had accused Jammeh of rape under a pseudonym in the Human Rights Watch investigation had also testified already. She'd been a protocol officer for Jammeh for three years, during which time he'd repeatedly assaulted her. Her closing statement had been riveting.

"Yayha Jammeh was powerful and cunning," she'd said. "Using his position of authority, he put a system in place, using state institutions and resources to ensure that women would not or could not say no. For me, his system was wicked. And he targeted young, vulnerable women from vulnerable families. Most of the times, these young women were the ones supporting their entire family. He sometimes even directly supported the families, appearing as a generous benefactor. He made you believe he was a father to you or a mentor. He made promises of education and scholarships. And we all longed for a better life. It is at that time, when that confidence was built, that he made his sexual demands in return. If you said no, he makes sure you suffered, humiliates you and makes others belittle you. This is my story. Others felt that they had no choice but to accept his advances and become his sexual slaves."

Her words rang in my ears as I ran through what I wanted to say, again and again. I am terrible with dates and numbers in general, and I'd written down the dates of my schooling and used photos I'd transferred from my phone to my computer to help me figure out what had happened when, from winning the pageant until I left The Gambia, using the time and date stamps on the images to guide me. Mum had been surprised when I'd even written my birthday down, worried that I'd get something even that basic wrong. "You know how bad I am with dates!" I told her, and we had laughed about it. I'd printed it all off in a document organized sequentially.

Now as I flipped through the pages, looking at the pictures, I was struck by the naïveté of the young woman captured there. I was so happy in those early photos. The doors to the world were open in front of me, with the prospect of a paid education anywhere I wanted to go. My family and community were so proud of me. The president of my country had called me a brilliant young woman and was listening to my ideas. My eyes shone with the possibility of a future that was mine to create. I was so confident, so sure I had the right to decide where that future would take me, the right to say yes to what I wanted, to say no to what I didn't.

So much had happened since then as I rebuilt my life, some of it beyond my control, and so much else I had worked hard to achieve. Jammeh had done what he could to crush the spirit of the girl whose eyes shone so brightly in those photos. He hadn't succeeded. I was strong. I'd found the support I needed. And I'd been lucky. But as much as I'd worked to rebuild myself, I couldn't help feeling some sadness for the Toufah in those photos. I was still Toufah, but I wasn't *that* Toufah; I could never be that girl again.

When morning came, I was dressed early and had my bags packed, since we would be moving locations after my testimony. Just before we set out for the hearing hall, my phone rang. It was Mum. She was certain these hours of testimony would silence those who disputed my claims: How could they not believe me once the facts were laid carefully before them and the commission?

"Are you okay?" she asked when I answered her call.

"I don't know," I told her. "How are you?"

"I feel like I am sitting on an egg," she said. "I wish we'd spent last night together."

Me too, I told her. I couldn't believe it was finally time for me to testify.

"You'll be fine," she said, her voice filled with her belief in me. "We will get through it like we have before." She paused. Would I do one thing for her? she asked. Would I recite some verses from the Qur'an on the drive to the TRRC hearing hall?

At other times I might have resisted her request, but I knew agreeing to say the prayers would ease her mind, her effort to comfort me a way for me to comfort her in return.

I hung up. And then the driver was there.

From the back seat of the car, I watched as people went about their business on the streets of Serrekunda. Girls hawked mangoes. Office workers bought breakfast from street vendors. I knew the people of The Gambia were tuning into the TRRC hearings every day, listening on radios, watching on their smartphones and televisions. "Now Streaming on YouTube" a *New York Times* headline had declared just a few weeks earlier in a story describing The Gambia's TRRC as "the most accessible truth commission in history" with "a live feed that sends testimony through YouTube, Facebook, television and radio—directly into phones and homes around the country" with "listeners stretch[ing] from the capital, Banjul, into the countryside and abroad to the diaspora." In a few short hours, it would be my voice they heard, my face they would see.

The hearing hall was in a low-rise white building in Serrekunda's Senegambia neighbourhood, just a few intersections away from Palma Rima Beach on the Atlantic coast. The air here was a few degrees cooler, the breeze carrying the scent of salt and the grasses that grew around the building. When we arrived, a security agent led me from the back parking lot into a private witness waiting room, the room's air-conditioned chill noticeable in contrast to October's thirty degrees Celsius heat. Soon the commission's therapist joined me; an investigator, the lead counsel, Essa Faal, and deputy lead counsel, Horejah Balla Gaye, the woman who would be questioning me, all stopped in to see me as well. When Mum and Penda arrived, Penda was star-struck. She'd watched Horejah for hours on television as the lawyer calmly and methodically questioned both victims and those who had acted on Jammeh's orders. Penda confessed that she thought Horejah was the smartest woman she'd ever seen.

It would be a long day, Horejah told me, but anytime I needed a break, I simply had to ask for one. I felt almost outside of my body: functioning, engaging in small talk, but also not completely there. One minute, I felt overheated, sweaty. The next, I felt chilled to my core, as if blasted by the room's air conditioning. I excused myself again and again to pee; my bladder seemed to be trying to empty every bit of fluid from my body. In the background I could hear the translators testing the microphones; they would interpret my words into Fula, Wolof, Mandinka and other local languages, or into English when I spoke in any of those languages. I could hear chairs scraping the floor, news reporters doing their introductions. I opened Facebook on my phone and could see the viewer numbers for the commission's live feed climbing higher and higher. I remembered the therapist's advice from the day before. Don't think about who is watching, she'd said, just talk to the people in the room. But in that moment, it was hard not to think of those at the other end of the broadcast: my dad's extended family on Gambia's MacCarthy Island, people I'd grown up with and gone to school with, people I hadn't seen since before all of this had happened. They had known the Toufah from before, the one whose photos I had spent the night looking at. Now they would be meeting a Toufah who had been changed by what had happened to her. In that moment it felt like my testimony was a reintroduction to everyone I had ever known, as over the course of it, I would put myself out there, saying, "This is who I am now." Would they recognize me? Would they understand me? Would they believe me? Would they accept me?

I didn't know.

Reading my face, Mum said, "You've come this far, you'll be okay."

"I don't know about that," I replied.

Word came that the hearing would begin soon, and Mum and Penda made their way out to the hearing hall, where Dad and other extended family and friends were already seated. The witness room that had been filled with people now seemed to have exhaled them, leaving me alone with the therapist. I stood and stomped my feet and rubbed my hands together to bring warmth and circulation into them.

"Let's take some breaths," the therapist said, guiding me through some deep breathing exercises.

And I broke down. I started to scream as tears streamed down my face.

"It's okay, it's okay," she said. "Let it all out."

I don't know where it came from, but in unleashing those screams I wasn't just releasing the pain of what I'd been through; I was venting the pain I knew was about to come. I let the tears tumble out of me, pushing up from deep inside. At last I wiped them from my face, drew some more deep breaths.

It was time to go in.

It looked like any other office chair: square-backed and covered in what appeared to be black leather, positioned behind a brown-topped desk and microphone. But in The Gambia, the chair was famous. The vice-president of the country had sat in it. People who had cut off the heads and hands of others and buried bodies in unmarked graves had sat in it, vividly describing what they had done. People who had been tortured had sat in it, detailing their agony. And now it was my turn. I dropped my handbag at its foot, placed my folder of notes and photos on the desk next to the bottle of water and box of tissues already there. An usher held a Qur'an before me, and I put my hand on it, swearing to tell the truth, the whole truth and nothing but the truth.

Across the room from me sat the commission counsels, the lawyers who had come to see me in the waiting room. Behind me, translators in their booths readied themselves, a sign language interpreter sitting in front of them. To my left, behind a long table, sat the commission chair, Dr. Lamin Sise, a proper, grey-haired man who had spent his career at the United Nations, including as a senior adviser to Secretary-General Kofi Annan. On either side of him were nine commissioners, a Christian bishop at one end and an Imam at the other. The walls behind them were covered in signs: The Truth Shall Set You Free and #NeverAgain. To my right was the audience, where my family, Marion and a number of young women she'd helped to attend sat among the five rows of spectators and supporters, many in #IAmToufah T-shirts, alongside the camera operators who would broadcast my testimony across the country and around the world.

In preparation for my appearance, I'd thought about how I needed to sit. I wanted to be confident, open, direct. I planted my feet hip-width apart under the table, set my forearms on the desktop and held my head high with my shoulders back. I had a moment of unease as I wondered if the desk front was open or closed. I knew I jiggled my legs when I was nervous, and I didn't want those seated around me to be able to see my anxiety so easily. I snuck a look under the desk and was relieved to see it was closed on all three sides. I straightened again and looked across the room at the lawyers, as the lead counsel, Essa Faal, announced that Horejah would question me.

Horejah's voice was a calm beacon as we made our way through the evidence. Her opening queries were to elicit background: where I had grown up, where I'd gone to school, where I lived now, how I had come to participate in the pageant, the competition itself. Key to this first round of questioning was what I understood to be the point of the pageant: that I believed I was competing for an educational scholarship. An hour and a half after we began, the commission chair called for a break, and I retreated to the witness room. I was lying on the couch when Mum joined me. "You're doing a great job," she said. "You're not rushing it. You don't look nervous." Her reassurance meant so much. I knew she was nervous herself, and if she thought I looked confident, it must truly be so. *I just have to maintain this clarity,* I thought. It was easy to be clear about my childhood, about the pageant preparation. *Don't be scared to be this clear when it comes to the parts the world doesn't want you to be clear about,* I told myself.

As we were recalled for the second session, I entered the hearing room a bit more relaxed. But still, I ran through what I had come to think of as my woman's apology self-check. Was my tone of voice all right? I didn't want to sound aggressive, but I didn't want to sound pitiable either. I wasn't seeking sympathy, because I knew sympathy could turn quickly into contempt as people tried to distance themselves from acknowledging the more uncomfortable facts I was going to have to disclose. I needed to own my space and speak with firmness, clarity and honesty.

Now Horejah's questions focused on my contact with Jammeh—when we had met, where, how he had behaved. It would have been easy to paint him as a monster from the outset, but the truth was vital here: in those first meetings, Jammeh had not been a monster. His interest had seemed fatherly. His behaviour had seemed proper. I had believed I was a pageant winner, not prey.

After another hour, we broke for lunch. My family joined me again in the waiting room. My phone was nearby and I couldn't stop myself from checking what was being said on the Facebook Live feed of the hearing. The comments were what I had come to expect: a mixture of support and accusation.

She's lying, said one comment.

What is she lying about? someone else asked. *Where she went to school?*

No, responded the original poster. *About what she's about to say.*

There were comments from men, focused on how I looked. *When all of this is done, can someone give her to me as a wife?* one man had written. I shook my head. Here I was as a survivor of sexual violence, and the response was to treat me as a sexual commodity.

Another commenter, a woman, had simply filled her comment field, over and over, with dog emojis, her message apparently that I was a bitch. Penda looked at it over my shoulder.

"I should just message her right now," I said to Penda. "I should write, 'I think you should adopt a dog, you seem to like them so much.'"

"Don't let them know you're watching their craziness," she said.

As I was recalled to the stand once again, I knew this would be the most difficult part of my testimony. My country was watching, and I was convinced Jammeh was as well. When he'd summoned me to private meetings at his residence, the big screen television had always been on in the background. He was too much a narcissist to resist watching when he was the subject of the broadcast.

You are speaking to him, I told myself as I made my way back to the witness chair. *This is your chance to tell him what he did to you.*

Horejah first questioned me about more pageant-related events, filling in the timeline from January to June of 2015. And then we were talking about that night. I described Jimbee's phone call requesting my presence at the Ramadan ceremony, how she had taken me from one room to the next before leaving me on my own. How Jammeh had burst into the room, filled with anger.

Tears filled my eyes, and I paused.

"Just take your time," Horejah said. "There's a bottle of water next to you in case you want to drink."

I drew a breath. "He said, 'Let's see if you are a virgin.' I swear to God I was scared. I started to apologize. 'I am sorry, I am sorry, please don't do this.' Because he appeared very angry. I don't know what I was apologizing for." As I described his actions, how he jabbed the needle in my arm, rubbed his penis in my face, pulled my dress up, I stopped.

"I keep saying 'he.' I would say his name," I said. I wanted his name associated with these acts, what he had done to me. "Yahya Jammeh decided to penetrate me. Yahya Jammeh did not want sex with me or pleasure with me. What he wanted to do was to hurt me. What he wanted to do was to teach me a lesson."

Yahya Jammeh couldn't believe an unknown girl from an unknown family would have the audacity to say no to him, I said, a man whose position meant he probably didn't hear very many noes. "My noes were very clear, even as I pleaded and said I was sorry," I continued. "Yahya Jammeh was sweating. I don't know why. He was sweating a lot. My face was smooshed into the bed, crying for help. When there was none." My voice broke and I sobbed. "You know?"

Horejah waited for a moment for me to collect myself. "If you need a minute or two we can take a short break," she said. The therapist came over to ask if I needed a break as well.

"I have to continue," I told the therapist quietly, my microphone turned off. "He's watching. I cannot stop, because he would like that." And so I pressed on. I focused on Horejah, not looking to my left at the commissioners or to my right where my family and friends sat. I had promised myself I would be clear here. I would not cloak Jammeh's violence with vagueness. I needed to say it, directly, to everyone. And I couldn't do it if I looked at my family.

"He sodomized me," I said. "And what that means is that he took his penis and he put it into my anus instead of my vagina. That's what sodomy is." In a country where these words were never spoken in public, let alone broadcast, I knew what I was saying was echoing on every radio, on every corner, my voice heard in cars and homes and offices. It was all about hurting me, I said. And he knew he would get away with it, as the Imams' voices read the verses from the Qur'an over the loudspeaker in the garden outside the room where he was raping me. Because he was a president. And because no one would believe a girl like me.

"This is what happened on the night that Yahya Jammeh raped me. And that is how he did it," I said.

There was a pause before Horejah spoke. "What you have explained quite clearly is rape, so I'm not going to belabour it by asking you additional questions just to get more information," she said, enumerating the factors that indicated rape: the use of force, the absence of consent, the injection of drugs, the forced removal of clothing, the anal penetration. "I want simply to ask you how you felt at that point, when all of this was happening and immediately after that, how you really felt."

I struggled to find the words to describe it. "I just lost a part of me," I said, using the Mandinka words "suun nu sayaa." She asked what the phrase meant. "It's like a sense of grief and loss of self," I said. "I wasn't sure of who I was anymore. I lost a part of Toufah." I wiped tears from my eyes. I still couldn't look at the people seated in the audience, but later others would tell me there were tears there as well.

Horejah continued, asking about Jimbee's role. "Do you believe she knew what happened?"

"Yes." I described Jimbee's role: calling me to the State House, meeting me at the door, bringing me into the first room, shifting me to the second room, disappearing just before Jammeh arrived, being there when Landing drove me home. "Jimbee was the one who made all of this accessible to him," I said. "If she had just let me go and sit in that crowd on that night, maybe it wouldn't have happened. It was pre-meditated by her."

Horejah then led me through my escape and move to Canada, before circling back to ask again about the impact of Jammeh's actions on my life, on my family's life.

"One minute I am a teenager going to college in Gambia and the next minute I am a refugee in Senegal who cannot talk to anybody that I love," I said. From there I'd travelled to a country where I knew no one, had to figure out how to survive on my own, isolated from even the Gambian community in Canada because of the rumours that swirled around me, after my family was questioned by police and targeted on social media. I had struggled with depression, filled my hours with multiple jobs so I wouldn't have to be alone with my thoughts, "waking up some days and not wanting to be here," I said as a sob rose in my throat. And it had taken four years of work on my part, of counselling and effort to find my way to a place where I could speak out— even knowing that as I did I was putting my family through the agony of reliving all of this again.

"Counselling did not give me back the part I lost, but it gave me back a new part of what I can be," I said. "I can still be a Fula girl, a proud one from a Wolof mother and a Fula father. I can still be a Gambian. Yahya Jammeh is not more Gambian than me."

As the questioning finished, commission chair Sise offered me the chance to say some final words. I opted to speak first in Mandinka, as I talked about how our culture could find strength in change, as difficult as change might be, that we could do away with the secrecy and silence that protect perpetrators of sexual violence, and shift the shame of abuse from victims and onto those who committed the crimes instead. I switched to English to talk about how Jammeh had cloaked his crimes behind a pageant aimed at empowering women, how our country had held women up as symbols of our progress while continuing to block them from real power and influence. I called for greater access to counselling for victims of sexual violence, for the addition of social work programs to our universities to train people to support victims.

"I know usually when we are done speaking, we say, 'I am sorry if I offend anybody,'" I said, referencing our Gambian custom of offering apologies to those who might disagree with one's point of view. I know who my testimony might offend, I said. "It offends Yahya Jammeh. It offends men like Yahya Jammeh. It offends men who want to sympathize with perpetrators. And to those people: I am not sorry. Thank you."

There was a moment of silence in the room, and then, though it was not permitted, the spectators began to clap. I looked over to where Mum and Dad and my family sat. I could see the relief on their faces, that we'd all made it through this day. And I could see they were proud of me.

As the cameras stopped recording, an Imam approached me to thank me for my testimony. "You are so brave," he said to me in Wolof. "You know, I have a son. He is a doctor and he needs a wife." I understood this was his way of celebrating me, to suggest I was worthy of being his son's wife. But it also brought home to me again how far we had to go in order for my worth, for any woman's worth, to be seen as residing in her *self*, not in her role as a wife or prospective wife, or as a mother, a daughter or daughter-in-law.

Later, it struck me that the Imam's response was similar to when people try to get men to understand the impact of sexual harassment by saying, "Would you want someone to do this to your mother or your wife?" What we should be saying is, "No *person* should be subjected to this." If a woman's value, a woman's autonomy, her right to be free from assault, is dependent on her relationships as a mother, wife, sister or daughter to the men in her life, it means she is only as human as the strength of her relationships to the men around her—that women are only conditionally human.

As I struggled to respond to the Imam, the female security officer who had been assigned to travel with me back and forth to my accommodations moved forward. She'd overheard the exchange. "We need Toufah over here," she said, as she pulled me away, one woman rescuing another, as women have done forever.

I tried to speak with Mum and Dad, but the scene was like a bad version of a business networking event—and without a buffet for distraction. People milled awkwardly, and there was no chance to speak with my family privately. Drivers

responsible for getting Mum and Dad, me, the commissioners and others to our respective destinations tried to find
their passengers and direct them to the proper cars. "We will
see you when you come home," Mum said to me as the security officer led me toward the witness waiting room and the
driver ushered her and Dad to the car that waited to return
them to Mum's house.

Exhaustion washed over me as I sat alone on the couch in
the small witness room. My whole body ached from the tension of sitting in that chair for hours, of holding myself up
straight under the burden of my story. *I did it*, I thought, as
tears streamed down my face.

The door opened and the security officer returned. "We
need to get you to your hotel," she said.

"I'm not going to the hotel," I told her. "I'm going to a
spa." I pulled my phone out of my bag and texted Marion.
Did she think there was a spa we could go to? It was already
early evening, and most spas would close by 9 p.m., but
within minutes, Marion had found a place willing to stay
open long enough to provide the treatment my aching body
so longed for.

The security officer cleared my departure with her bosses,
again instructing me to remove my jewellery and cover my
hair so I didn't look quite so much like myself, and Marion
and I climbed into a cab. I turned off my phone, shutting out
the conversation that continued to rage online about my
testimony. As we drove through Serrekunda's streets, from
the radios in other taxis, from the smartphone speakers of
the people sitting at the intersections brewing green tea and

chatting in front of restaurants and bars, I could hear my voice echoing through the air.

The next day I made my way to Mum's house. The online news sites were still filled with my testimony, and Mum's phone was ringing off the hook as friends and family called. This time, though, their calls communicated more celebration than sadness, and conveyed their pride in the way I had presented myself and told my story at the hearing.

The tone of the online comments had shifted subtly too, as I watched another real-time demonstration of rape culture in action. The *she's too ugly to be raped* comments were mostly gone, as were many of the suggestions that I wasn't truly Gambian or was a puppet of some foreign power. But even as some conceded perhaps Jammeh wasn't as pure as they'd thought he was, the conversation now shifted to *They were dating and she got mad when he wouldn't give her more.* He may have had sex with me—but I'd wanted it, asked for it. For Jammeh's allies, no evidence would ever be enough. And even for some who were not his supporters, the cultural barriers to believing a victim of rape were still difficult to break down.

But theirs were not the only voices. Women continued to come forward to tell their stories, using the #IAmToufah hashtag online, and sharing their experiences in conversations privately as well. Women were speaking up and speaking out.

My whole family gathered at Mum's house, including her parents, my grandma and granddad. I had never spoken directly to my grandparents about what had happened, and even now, our conversation was oblique. Granddad grasped my hands as I sat next to him and bowed his head in prayer. "May you be content," he prayed, his words aimed at God and at me, constrained by his culture from speaking about what had happened to me, "and may that man be punished by God."

It was clear my grandma didn't understand why I had felt compelled to so publicly share what had happened—and especially to share it for a second time, after the memory of my first public statements had started to fade. She said nothing to me directly, but I could see the expression on her face as Mum answered phone calls from well-wishers. "Your mother has suffered so much," I heard her say to one of my siblings. I could see the generational differences: my grandmother wanting to bury what had happened, my mother hoping all would be fine now and everyone would be convinced I had told the truth, and me relieved to no longer be burdened by the shame of the secret but accepting there were some who would never believe me. We were all strong women, each coping in our own ways.

My baby sister, Ida, hadn't been at the hearings but had clearly seen at least some of my testimony on television at home; she marched through the room declaring, "I. Am. Not. Sorry!" an echo of my final statement. Nogoi joined in, teasing me about how I had declared who I was at the beginning of the hearing: "I am Toufah Jallow," she repeated. Another generation of women, learning a new way of moving through the world.

As Granddad and I shared a plate of food, I joked with him that they should have cooked the meat so that it would be softer for his new dentures. "My teeth are strong and fine!" he declared. "I don't know who told you I have dentures!" The air was filled with laughter and relief. Joy filled us. Joy filled *me*, an emotion I'd worried I might never feel again. Just four years earlier, I had been alone in a basement apartment in Toronto, sliding into despair, convinced I might never see my family again, sure I had lost everything important to me. I could never have imagined this moment, never have imagined the Toufah I was now. Not the same girl who had competed for the chance to go to university. But not the same girl who had shivered in that cold basement room either.

A different Toufah, whose voice would not be silenced by a secret but rather raised to speak her truth.

12

A LIFE IN TWO HALVES

"Just a little bit more to your right," the photographer directs me. It is December 2019 and I am at the United Nations, standing with three other youth activists, all amazingly talented, brave people: Feliciana Herrera Ceto, a young Indigenous leader from Guatemala; Alexus Lawrence, a youth activist from New York who completed high school while homeless; and Carl Smith, an environmentalist from the Yupiaq tribe in Alaska. We've all been invited to take part in a youth panel for Human Rights Day. Now we stand arranged in front of a mural, two of us on either side with a gap in the middle, waiting for UN Secretary-General António Guterres to arrive and literally step into the centre of the picture.

"Can we get a photo of just the four of us?" one of us asks. The UN photographer doesn't want us to move, and so Marion captures an image of us standing awkwardly with a secretary-general-sized hole in the middle. Just as Marion finishes snapping our photo, Guterres and his aides arrive.

He moves into the middle of our group, stands for the photo, shakes our hands—and then disappears. It occurs to me the mural has probably been used many times as the perfect backdrop against which to arrange and frame people for similar click-and-run photos with him.

I'd returned to Toronto after my TRRC testimony in early November, and not long after, I was invited by the International Criminal Court (ICC) in The Hague, Netherlands, to speak at a session on sexual violence, and by the United Nations to take part in this youth activism panel on Human Rights Day in New York. Both are exciting opportunities to promote awareness about the needs and rights of victims of sexual and gender-based violence. But while my travel expenses are covered, neither event pays speaker fees and they both mean more time away from work, which means losing income I can barely afford to give up. I am learning activism isn't cheap, and organizations—including some of the world's most high-profile ones—sometimes expect people working to change the world to do it for free. Expectations like these shut many people from marginalized communities out of conversations affecting their lives, and as a result, limit the perspectives and solutions proposed.

In New York I enjoyed meeting and talking with the other activists, but it wasn't lost on me that we "leaders of the future" had been largely speaking among ourselves. We had sat through presentations by senior UN officials and had been officially welcomed and introduced by similarly high-ranking bureaucrats, but when it came time for our panel discussion, the "adults" disappeared, leaving us to talk to a room full of students in their teens and early twenties. I was happy to have the chance to speak with other young people, but equally disappointed the senior decision-makers didn't feel it necessary to listen to what we have to say.

Just a few days earlier, I'd been in the Netherlands capital to speak at the annual assembly of the International Criminal Court. There, representatives of human rights organizations, legal groups and governments had listened to victims' rights advocates from around the world. Based in The Hague, the ICC was established in 1998 and, in situations where countries are unwilling or unable to prosecute, the court tries individuals for genocide, war crimes, crimes against humanity and aggression. Over 120 countries have signed on to the ICC, including Canada, the United Kingdom and The Gambia. (While the United States was active in the formation of the ICC, it hasn't yet officially signed on.) From its earliest days, the ICC has been described as the victim's court, because it sought victim input and participation as its proceedings and processes were developed and established. Still, the court's track record in successfully pursuing cases involving sexual violence has been low, and it has been criticized for dropping charges of rape from cases where other crimes such as murder or torture—often perceived to be easier to prove—were involved, and for requiring what appears to be a higher level of proof in rape cases when compared to other charges.

My appearance before the ICC's Assembly of State Parties was part of a session designed to seek input from survivors of sexual violence about the laws and policies affecting them. I'd been sponsored by Africa Legal Aid, a group that works to ensure African voices are included in ICC discussions. My formal statement to the group was straightforward: Jammeh needed to be prosecuted for all his crimes—murders, torture *and* rapes—and I hoped eventually that would happen with the ICC's support. At a later panel, I returned to ideas and themes I'd been speaking about since first coming forward: we need to be clear in naming sexual violence and the acts involved, and we need to work to overcome cultural barriers that silence victims of sexual assault. Listen to victims, I urged the panel and attendees—and work side by side with us, empowering us as activists, fighters and advocates for ourselves and others. "Our intersectionality matters," I said.

Were my speeches at the ICC and UN effective? I'm not sure. It seemed important to have a presence on these international stages, even if the most tangible outcome was a photograph of me standing next to the UN secretary-general. After all, both are important international organizations. But talking to politicians and bureaucrats—or in rooms politicians and bureaucrats had just left—didn't feel like enough. Maybe this kind of profile-raising needed to be part of my activism, but these meetings weren't reaching the women— and men—whose attitudes I wanted to change. And while speaking in these venues might make potential funders take The Toufah Foundation seriously, on their own, these appearances seemed unlikely to lead to the real change I craved.

Marion had accompanied me to New York, her travel expenses covered by a small grant from the Swiss embassy in

Dakar. While we were together there, we talked about what projects we could propose that might open people up to new ways of looking at the behaviour and cultural norms that permitted sexual violence. I kept thinking about all the points along the way where I'd been let down, using my journey as a lens to identify what conversations were needed, what services could have helped—everything from open discussions so victims knew how to name what had happened to them, to better support services for reporting crimes and healing from trauma, to shifting cultural attitudes so victims weren't blamed.

But I knew from my time in North America there was no quick fix for attitudes. Laws against sexual assault weren't enough if police—and others—didn't believe the victims who reported crimes. When U.S. Supreme Court nominee Brett Kavanaugh was accused by Christine Blasey Ford of having raped her, then-president Donald Trump spoke in Kavanaugh's defence, suggesting women routinely accused men falsely. (Trump himself had been publicly accused of assault by at least twenty-six women.) In Canada, the *Globe and Mail* newspaper published a major investigation of how in one in five sexual assault cases, police refused to move cases forward, classifying them as "unfounded." In some Canadian cities, the "unfounded" rate was as high as one in every two cases, meaning that even after a victim worked up the courage to report an assault, there was a fifty-fifty chance police wouldn't move ahead with the case because the investigating officer didn't believe a crime had actually happened. In the United States, FBI data showed that in cities such as

Baltimore, Louisville and Pittsburgh, there had been years where almost one in every three rape complaints wasn't investigated by police, with a *Baltimore Sun* investigation finding the local police department had routinely ignored rape cases over a number of years.

The irony in all of this is that women are far more likely to *not report* being raped than to make a false accusation. Studies in the United States estimate more than 75 percent of rapes are never reported to police, and of the assaults that are reported, 2 to 10 percent are false claims. When you follow the cases further, to actual convictions, the numbers get even smaller. And for members of the queer community, the numbers are even worse, with even lower reporting and conviction rates.

A false accusation is terrible for the person accused. "Think of your son. Think of your husband," Trump said when Kavanaugh was accused. But think too of the exponentially larger number of daughters, wives and other victims who have been raped and didn't report it. And these are the numbers in a country—the United States—where there have been decades of public education and lobbying for rape victims' rights. In countries like The Gambia, the percentage of unreported assaults is much higher and unaccounted for.

I knew it wasn't a simple thing to change attitudes and results for victims. But we needed to start somewhere. Victims in The Gambia and West Africa often didn't have clear words to describe rape, and so that needed to change. The conversation about what was acceptable behaviour for men and what women should just "put up with" had barely started in my home country, and young women needed to be empowered to speak up for themselves, to have a voice equal to that of the men around them in determining their futures. I knew services were needed to help women survive and heal from the trauma of sexual assault, and that the justice system needed to support women in reporting assaults and ensuring cases would be properly prosecuted. And I knew women needed a safe place to live for themselves and their children if they were being abused at home. So many necessary changes, all pieces in an interconnected puzzle.

As I brainstormed with Marion, Retsam, mentors and others about possibilities for the foundation, the ideas bubbled up. Public education to introduce language about rape and rape culture and the idea that women had a right to say no, as well as showing how women's lives are affected by casually sexist attitudes and actions. Programs for young women to help them develop their voices and dreams. Opportunities for survivors to speak about their experiences. Proposals for changes to legislation. A shelter for women and their children to escape and heal from trauma and violence. All were essential. I knew from my own experience that simply focusing on one aspect—telling young women they can be what they want to be, say no if they want to say no—was actually dangerous if those shiny ideals weren't backed up with practical supports, effective laws and societal structures to hold abusers accountable.

Though we had started the conversation about rape in The Gambia with the Human Rights Watch report and later with women placing their stories on the record with the

TRRC, sexual violence remained a kind of side note, an after-thought, to the investigation into Jammeh and his regime. In January 2020, an expert witness testified at the TRRC about the overall impact of Jammeh on our country. While he briefly mentioned that Jammeh had raped many women, he went on to say that "Jammeh should be credited for having promoted many women to important positions of power." But some would say that was just posturing, replied the commission's lead counsel. The expert's reply? "I want to see Jammeh as having at least made an effort in some regard. I don't want to see him or paint him as totally irredeemable." It was as if he believed Jammeh's rapes were erased by pro-moting a handful of women within his government. And the larger issue, of how Jammeh's behaviour created a climate that permitted other men to rape and discouraged their vic-tims from reporting, was almost completely ignored. Rapes by soldiers were glossed over, rapes of women prisoners at the notorious Mile Two Central Prison were unacknowl-edged, gang rapes by men in uniform were hinted at with no follow-up questions asked.

This wasn't a sprint. It was a marathon, or maybe more accurately, a relay marathon, where we needed to build a community of survivors and allies to make the journey together, each of us contributing our skills and our strengths to help all of us reach our goal.

Marion and I continued to develop ideas for projects that would be the first steps in our marathon, texting and talk-ing and writing back and forth. I had returned to my call centre job, and so our work together filled my evenings and weekends as I scrambled to catch up on the earnings I'd lost by travelling to the TRRC hearing in The Gambia and then to The Hague and New York. My budget was always tight, now even more so, but my work with The Toufah Foundation and its allies energized me. Already, it felt as if 2020 would be a year of possibilities.

Something was up. I was technically an employee of a temp agency, but in practical terms, I'd worked for the same telecom company in their call centre steadily for seven months. I'd had good feedback from my supervisors; I regularly met my targeted number of sales. When new employees ended up in the cubicles next to me, I tried to help out, answering their questions about processes and policies. Yes, I'd taken time away: vacation time for the trip to The Gambia for the release of the Human Rights Watch report on Jammeh; and unpaid time away for the TRRC hearings, and the International Criminal Court and United Nations presentations, when I'd also arranged for someone to cover my shifts.

Part of it was that I felt different. Speaking out about Jammeh, leading marches in the streets, being interviewed by major media around the world, testifying to my country at the TRRC hearings: this felt like the work I was meant to be doing. And then back home in Toronto, I worked call centre shifts for sixteen dollars an hour, trying to earn enough to pay my bills. I felt as if I was a character in a video game or an episode of *Black Mirror*, where I got to be a superhero activist for a few weeks and then had to go back to under-cover life as a call centre operator.

But it also felt as if I was being treated differently. When no one at work had known about the other part of my life, I'd been just another face in the call centre crowd: someone who came in, did a job and went home. But once my boss saw the *New York Times* article, it seemed as if the shift super-visors were all paying a bit more attention to my comings and goings. In the past, being a few minutes late or having to leave early for an appointment didn't get remarked upon if it didn't happen too often or you made up the time from your breaks. Now, though, it seemed as if I was being specially noticed by the all-male supervisors—and not necessarily in a good way. If I was late, they told me, "You don't get to be an exception to the rules." Except that everyone was given a little bit of flex on the rules. I wasn't asking for special treat-ment, just the same bit of wiggle room we'd all usually had. On top of that, suddenly, they told me that customers were complaining they couldn't understand my accented English, which had never happened before.

It was a Friday in mid-February, just before a long weekend. I'd left work and was on my way to catch my bus when my phone rang. It was the HR department at the call centre. "Hi, Toufah?" the woman asked when I answered the call. "I'm just calling to let you know there's no need for you to come back in on Tuesday. When we need you again, we'll give you a call."

As quickly as that, she hung up. I called some of my co-workers from the temp agency to see if they'd had similar calls. No: they all still had jobs. I called my immediate super-visor. "I just got a call that I'm not needed on Tuesday. Does that mean I should come in on Wednesday or Thursday?" I asked, deliberately playing a bit dumb to see if anyone would tell me directly that I'd been fired. He had no idea why I'd gotten the call, he said. He'd check with HR and get back to me. Tuesday passed without a call, and Wednesday too. On Thursday he texted me: my services weren't needed right now and they would call me when they needed me again.

Superhero activist one day. Undercover and unemployed the next.

I needed another job. If I didn't find something soon, I wouldn't be able to pay my rent. I needed a new resumé—but what would I say on it? My life—and my resumé—felt like it was made up of two halves that didn't fit together any-more: unpaid advocacy work that put me on the pages of the *New York Times* and at the podium at the UN in one half, and a list of poorly paid, relatively unskilled jobs in the other.

"Why are you here?" asked the YMCA youth employment counsellor as I sat down in her cubicle a week after being told my services were no longer required at the call centre.

I still feel guilty about what happened next: I started talk-ing and I couldn't stop. She must have thought I was insane or lying, as I vomited my life into her lap. I told her I had been raped by the president of my country and came here as a refugee. I told her about the jobs I'd had and how the last one had ended. I told her I'd been interviewed by major media around the world, had testified at my country's Truth, Reconciliation and Reparations hearings. I told her I didn't want to work crappy jobs anymore. I wanted to go to school. I'd missed out on college because of what had happened to me, and I wanted the chance to be young and normal. I was sobbing through it all.

"Why don't you leave it with me and I'll work on your resumé for you," she said gently, when I finally stopped talking. "Why don't you go home and get some rest?"

I nodded, numb, wiping the tears from my face. As we both stood up, I don't know what possessed me, but I hugged this woman, this stranger. And I left.

What the hell just happened? I thought as I walked away. Part of me was embarrassed, but there was also a kind of physical relief at having let my emotions overflow. I started to laugh: I kept picturing this poor woman going home and saying, "You won't believe what happened to me today!" Later that night I emailed her an apology, which she graciously deflected when she responded with a draft resumé for me. It was the beginning of March 2020, and it was time to start job-hunting.

In mid-March COVID-19 shut the world down. Borders closed. Employees were sent home: some with paycheques and work to do in their quickly improvised home offices, others with no pay, no work and nothing but worries. In Canada we were lucky. The federal government announced an income support program that paid those of us without work two thousand dollars a month for the initial months of the pandemic. It was almost as much as I'd made at the call centre, enough to cover my rent, bills and groceries. Enough to let me breathe. Enough to let me figure out how to make the two halves of my life fit together again.

When I'd been sobbing in the YMCA job counsellor's office, I'd told her I didn't want to work anymore. It wasn't exactly true: what I wanted was to work at things that were meaningful to me. And I wanted to go to school. That goal wasn't just to make my mother happy. From the beginning of all of this, I'd wanted to go to school, to study something I could devote my life to. When I competed in the pageant, I thought perhaps the scholarship I'd been promised would allow me to study drama or the arts. But my life had changed, and with those changes, so had my passions. I wanted to learn to help people who'd been through what I'd been through, wanted to learn to create programs aimed at preventing what I'd gone through. With The Toufah Foundation, I knew we had the chance to make change—but I wanted to be sure what I was doing was grounded in the best anti-oppression practices, most current research and a solid knowledge base. I wanted to continue my social work studies.

I knew Solomon had taken a college program that gave him training as a community worker—he now worked at the resettlement centre where we met. His wasn't exactly the path I wanted to follow, but something like that—an intense, focused program that could be a stepping stone to university—seemed ideal.

As I searched for a program that fit my future plans, we received some good news on one of our first project applications: an American NGO called the International Coalition of Sites of Conscience had approved a small amount of funding for The Toufah Foundation to produce a series of educational radio programs about sexual assault, recorded in the five most common tribal languages in the region. Audio content was relatively cheap to produce, and it was easy to distribute. The Gambian national radio network would air it, and it was also possible to share it as a podcast, requiring relatively low data usage to download it to a smartphone. An expert witness at the TRRC hearings had provided some excellent content in English on this subject, and so I worked in my Toronto apartment to condense the material to a shorter audio script. We recruited translators and hired an audio production person in The Gambia to record the voice talent and help bring the scripts to life with sound effects. Mum got involved and the audio producer, translators and I shared files back and forth online between Toronto and The Gambia.

The world was in lockdown, but our work carried on. Ironically, though health care in The Gambia lagged behind that of Canada, the United States and many European countries, the virus seemed to have less impact in my home country's well-ventilated houses, in communities where so much of daily life happens outdoors. In the first wave, at least, infection rates in The Gambia were low, and life there remained relatively normal.

As summer approached, there was more good news. I'd been accepted to a two-year Assaulted Women's and Children's Counsellor/Advocate program at Toronto's George Brown College. It seemed perfect for me: grounded in a feminist, anti-oppression approach, it was geared to equipping

students for work in counselling, community education, political action and law reform. And because of COVID-19, the
program was even more perfectly suited for my two-halves-in-
two-countries life. It would be entirely online, which meant
I could do it from anywhere I had an internet connection. At
about the same time, the foundation received word that
the Swiss embassy in Dakar would fund us to produce four
videos we had proposed on sexual and gender-based violence
that included the voices of other survivors. I would need to
go to The Gambia to work on them, and so I started making
travel arrangements, navigating pandemic travel guidelines
as well. The halves of my life were starting to fit together.

I watched as the manager stepped behind the assistant, mas-
saging the employee's shoulders, a leer on the face of one,
discomfort evident on the other. "Great!" I said as we ended
the shot with the assistant bolting from the office. Later, we
took our cameras outdoors and filmed as a trio of green-tea
drinkers lounged on a Yundum sidewalk around an outdoor
burner and kettle, catcalling as the assistant hurried past.
Next we squeezed into a taxi, where the assistant was harassed
again by two other passengers in the cramped back seat.

It was uncomfortable shooting these scenes. But it was
also deeply, weirdly funny. I couldn't help laughing as we
worked to edit the material into a nine-minute depiction
of a Gambian homemaker's day, from waking up before
dawn to clean the house and prepare meals for the family,
to dealing with sexist bosses and strangers on the street and

in taxis, to working late into the evening while the spouse played video games and then expected bedroom romance from the exhausted homemaker. The reason for my discomfort was obvious. But the humour? We'd swapped gender roles, putting a man in the role of homemaker, assistant and caregiver, and women in the roles of video-game-playing spouse, boss, catcallers, taxi passengers and driver. What was so often shrugged off as the normal male behaviour that women just had to learn to navigate seemed shocking—and absurdly funny—when the tables were turned and men were subjected to it. I couldn't wait to see how viewers responded.

It was autumn 2020. A full year had passed since my testimony at the Truth, Reconciliation and Reparations hearings. I'd been about to start my college courses when we received word that the Canadian government had approved funding for The Toufah Foundation to create a documentary about Gambian survivors of sexual assault. We'd already begun production on the videos the Swiss embassy had funded, which included the "role reversal" videos. We were nearing completion on our educational radio broadcasts. And we were supporting those who were victims of sexual and gender-based violence, including cases connected to the new government: a prominent lawyer at the Ministry of Foreign Affairs had been accused by multiple women of assault, and a close supporter of President Barrow had been accused of raping his wife's fifteen-year-old sister (the teenager later gave birth to a child conceived as a result). Leaked police files showed that old attitudes die hard: one of the lawyer's victims, police had noted, was not a virgin. And the family of the fifteen-year-old

schedule straight by using sticky notes stuck to my wall with deadlines and appointments. But it was Penda, Retsam and other members of the foundation who really helped keep me on track. My days were packed, but thanks to the team around me, it was manageable. At night, I collapsed into bed, ideas and to-do lists filling my brain until sleep came.

Exhausted. But happy.

It wasn't all school and foundation work. For the first time since I'd escaped from Jammeh, I was able to spend long, normal stretches of time with my family. Yes, I'd visited before, but the trips had either been too short or, more recently, taken over by my public efforts to hold Jammeh accountable. Now, with weeks and months of time together, I was again part of the normal ebb and flow of our family life. As we caught up with each other, I realized that, just as I had hidden many of the challenges of my daily life in Canada from my family, they had also edited their lives to avoid burdening me with what seemed to them to be their smaller problems and irritations.

One evening, as we sat chatting, someone joked about the few months during which everyone had been electrocuted. "Whaaat?" I asked. The details spilled out: when it rained, the barbed wire we'd added to the exterior wall around the house kept coming into contact with electrical wires running to the house. No one had noticed the source of the problem, and for months, after it rained, people had gotten shocks when they touched the house's metal doors, the metal gate to the road, metal downspouts, the metal clothesline posts. It was awful, but as one family member after another shared their jolting experiences, we all collapsed with laughter:

Penda shocked while hanging out the laundry; Ida zapped trying to open the door; Muhammed, Ida and Nogoi trapped inside the courtyard and unable to get to school because the gate was buzzing with electricity.

"So you're telling me you were basically living inside an electric box and no one told me?" I said between gusts of laughter.

"We didn't want to worry you!" said Mum. Electrician after electrician had been unable to spot the problem until finally one noticed the sagging wet cord in contact with the barbed wire.

"Worry me? You were being electrocuted!" I said as we dissolved into laughter again at the absurdity of it, shared laughter helping to heal us all.

Other bonds were strengthened too. After I left The Gambia, I'd felt deeply alienated from my home country, isolated because of the secret of what had happened. Once I spoke out, I'd been accused of not really being Gambian, of turning my back on Gambian values by talking openly about sexual assault. *If staying silent is Gambian, then maybe I don't want to be Gambian,* I had angrily thought. But I was Gambian, am Gambian, and no one—not Jammeh, not his defenders—had the right to take that from me.

Now, as I reconnected with my family, I also reconnected with my country, learning to navigate its idiosyncratic bureaucracies and processes as we developed The Toufah Foundation and our programs. As I drove to location shoots and travelled to meet people, I reconnected with the Gambian landscape as well, rebuilding an internal topography of my country's beaches, the grassy flood plains of the Gambia River and the inland savannas, its boisterous city roads and quieter rural routes. The Gambia is where I am from, it is part of who I am, and my connection to my country is something I won't let rape apologists, Jammeh and his followers take from me again. They can't un-Gambianize me.

As I looked ahead, my plan was to stay in The Gambia until early 2021, and then return to Canada for a few months, moving back and forth between the two countries as circumstances, school and foundation projects demanded. Canada had been the place that had offered me refuge as I rebuilt myself, the country where I had reimagined my life and begun again. It was the place where I was getting the education both Mum and I wanted me to have, the analytical and intellectual framework I needed, alongside my lived experience as a survivor, a woman, a Gambian.

I had imagined as a child that I would live my whole life in Gambia. As a nineteen-year-old I had believed I might never see Gambia again. Now, at twenty-five, I hoped to create a life as a citizen of two countries on opposite sides of the Atlantic Ocean, two halves that had helped make me whole, two countries both home to me now.

It is a sunny afternoon as thirty of us sit on Kasumai Beach: a group of teenaged girls, myself and the facilitator who coordinates the group for The Toufah Foundation. They are young women I've been in touch with for more than a year, some as young as fourteen or fifteen, others about to graduate from senior secondary school. I'd first met with the girls virtually in the time between the Human Rights Watch report release and my return to The Gambia for the TRRC hearings. They were teenagers who'd contacted me online, along with some who had been put in touch with me by my former teachers, and others invited by the girls themselves. I wasn't sure at first what shape our gatherings would take, and so in that initial online meeting I'd asked the girls what we wanted from each other. The jumble of voices made it a chaotic conversation, but what emerged was a desire by the young women to talk about strength, survival and how to raise their voices so that they would be heard.

When I came home to testify at the TRRC, some of the girls attended the hearing, wearing their #IAmToufah T-shirts. After the hearings, as Marion and I unwound at the spa, I'd group-messaged them to see if they wanted to meet in person, and we'd had our first face-to-face gathering before my return to Toronto. Over the next year, they met in person and I joined them virtually when I could. The program was developed in partnership with the girls: they directed the content and activities, with support from me and two other facilitators. We had frank conversations about the challenges women and minority groups faced in The Gambia, we talked about personal safety and sexual violence, and the girls brainstormed strategies and projects for improving their safety. One of their first projects was an online e-safety kit they were authoring themselves to share with other girls, filled with strategies and advice for young women about avoiding and reporting harassment online.

Now back in The Gambia, I was able to see the girls in person again. I'd been thinking a lot about the role models they were exposed to—especially women who looked like them, Black women, women of colour, African women. Most of them knew of Nigerian novelist Chimamanda Ngozi Adichie. Former American first lady Michelle Obama was someone the girls admired as well, and actress Lupita Nyong'o too. Closer to home in The Gambia, there were female school principals, doctors, lawyers, activists, businesswomen and artists such as educators Dr. Isatou Touray and Harriet Margaret Ndow; Jaha Dukureh, a Nobel Peace Prize nominee for her work to combat female genital mutilation; and environmentalist Isatou Ceesay.

We'd faced some pushback from people in the community who didn't think we should use a feminist framework to learn from and teach the girls—that such views were Western, only for white women. And it was true that so many of the words we used to explore concepts and topics were in the languages of those who had colonized Africa, languages that had been used to oppress and suppress.

But as African women, we have our own matriarchal history to draw on for examples of female leadership and strength. I have always drawn strength from the examples of my mother and grandmothers, and there are other African women who are part of our shared history, women I have only recently begun to learn about. Lupita Nyong'o's role in the movie *Black Panther*, as Nakia, a spy for Wakanda's all-female Dora Milaje army, had its roots in the real-life Agoji, an all-woman army in the African Kingdom of Dahomey in what is now Benin. These were the female soldiers Western writers named "Amazonians." Some sources suggest the Agoji originated in groups of female hunters called Gbeto, known for their skill in hunting elephants, a challenging quarry. In past centuries, women traders known as Signarés had used family networks reaching into The Gambia's and Senegal's interior to bring products to market at home and abroad. And one of the most celebrated poets in pre-nineteenth-century America, Phillis Wheatley, was born in The Gambia before being enslaved.

There were female African rulers as well. Two thousand years ago, Queen Amanirenas ruled Kush, now Sudan, and led her army in a five-year war against the Romans. In the sixteenth century, Queen Amina, renowned for her cavalry skills, was a Hausa Muslim ruler of the city-state of Zazzau in what is now Nigeria. For more than three decades, Queen Amina successfully expanded her territory, surrounding her new cities with earthen walls. More than four hundred years later, many of these ganuwar Amina, or Amina's walls, still stand. Njinga Mbandi of Ndongo and Matamba ruled what is now Angola in the seventeenth century, fighting the Portuguese who sought slaves for their colony in Brazil. At the end of the nineteenth century, Sarraounia Mangou led troops against the French during the Battle of Lougou in present-day Niger. Into the twentieth century, Queen Ngalifourou ruled the Téké of Mbé in what is now the Congo. And more recently, there are political leaders such as past president Ellen Johnson Sirleaf in Liberia, President Sahle-Work Zewde in Ethiopia, Prime Minister Rose Christiane Ossouka

Raponda in Gabon, and Prime Minister Victoire Tomégah-Dogbé in Togo.

Still, even in gathering a list of notable African women leaders—and especially for those of the more distant past—it is hard to see these women through eyes unclouded by the colonial gaze. So many of the recorded stories about them come to us through the works of those who sought to conquer our continent, enslave our people and strip our resources; our own oral histories were interrupted by colonization and narrated by those with power for others with power. It makes it hard to untangle their stories from the biases of the conquerors and patriarchs who committed those stories to paper. So yes, we wanted the girls to see women who inspire them—but we wanted them to question the sources who tell them what to see in those role models, who try to dictate the acceptable interpretation of the roots of African feminist resistance.

The values of self-determination and resistance to injustice are not uniquely white: they have deep roots in African culture. But colonialism and patriarchy both contribute to "keeping women in their place." Some Black African men use the belief that women advocating for their own rights and for the advancement of their communities are adopting white values as a way to accuse them of being less Black, less African, when they challenge male power structures, and so we are asked to choose between our Africanness and our quest for equality. It is another way to silence us.

Now, on the beach, as the Atlantic Ocean breeze carries our voices through the air, we pass around a historical drawing of an African woman holding a spear, an image that some say is simply a woman prepared to hunt small prey and that others suggest is a warrior woman, ready for battle. We ask the girls what they see.

"She has strong legs and arms," says one girl.

"That's a bigger spear than you need for small animals," says another.

"She looks powerful!" says a third.

"She looks like us," says one of the older girls.

Their enthusiasm energizes me—and challenges me too. We all need to see strength in ourselves, to make ourselves into people who would inspire others. I know from my own experience the necessity of being able to imagine a future for yourself, as well as the importance of finding support in navigating through the challenges of one's past and present circumstances. But I know too that girl-power slogans and feel-good quotes aren't enough. It causes more harm than good to build strong girls who, as women, are blocked from expressing their strength. We need to transform society so it makes room for the women those strong girls become. Otherwise it is no better than teaching people to sing and then pushing their heads under water: no one will hear their songs as they drown.

I recognize the girls' energy, their spirit. I saw it in the eyes of the girl in the photos on my phone I used to help me in my testimony at the TRRC hearings, the girl who'd believed her future promised a scholarship and world travel, the Toufah I'd been. I do not want these girls, or anyone, to go through what I'd experienced. I do not want them to drown while singing girl-power songs.

As I look at the girls on the beach, I think of the women in my family. I know the compromises my mother and grand-mothers made: strong women who needed to feed their children and survive within the societies they'd been born into, even as those societies changed ever so gradually. I had seen, too, the compromises women in North America made, as they managed their lives in their imperfect worlds.

Women everywhere still find themselves forced to choose to live with abuse, if it means their children will be fed. Women everywhere still find themselves forced to choose to ignore harassment at work, if it means keeping the job that pays their rent. Women everywhere still find themselves forced to choose to not report sexual assaults, because they know the legal system—and the society around it—will blame them more for the crime than the person who committed it. I want something different for the girls in our group, for the women in my country and beyond, for Penda, Nogoi and Ida—and for Muhammed and the men and boys too as well as those who do not see themselves represented in these binary roles.

We live in a world where the two halves don't fit properly together: the half where we promise women they can be whatever they want to be, and the half where we make it impossible for them to be fully who they are. But the answer isn't to stop making the promises; the answer is to change the world to make the promises possible. To change the world for these girls, *with* these girls who sit with me on the beach, as we create the next chapters in our stories, the stories that come after the headlines and the witness stand.

I am Toufah. And I am changing our world.

TIMELINE

Early life:
April 1996: Born
2011: Brother Pa Mattar dies

Pageant and escape:
November 2014: Pageant competition and win
December 2014: Additional pageant ceremony
June 2015: Raped by then-President of The Gambia,
    Yahya Jammeh
June 2015: Escape from The Gambia to Senegal
August 2015: Leave Senegal for Canada
8 August 2015: Arrive Canada

Life in Canada:
December 2015: Move from Toronto to Vancouver
July 2016: Move from Vancouver back to Toronto

Change in Gambian government:
1 December 2016: Election in The Gambia, Jammeh loses,
    Adama Barrow wins; Jammeh initially concedes defeat
    but then reverses decision and says he will stay in power

18 January 2017: Adama Barrow sworn in as president of
The Gambia at the Gambian embassy in Senegal.

21 January 2017: Jammeh leaves The Gambia

November 2017: Toufah returns to The Gambia for the first
time since fleeing the country; visits family

Speaking out:

2018: Toufah begins conversations with Human Rights
Watch about going public

Early 2019: Meeting with Human Rights Watch; Toufah
decides she wants to accuse Jammeh publicly, using her
own name

25 June 2019: Human Rights Watch report released

26 June 2019: press conference in Dakar, Senegal

June, 2019: press conference in The Gambia

31 October 2019: Toufah testifies at The Gambia's TRRC
hearings

3 December 2019: Toufah appears at International Criminal
Court Assembly of State Parties meeting in The Hague

10 December 2019: Toufah appears at UN Human Rights
Day in New York City

March 2020: COVID-19 pandemic declared

Building The Toufah Foundation:

September 2020: Toufah returns to The Gambia to work on
public information and advocacy programs developed by
The Toufah Foundation

April 2021: Toufah returns to Canada; plans to split her time
between Canada and The Gambia

ACKNOWLEDGMENTS

Many have supported me on my journey, more than I can name.

My mum and Aunty Marie, my first and forever role models of both strength and love.

Omar Topp, who was the first to hear me and believe me.

The therapists who walked with me through my most difficult stretches: thank you for holding space for me.

Activist Jereh Badgie, who did what needed to be done, from marching to working alongside us to create the foundation and all that has come since.

All who marched with us under that hot sun.

Canadian diplomat John Crysler, who in a hotel restaurant in The Gambia planted a seed by saying, "It would be great to read your story in a book."

All of the women, female-identifying people and oppressed who have walked this path before me and whose stories and voices have come together in a global #MeToo movement.

To young people such as Emma Brandau, whose pen sketches of me keep me grounded.

Thanks to the publishing teams at Random House Canada and Steerforth Press. I am grateful to Kim Pittaway for helping me focus my voice, and also to my agent, Marilyn Biderman.

In April 2021, I sat at the grave of a Gambian teenager, a victim of rape and murder. I felt the coarseness of the soil under which she lay with her unborn child and knew that, whatever hardship I face, it is both my responsibility and privilege to speak for those who have been silenced. I will not rest.

If you are traveling this road: Remember you are worthy of compassion, of visibility and of joy. Honour our ancestors for their survival, and for all they have done for us, regardless of how they did it and where you come from.

INDEX

TOUFAH JALLOW is an African anti-rape activist who inspired a #MeToo movement in West Africa. A compelling and poised speaker, she has told her story to her nation on live television, as well as to reporters from the BBC, CBC, NPR, *New York Times*, *Globe and Mail*, *Guardian*, *Al Jazeera* and more. She has spoken before the United Nations, presented at the International Criminal Court at The Hague, and given testimony at The Gambia's Truth, Reconciliation and Reparations Commission. She lives in Toronto, Canada, where she is studying to become an assaulted women and children's counselor, and travels frequently to The Gambia, where she heads The Toufah Foundation in support of survivors of sexual assault.

KIM PITTAWAY is the Executive Director of the MFA in Creative Nonfiction program at the University of King's College. She is an award-winning journalist, former editor-in-chief of *Chatelaine*, and a recipient of the Outstanding Achievement Award from the Canadian National Magazine Awards Foundation. She lives in Halifax, Nova Scotia.